W9-ASF-078

Psychological Interpretation

LEON H. LEVY
INDIANA UNIVERSITY

Psychological Interpretation

HOLT, RINEHART
AND WINSTON, INC.

NEW YORK

CHICAGO

SAN FRANCISCO

TORONTO

LONDON

ST. PHILIPS COLLEGE LIBRARY

132.075
L 668

Copyright © 1963 by Holt, Rinehart and Winston, Inc.

ALL RIGHTS RESERVED
LIBRARY OF CONGRESS CATALOG CARD NUMBER: 63–8490
25240–0113
PRINTED IN THE UNITED STATES OF AMERICA

To

STINE, and to

PAUL, CLAIRE, and JUDY

25309

Preface

CLINICAL psychology today is a field beset by conflicts. Commentary appearing periodically in the *American Psychologist,* as well as the content of conferences given over to the consideration of the proper training of clinical psychologists, makes this only too obvious. At one time the conflict is seen in role-theoretical terms, between the demands of the roles of the professional and of the scientist; at another time in trait-theoretical terms, between the traits of empathy, intuitiveness, and daring on the one hand, and those of objectivity, rigor, and discipline on the other; and, at yet another time, at the level of the polite epithet, between the artist and the scientist.

At no point in either the teaching or the practice of clinical psychology does evidence of these conflicts, however they may be conceived, become more acutely apparent than in connection with the act of interpretation as this is carried on in psychodiagnosis and psychotherapy. Here, it has been my observation, the clinician striving to maintain an image of himself as a scientist becomes most uncomfortable; here his non-clinical colleague points to what he believes to be prime evidence of the irrational lapses that characterize the thought-process of the clinician and that therefore represent, at the very least, a blemish upon his scientific escutcheon.

Where conflict dwells, confusion cannot be far away. Thus we often find students, as well as some practitioners, confusing interpretation of any form with subscription to a particular theory of personality. It is not uncommon, for example, to hear an interpretation prefaced with "Well, if we want to be psychoanalytic about it, . . ." or, "Psychoanalytically, I guess you might say that . . . ," when in many instances what follows bears little or no relationship to psychoanalytic theory. In other instances we find interpretation being confused with license for absurdity, obscurity, or intellectual exhibitionism.

Interpretation is the most important single activity engaged in by the clinician. Whether engaged in overtly or covertly, intentionally or unintentionally, interpretation underlies every decision, diagnostic formulation, and therapeutic act. Without interpretation, the clinician must take the data furnished him at face value; without interpretation, the clinician is not much further ahead in understanding his patient's behavior than is the patient himself; without interpretation, the clinician is at best a technician who must record whatever is presented him and then hope that some of the data will appear in actuarial tables or cookbooks so that he can find out what to do next.

Interpretation begins when we ask the question: What does this mean? It ends when we no longer feel the need to ask this question. What transpires between these two states is the subject matter of this book. I propose to treat interpretation as an activity or behavior and to determine, through an analysis of the conditions of its occurrence, its form, its content, and its consequences, those assumptions and principles that guide or are implicit in it. In taking this approach, it will be apparent to some, I am following the logical-empiricist approach of modern philosophy of science. While this is true, my purpose is not to present an essay in philosophy of science. As I pursue this approach, it will also appear to some that I am attacking many time-honored concepts and beliefs subscribed to by clinicians engaged in interpretation. While this is true, my purpose is not to be iconoclastic.

Although I disavow iconoclasm as my purpose, I think it only fair to warn the reader, before he goes any further, that if he should subscribe to the point of view presented in this book he will do so at the peril of losing some of the rituals, beliefs, and household gods upon which he may have relied for support and reassurance. This demands courage and the reader is perfectly within his rights to ask what he may expect in return. To answer this is to give my reasons for writing this book.

Having both observed and experienced the conflicts and confusions associated with the practice of clinical psychology, and of interpretation in particular, and being involved in the education and training of future clinical psychologists, I began writing this book as an attempt at working through both my own problems in this regard and those of my students. Evidence abounds that confusion over one's identity provides fertile ground for a wide range of forms of maladjustment; if some of this confusion could be reduced it seemed clear that the professional efficiency and competence of my students, not to mention myself, would increase greatly. The question with which I began was therefore whether one can engage in psychological interpretation and still maintain his sense of integrity and self-respect as a scientist and rational human being, or whether one must be willing to tolerate some kind of schism in his perception of himself. What follows indicates, I believe, that this schism is not necessary, that there need be no break in continuity between one's functioning in the laboratory and in the consulting room, that interpretation is of a piece with experimental observation, hypothesis-forming, and theory-construction.

To be gained by acceptance of this point of view is not only an integration of an important clinical activity with other activities engaged in by the psychologist, but also a greater flexi-

ST. PHILIPS COLLEGE LIBRARY

bility in the use of interpretation, a greater willingness to entertain alternative interpretations in a given instance, and a greater awareness of the needs and possibilities for research in this area. Further, if the clinician in adopting this point of view should feel less alienated from his nonclinical brethren, the reverse should also be true, and so the increasing fragmentation which we see in psychology, both as a body of knowledge and as a body of scientists, may at least be retarded.

The development of islands of knowledge is a danger against which every science must guard. We find in interpretation a situation where we have islands within an island. Not only has interpretation been treated as of a different order of activity or status from other functions of the psychologist, but it is frequently taught and practiced as though there were different processes or principles involved when interpretation is applied to dreams, TAT protocols, artistic productions, and social interactions. The result is a hobbling of both the intellect and the activity of the clinician.

In this book I shall attempt to demonstrate that a single set of principles guides interpretation regardless of the material involved, and that the process of interpretation is the same regardless of the material treated by it. Thus, having grasped these principles, the student should be able to deal with dreams or conversations, TATs or figure drawings, with equal confidence. His concern is no longer that he has not learned how to interpret a certain type of content, only (a) whether the means by which the content was obtained or the content itself is likely to be *useful* for his purposes, and (b) whether his chosen theory and language are meaningful—two concerns which will be discussed at length in the text.

A word would seem in order about my intended audience. In keeping with my personal orientation toward psychology as a science and profession, I have written this book with both the clinician and non-clinician (especially at the graduate and postdoctoral levels) in mind. I would be disappointed if the clinician read this only as a "how to" book, although I do believe that it will implement his clinical skills; if clinical psychology is ever to fulfill its promise, its practitioners must accept as one of their responsibilities the development of more sophisticated conceptualizations than now characterize the field and the development of a much more extensive and reliable body of knowledge than we now possess. For the non-clinician, my hope is that this book will suggest areas of research to which he may turn his energies. For any psychologist to see the problems involved in interpretation as exclusively clinical is a dangerously narrow view, which reflects poorly on his training and bodes ill for the entire field. It is doubtful whether any problem is ever profitably thought of as belonging within one province or another; rather, it is only as we abandon such provincialism, as we cease to see problems as belonging either to learning theory, or to psychophysics, or to clinical psychology, that we are likely to achieve anything like a creative approach to the problems of psychology.

ACKNOWLEDGMENTS

One's acknowledgments could easily read like an autobiography if he attempted to do full justice to all of those people and circumstances contributing to his work. I shall stop far short of this. Nevertheless, I feel that I must acknowledge my intellectual debt to two of my teachers, George A. Kelly and Julian B. Rotter, who each in his own way contributed to the intellectual orientation represented in this book. Whether they would subscribe completely to the form which it has taken I am not sure. But together they helped instill the idea that to be a good clinical psychologist one need not forsake the canons of science, rationality, or common sense. This I have tried to convey in these pages.

Dr. Hanna N. Colm read this manuscript through in its entirety and made many cogent criticisms and suggestions. Had

I the wisdom and sensitivity represented by these, this would undoubtedly be a better book. Dr. T. R. Sarbin also read the entire manuscript and has made many helpful substantive and editorial suggestions. Of no small help has been the interest and encouragement of my wife, Stine, who not only did much to make my syntax more conventional, but who also kept constant vigil over her husband's penchant for the prolix and the ponderous.

Lastly, without the very able secretarial assistance of Lynn Nickels this book would have been much longer and more frustrating in the making.

L. H. L.

Bloomington, Indiana
November 1962

Contents

Psychological Interpretation

CHAPTER 1

The Nature of Psychological

Interpretation

CONTRARY to some widely propagated and widely held notions, psychological interpretation does not in any way depend upon some arcane wisdom on the part of the interpreter. On the contrary, it can be shown that psychological interpretation of all content, whether of expressive movements, dreams, projective test protocols, or interviews, follows a small number of principles that can be made explicit and that constitute the logic of psychological interpretation. Once this logic is grasped the interpretive process loses its aura of mystery and can be treated as merely another means of transforming data, which in fact it is. That is, it can then be taught, examined, and revised. Until this is accomplished—until the notion is dispelled that interpretation depends upon some obscure ability possessed only by the initiated—the psychological interpretation of content will persist as variously a source of wonder, frustration, or ego enhancement, or as an object of suspicion, but never as an instrument of science.

There is good reason why efforts to explicate the interpretive process should meet with rather stiff resistance. For those whose prestige rests upon the claim to skill in this area, disclosure of the logic of psychological interpretation threatens at the very least to make common their once exclusive preserves. Skills possessed by many are not likely to contain the seeds of eminence. But this, as we shall see, is an unwarranted fear. For as Barzun (1959) has pointed out in another context, understanding is not identical with professional skill.

Laying out in public the principles of psychological interpretation may be not only disenchanting. Because this makes them vulnerable to empirical research, it may be also disabling. The interpreter who, for example, has been blithely inferring problems in sexual identification from certain misperceptions in the TAT may begin to feel some apprehension at continuing in this practice after studies begin to appear that cast doubt upon the validity of such inferences. As the evidence mounts, with regard not only to this interpretation but to others as well (some of it positive to be sure), he is likely to become somewhat less fluent with each succeeding protocol handed him. His statements contain an increasing number of qualifiers; flat assertions disappear from his reports. Ex-cathedra pronouncements give way to tentative inferences. Those who receive these reports may begin to think of him as less of an expert than before, as he himself may, and he may even begin to wonder whether his true talents don't lie within physiological psychology where surely no one can accuse him of casuistry.

By those who hold that psychological interpretation constitutes an art any attempt such as the present one is viewed with horror. The specter of mechanization and automation lurks in the background when we begin to speak of principles, rules, and logic. For these people this presages a devaluation of the individual. To those who luxuriate in obscurantism and esoterica the present enterprise is undoubtedly an abomination. There is within the field of psychology, as within many other areas, a romanticism with which some are afflicted that seems to render its victims either insensitive or antagonistic to any attempt at rational analysis. To these people, little solace can be offered. To this writer's way of thinking, rationality and human dignity are not antithetical to each other; nor are science and art for that matter.

It may be well to consider briefly the types of arguments that these people are likely to marshal against an undertaking such as the present one. It is rare that one will simply say, "You can't do that!" Rather, epithets such as "atomistic," "mechanistic," and "superficial" are dusted off and thrown into the breach. A rather frequently used riposte, particularly when all else has failed, is that the clinician does something more in his interpretation of content, which cannot be stated in a few simple rules. There is nothing wrong, the argument goes, with what we have said, it just doesn't do complete justice to the interpretive process. This may be true. But it is not the issue. Something is always lost when we use words, when we abstract from the situation. This is inescapable and has been admitted as long as lovers have been trying to describe their feelings to each other and general semanticists have been exploring the vast difference between the word and its referent. But the issue is an empirical one and simply stated is this: can a set of statements be formulated about the process of psychological interpretation that will be communicable, useful in accounting for this process, and subject to verification by empirical research? It is with respect to this issue that the present work is submitted for consideration.

When do we interpret?

In understanding the nature of psychological interpretation it will be helpful to consider it as a kind of behavior engaged in at certain times and not at other times, and to ask what the common characteristics are of those times when it is engaged in. By setting a behavior into some context, by noting consistencies in the contexts or patterns of instances in which it occurs, we are able to make reasonably good guesses about the purposes it fulfills or is presumed to fulfill. By classifying psychological interpretation as a behavior we are implying that it is observable, that it has certain antecedent and consequent conditions which may be worthy of consideration, and that it is only one of several kinds of operations or behaviors engaged in by the psychologist. Therefore we might also ask when it is that the psychologist engages in this operation rather than some other, and also, perhaps, when he should engage in this operation rather than some other.

Let us consider instances in which material, either verbal or nonverbal, is likely to be subjected to interpretation. A patient has just told his therapist that he cannot get along with his wife, try as he will. He goes on to say that he finds her nagging, arbitrary, and unloving. He sees no future in his marriage with her. The therapist recalls that many of the characteristics the patient attributed to his wife were also attributed by him to his mother. Depending upon a host of other considerations which need not concern us at this point, the therapist may hazard the interpretation that the hostility the patient feels toward his wife is actually a displacement of feelings he has toward his mother.

Consider the case of a group of young adolescents who were masturbating openly in the classroom (Stirt, 1940). The teacher was at a loss in finding a way to control their behavior. After two one-hour sessions in which the "meaning" of this behavior was interpreted to the boys, a complete cessation of the activity was reported.

Another instance: a person presents himself at an out-patient clinic and complains of anxiety and obsessive thoughts. After an intake interview, projective tests are administered and these are subjected to interpretation.

Of course the number of situations in which interpretation is undertaken could be increased one hundred-fold with little effort, and it may appear to the reader that interpretation as a behavior is of such ubiquity that little can be said about the instances in which it occurs which would be of much significance toward understanding its nature. But this is not the case. All the instances that have been described as well as all other instances in which we professionally engage in psychological interpretation appear to have one feature in common: *someone is in a bind.* It may be the patient, it may be the therapist, or it may be both. We have reached a point where progress by whatever measure we are using appears to have ceased. We have run out of alternative courses of action. We are looking for a different tack to take with a client or to suggest to a client and we seek to accomplish this through the interpretation of certain material. In other words, when we engage in psychological interpretation we are, in effect, saying: "The way in which we have been looking at this situation has led us to a dead end. Let's see if there isn't some other way of looking at this thing." And this is precisely what the psychological interpretation of content consists of: *a redefining or restructuring of the situation through the presentation of an alternate description of some behavioral datum.*

More specifically, interpretation occurs whenever a new or different frame of reference, or language, is brought to bear upon some problem or event. What the patient described as concern about his child's health, he "learns," may represent hostility toward the child. Where a woman saw her fear as due to altitude, she is told that it represents insecurity about her social status. What the Don Juan saw as a problem in being "oversexed," might, his therapist suggests, be better described as concern about being "undersexed." And so it goes. In psychological interpretation, most simply stated, one language system is pitted against another.

While fixity is the state of conditions prior to the onset of interpretation, change characterizes the situation after the interpretation ceases. The parent no longer worries about his child, at least not in the same way. The young lady is now employed as an airline hostess. And our much-maligned Don Juan has settled down to a state of single blessedness. At least these might represent the ideal outcomes of the situations I have described. And they would appear to justify whatever the interpretations were that resulted in these outcomes. Having achieved these outcomes the situation has changed and the need for further interpretation diminishes. Where these or analogous consequences do not follow, it is likely that interpretive activity will continue. Thus we see fairly clearly that the ultimate purpose of interpretation is to bring about change in some state of affairs. How interpretation accomplishes this has not as yet been thoroughly investigated, and discussion of this will be deferred until a later chapter. To be sure, interpretation is not the only procedure used in bringing about change, but it is certainly one of the major ones, and quite likely one of the most powerful ones.

It might be argued that interpretation serves other purposes than that of instituting change. In particular, it might be contended that interpretation, especially with respect to projective test protocols, serves simply as a basis for better understanding the individual's behavior and personality. It may, perhaps, be suggested that it serves as a basis for prediction. With this there can be no argument. Predictions are frequently made on the basis, at least partly, of interpretation of diagnostic test material. However, it should be recognized that when we speak of understanding and prediction, we are simply speaking of certain preconditions for the institution and management of change; these are never ends in themselves except for the dilettante. When we turn to projective tests in our work with an individual we are saying in effect: "We will be better able to predict this person's behavior in a given situation if we can bring a different frame of reference into play. We feel that in order to do this we will have to draw a different sample of behavior from that available to us now. Specifically, we want a sample of behavior that is amenable to description in our frame of reference, one that was designed with our particular language system in mind."

Finally, it might be observed that change is still the ultimate problem, even where diagnosis is the ostensible one. For we only see persons professionally when they are involved in a set of conditions that in some way, to someone, cannot be tolerated. The conditions in question may not have occurred yet, but may be anticipated. For example, the question might be whether or not a patient will be assaultive to his wife if he is released from the hospital. It might be whether or not a particular candidate with a history of alcoholism should be hired by an advertising agency. It might be why a student becomes ill every time he enters a certain classroom. In each of these instances there is a set of conditions we wish to avert, to assure, or to mitigate, and we seem unable to accomplish this without recourse to a new frame of reference, to psychological interpretation. Whether in all instances this is justified is of course open to question, but that is beside the point for our present purposes.

To sum up, psychological interpretation, viewed as a behavior, is engaged in whenever a state exists that seems refractory to other efforts at mitigation or understanding. In essence it consists of bringing an alternate frame of reference, or language system, to bear upon a set of observations or behaviors, with the end in view of making them more amenable to manipulation.

Events and their interpretation

The term *event* is to be thought of in a generic sense as meaning any occurrence, behavioral or environmental, in a free field or under structured conditions such as interviewing or testing, of which we are aware or which has stood out as figure. Our position regarding the interpretation of events is essentially that of Kelly's (1955) when he says, "We assume that all of our present interpretations of the universe are subject to revision or replacement" (p. 15). And again, "A clinician chooses his constructs according to what he wants to accomplish" (p. 782). Events, in other words, do not carry with them their own interpretations. They are innocent of any meaning except insofar as we impose it upon them. The meaning with which we invest them, our interpretation of them, will be determined jointly by their own morphology, our purposes and interests as regards them, and our background and experience. While such a statement may seem innocuous enough—and perhaps even platitudinous to some —it has implications that may not be similarly construed by all and that are of particular importance in defining our position concerning the nature of psychological interpretation.

When we say that the morphology of an event enters into the interpretation we place upon it, we merely wish to recognize that within rather broad limits the form or structure of an event increases the probability that one significance rather than another will be attributed to it, that it will more likely be seen in one way than another. But we stress that these limits are broad. It would be easy to lapse into a metaphysical fugue on this point but we shall resist the temptation. It is, for example, simply an empirical fact that certain statements when made about another person are considered derogatory, and further that the person making them is considered in some way hostile toward their referent. Similarly, tears appearing upon being told of the death of another person would most likely be interpreted as an indication of sadness. But these are perhaps modal interpretations, in particular instances other ones may seem more appropriate.

With a modicum of effort and a few well-chosen symbols, it would be possible to conjure up a recondite and impressive diagram purporting to demonstrate how, through learning, this broad band of significance becomes associated with a given event. We shall forego this exercise, however stimulating it might be, and simply assert our belief that such a process can adequately account for the relationships we observe between events and their interpretations. In doing so, we are, of course, rejecting a realist position with regard to knowledge and ranging ourselves on the side of logical positivism, or of what Kelly (1955) prefers to call "constructive alternativism."

If its morphology sets certain broad limits upon the possible interpretations of an event, the purposes and interests of the clinician, together with his orientation, usually help to reduce these limits to manageable proportions, often to the point where it appears that only one interpretation is reasonable. If, for example, the therapist is intent upon helping a patient "recognize" his competitiveness with others, he may interpret the patient's rejection of a particular interpretation as an instance of the patient's competing with him, the therapist. The rejected interpretation, if accepted, would have represented to the patient that he had been intellectually bested by the therapist; the rejection, in other words, was just another act in a continuing power struggle between the patient and his therapist. If, on the other hand, the therapist is attempting to help his patient gain "insight" into his own defenses, the same rejection might be interpreted to the patient as another instance of his use of resistance or denial to ward off anxiety. Yet another therapist, whose orientation predisposes him to view human problems in terms of ability to give and receive love, might interpret the same rejection as reflecting the patient's fear of closeness: the rejected interpretation represented a gift from the therapist and would therefore commit him to reciprocate in some fashion—a commitment which he could not adequately fulfill. Clearly, in this illustration, truth value cannot be the basis for making one interpretation and not the other, and the making of one does not imply that any other one is untrue; the choice is made simply on the basis of consistency with the interpreter's orientation and purposes at the moment.[1]

The present position has several advantages. Paramount is its loosening of the tie between events and their imputed significance. We begin to ask if this interpretation is the *best* one that might be made. We consider others. We are freed from the belief that the interpretive process is a search for truth (a notion to which we shall return later). We begin to ask what the possible implications are of the various alternative interpretations that might be made of an event, and we feel freer about including these considerations in our final decisions. And finally, we recognize the essential role played by the person in psychological interpretation and are less dogmatic or tenacious when we engage in the interpretive process.

To recapitulate, the interpretation of an event is not a search for the true meaning of the event. Every event is subject to a vast range of interpretations. In psychological interpretation we apply that particular construction which we believe will best suit our purposes and which is consistent with the theoretical frame of reference we bring to the situation.

Modes of interpretation

The reader may wonder how the process of psychological interpretation differs from the activity that everyone engages in continuously and that goes under such headings as perception, construction of events, or cognition. In form there is no difference; in substance there may be.

Man is continuously striving to make sense out of his experience, to impose structure, to anticipate events, and to communicate. For this purpose he develops highly elaborate systems of coding events and hypotheses regarding the various contingencies in his experience that his particular coding

[1] It should be noted that only the most "insecure" or "inexperienced" therapist would be likely to consider the possibility that his interpretation was incorrect and warranted rejection by the patient!

system has produced (Kelly, 1955; Whorf, 1956). The psychologist *qua* psychologist is no exception.

Psychological interpretation differs from other modes of interpretation only to the extent that it brings to bear upon the situation a unique way of looking at it. More specifically, it consists of a language that was developed specifically for the theoretical description of behavior. Thus it contains terms not shared with other languages, and thus it *creates* contingencies not present as a result of the use of other languages. Of course there is no single language system used in psychological interpretation. There are several, each going by the name of some different personality or behavior theory (Rotter, 1954). Depending upon one's theoretical orientation a single event may be described in terms of prior reinforcements, expectancies, sublimation, compensation, or self-actualization. We cannot order such descriptions hierarchically on the basis of priority nor can we order them on the basis of truth values. We can only ask which serves our purposes best.

While psychological interpretation makes use of a language specifically developed to deal with behavior, it must be recognized that there are other languages of other disciplines also developed for this purpose and that there are many instances where behavior is better or more helpfully described by one of these other languages. Thus if our interest happens to be in the behavior of consumers vis-à-vis the new car market we may more fruitfully make use of the language of economics and market research. If our interest is in an individual's disturbance in locomotion we may find that the language of neuroanatomy best serves our purposes. In planning the defense of a client being sued for libel, we would find the language of the law most necessary in discussing his behavior. Again, we cannot order such descriptions hierarchically on the basis of priority nor can we order them on the basis of truth values. While some events seem to resist description in more than one language system, others are not so recalcitrant. In each case however, we select that language which we expect will maximize our ability to deal with the problem at hand; the choice is a pragmatic one whether we are aware of it or not.

There are those who, in the interests either of proprietary rights or of good housekeeping, have concerned themselves with the questions of when a psychologist is speaking as a psychologist and what the unique aspects of psychological interpretation are. Unfortunately, like so many questions that can be posed, their mere existence does not insure their meaningfulness or their significance. To ask such a question is to ask for a definition. While again, definitions can be generated ad infinitum, some of them very profound indeed, they remain simply definitions and are not statements of fact subject to verification by observation. To be sure, definitions have their place, but in regard to the questions posed above it seems that they are likely only to encourage boundary disputes and unlikely to serve any useful purpose. For example, Brunswik (1952), and Jessor (1958) after him, have suggested that psychology can be defined as a science concerned with organism-environment interrelationships. But surely such a concern is also shared with nutrition, economics, and sociology, to cite just a few examples. Marginal utility, for example, a concept of economics, would make no sense if we left either the organism, man, or the environment, supply, out of the question. There are times when definitions of boundaries serve some useful purpose in that they result in certain changes in behavior which would not occur otherwise. This does not appear to be one of those instances.

The evaluation of interpretations

If, as I have insisted, interpretations cannot be evaluated from the standpoint of truth or falsity, by what means can they be judged? Does this imply that all interpretation is arbitrary? How can one develop a training program and criteria of achievement from such a standpoint?

As the reader may have surmised, the situation is not so anarchic as it may seem at first glance. While the interpretive process is not a search for truth, any given interpretation can be judged as correct or incorrect. While interpretations cannot be ordered in terms of priority, any given interpretation can be judged as appropriate or inappropriate. The bases for evaluation are the same as those employed with any theory or theoretical statement.

As has been said before, psychological interpretation consists of bringing into play in a particular situation a new frame of reference, a new language system, a new theory. As a result of this, specific statements are generated about the situation. These we refer to as the interpretation. It is therefore possible to ask two questions: (1) Is the interpretation consistent with the theory from which it is generated? (2) Does it lead to, or facilitate, the change in state in which we are interested?

In answering the first question we first cast all the information we have about the event and its context into the terms of the theory in question and then ask whether, against this background, this interpretation makes sense. Is it consistent with the total situation in its transformed version and is it logically and psychologically consistent with our theory? If not, the interpretation is incorrect.

I am not, of course, suggesting that human behavior is a model of consistency. Far from it. But the purpose of theory is, in a sense, to transform raw data and, in so doing, to impose consistency upon it. Thus, to the layman, the hostility exhibited by a child toward his mother, who appears to spend her every waking hour ministering to his needs and protecting him from harm, may appear inconsistent. But when recast in terms of overprotection, domination, frustration, and aggression, we see no inconsistency. This is a contingency we have learned to expect.

The application of a consistency criterion necessitates the existence of a sufficiently articulated theory. And herein lies a present major weakness. Among the theories now developed to account for behavior and personality, there is none that has been so rigorously or so extensively developed that it can be applied to the whole gamut of human behavior and permit judgments of consistent or inconsistent to be rendered with absolute certainty. It seems to be the case that rigor of syntax and extensiveness of applicability are inversely related to each other. Consequently, our evaluations of interpretations by the criterion of consistency may be expected to vary in certainty depending upon the theory involved and the situation in question. But, except to disengage ourselves entirely from the interpretive enterprise, we have little choice.

An interpretation may be correct by our criterion but not appropriate. This involves the question of when to interpret. If interpretation is but one of several tools at the therapist's disposal, it follows that there are probably optimal conditions for its use. Considerations such as the threat of the interpretation to the patient, his ability to utilize it, the attitudes or behaviors it is likely to evoke are all of relevance when we judge the appropriateness of an interpretation. That the kind of relationship a man has with his wife appears to have a large competitive component involved in it may be a correct interpretation of all of the information at hand, but to communicate this to a patient who appears to be on the verge of an anxiety attack would be inappropriate to say the least.

Thus it may be seen that criteria for the evaluation of interpretations are readily at hand. Without being concerned with whether an interpretive statement is literally true or not—a judgment which we have long since recognized as being impossible to make from the standpoint of the philosophy of science—it is possible to determine whether the statement is

patient himself to offer. Let us now look at some samples of interpretation that purport to expose the nether regions of the personality. Do they have anything in common that will at the same time differentiate them from the ones we have just considered?

It is learned that the patient comes from a very moralistic home environment strongly dominated by his father, with whom he never got along. His anxiety symptoms are seen as due to a poorly resolved Oedipal problem resulting in castration anxiety. The pulling of teeth, being symbolic of castration, represents an all-too-possible likelihood for him. In the dentist's chair he would be too vulnerable. Hence his anxiety. This is a depth interpretation.

Again, the patient is unmarried, has few dates, and is attached to his mother. We also know that he has a poor relationship with his father. It takes but a small inductive leap to conclude that his anxiety is not actually due to a fear of pain, but rather to the activation of homosexual impulses as a result of the close physical proximity between himself and the dentist and the passive (feminine) role that he must adopt vis-à-vis the dentist. Again, it would be accepted by many that we are now working at the level of the unconscious.

With no intent of being exhaustive, we might consider one last example of interpretation in depth in this case. Knowing the moralistic home background of the patient, and knowing also that he has always been striving toward achievement and accomplishment, always grasping for responsibility, we might consider the possibility that he has strongly repressed dependency needs which threaten to come to the fore when he places himself as completely in the hands of another person as he does in the dentist's chair. For some this could be quite threatening; perhaps it is for our patient.

All the foregoing interpretations would appear to account for the symptomatology in the case in terms of certain aspects of the life history of the patient. But each interpretation makes use of different items of information, and some would be considered deep while others would not; some probing the unconscious, others not. What can we learn from this about the concepts of depth and the unconscious?

Clearly, all the items of information utilized are open to public scrutiny; none is hidden. Therefore, although the unconscious is presumed to lie hidden from public view we find that our statements about it are based entirely upon public referents, as are our so-called surface interpretations. The data are there for all to use.

Raush and his associates (Raush, Sperber, Rigler, Williams, Harway, Bordin, Dittmann, & Hays, 1956) attempted a dimensional analysis of the concept of depth of interpretation that is of some relevance to our discussion. They defined depth of interpretation as follows:

> Any behavior on the part of the therapist that is an expression of his view of the patient's emotions and motivations—either wholly or in part—is considered an interpretation. A patient has varying degrees of awareness of his emotions and motivations. Depth of interpretation is a description of the relationship between the view expressed by the therapist and the patient's awareness. The greater the disparity between the view expressed by the therapist and the patient's own awareness of these emotions and motivations, the deeper the interpretation.

Using this definition, judges were asked to rate excerpts from transcripts of recorded therapy sessions for depth of interpretation. On the basis of their analysis of their data Raush *et al.* concluded that while depth of interpretation as they defined it was the primary dimension governing judgments, secondary dimensions could be derived which were not clearly interpretable but seemed to vary with the judges and stimuli used.

Using this definition of depth in any strict manner would prohibit judgments about the depth of the various interpretations offered until we observed how they were received by the patient. If he acceded readily to the interpretation, or if perchance he offered the same interpretation himself, it would not be considered deep. But is this all that is meant by depth?

My view of the concept of depth is similar to that of Raush *et al.* with certain exceptions. If we view interpretation somewhat more broadly than they do, as any construction of a set of events, not necessarily affective in nature, it seems apparent from observation of its use that the concept of depth is invoked to account for *any* discrepancy between the patient's accounting for his situation and the therapist's, that is to say, for any discrepancy in the language systems brought into play in dealing with a given set of events.

Whorf (1956) long ago, and Bruner (Bruner, Goodnow, & Austin, 1956) and Kelly (1955) more recently, have pointed to the ways in which language makes one sensitive to certain stimuli and not to others, to the ways in which language seems to mold our ways of thinking and dealing with events. This, it would seem, could account for the fact that when different languages are invoked to deal with a problem, we find different items of information brought into the foreground. Therefore, from the present point of view it becomes questionable whether such concepts as depth, awareness, and the unconscious have much meaning apart from their denoting the presence of a discrepancy in sets of interpretations. Thus depth becomes an illusion, or at best, a play on words.

It may be of some interest to consider more closely how this illusion came about. It might first be noted that the concept of depth has been until quite recently the exclusive property of psychoanalysis. If our three examples of depth interpretations have anything in common it is that they reflect the concerns of psychoanalytic theory. Thus interpretations which deal with phenomena of prime interest to psychoanalytic theory are considered, prima facie, depth interpretations.

The simplest accounting, thus, would seem to run along the following lines. Psychoanalysis, having wedded itself to a substantive theory of personality with its tripartite division into the superego, ego, and id, was constrained to provide some locus of operation for each of these agencies. Since the ego seemed to be observable in its operation and the others not, it was reasonable to conclude that this was due to the ego being at the surface of the personality and others buried somewhere within its recesses. Personality acquired surface and depth as a result. Thus any statement within psychoanalytic theory referable to the ego was considered for the most part superficial, while any referable to either the superego or id was considered deep.

In effect, what the psychoanalysts and many after them had done was to equate "surface" with "observable" and "subsurface" with "inferable," and to fail to discriminate between observation and inference, so that they gave statements derived by either means equal factual status. Some facts required special techniques, special training, and the right frame of mind to discover; these were deep. Others made less stringent demands upon their discoverers; these were less deep. Interpretation was a search for truth and anyone who denied its findings was lacking in insight and offering resistance.

The concepts of insight, awareness, and resistance stem directly from the belief that the interpretive process is a search for truth, with the correlative assumption that the analyst vis-à-vis the patient is more likely to recognize truth when he sees it. Having made his interpretation, the analyst therefore checks with the patient to see whether he has made a similar one, or whether the patient is willing to acknowledge his (the analyst's) interpretation as correct. In the first instance he speaks of insight or lack thereof; in the second of resistance or lack thereof. But from our point of view it becomes clear that where insight is used we are simply asking about the extent to which the patient's construction of events matches our own, not whether he too has become privy to the truth. When we speak of resistance we are referring to the ease with which the patient will accept an alternate construction of a given situation, one which we think will be of more use to him than that which he has come up with on his own, not whether he is at last ready to acknowledge the truth. In neither instance is the question of truth an issue.

To sum up my position with regard to the concept of depth and its correlative concepts of awareness, insight, and resistance: if one does not adopt a substantive theory of personality—that is, if one views personality as an abstraction or construct, as I do—the concept of depth has no meaning. If one adopts my view of the interpretive process as that of offering alternate constructions of sets of events, with the question of the truth of either construction being both meaningless and irrelevant, then the concepts of awareness, insight, and resistance become of little value, at least as they have been traditionally defined. They may indeed be some value in having terms to denote the extent to which a patient's construction of events matches his therapist's, and the extent to which he is willing to entertain alternate constructions. But these must be recognized as being simply that and nothing else. To do otherwise is to invite mischief. If depth is to be retained as a term in our professional discourse, from the present point of view it can have only one defensible meaning: the complexity of the inferential link between the event and our statements about it.

The unconscious

To do adequate justice to the concept of the unconscious would be no mean undertaking, but I believe that one cannot properly talk about problems of interpretation without taking some stand on the question of the nature and existence of the unconscious. This belief is strengthened by recalling that Freud saw interpretation as making the unconscious

conscious, and noting Jung's (1933) statement: "We must recognize the unconscious if we are to treat of dream-analysis at all, for we do not resort to it as a mere exercise of the wits, but as a method for uncovering hitherto unconscious psychic contents which are causally related to the neurosis and therefore of importance in its treatment. Anyone who deems this hypothesis unacceptable must simply rule out the question of the practicability of dream-analysis." Neither of these statements can be considered the utterances of voices in the wilderness.

To put it simply and bluntly, nothing can be said, by the canons of modern philosophy of science, of the existence of the unconscious as a substantive entity: the assertion of its existence is in principle untestable and hence meaningless. To ask whether the unconscious exists is analogous to asking whether the soul or God exists: one either acts on the assumption that they do or does not. If we consider it as a theoretical construct, we simply doubt the utility or necessity of its existence.[2] The unconscious represents the outcome of interpretive analysis, and an ill-conceived one at that. But how did this come about?

It has long been recognized that the extremely flexible nature of our language is at once an advantage and a pitfall (Ayer, 1946). The concept of the unconscious is an example of this double character of language. The ease with which adjectives may become nouns and the primitive belief that because we are able to use a term as a subject in a sentence it must have real existence are to a great extent responsible for this state of affairs vis-à-vis the unconscious. But beyond that, in the case of the unconscious it seems also due to the belief that having named some attribute of an object, there must exist some substantive source from which this attribute derives which is apart from the object to which it is ascribed.

[2] For a more extended discussion of this point see Phillips' (1956) discussion of the question, "Is the concept of the unconscious necessary?"

Having labeled an act or thought as unconscious—that is, having ascribed this attribute to it—proponents of the unconscious as a substantive entity go on to posit a single source from which all events with this attribute must stem and use the attribute itself as the name of this source. And so, if an event is unconscious it is berthed in the unconscious; if it is conscious it resides in consciousness. We have created two realms and all the attendant problems of interchange between them.

Unconsciousness as an attribute leading to the unconscious as an entity is not the only instance of this occurrence in the history of psychology. Essentially the entire edifice of faculty psychology came about in the same way. Behavior was described as intelligent, and so *the intelligence* came into being; the attribute "imaginative" was bestowed upon an event, and *the imagination* came into existence. It would be interesting to speculate why certain attributes invited this treatment and others did not. Although we also describe some behavior as random, we seldom concern ourselves with the substantive existence of a randomness; although we describe an act as hostile, it has been some time since anyone has attempted to defend the existence of a "hostile" as an entity— although for some time the devil was a leading contender for this role; although we consider some behavior dependent and other behavior independent, neither of these attributes has been accorded the status of a substantive realm. The problem is intriguing but unfortunately one that would lead us too far afield to justify further speculation at this point.

To recapitulate our position, we have behavior and we have attributes that we find useful in describing this behavior. Where we engage in the psychological interpretation of behavior, instances occur where our constructions do not jibe with those of our patient. It is in these instances that we find the subject being described as unconscious of some motive (the one we believe best accounts for this behavior) and that we find the unconscious being brought in to provide a residence for this motive. This again clearly imbues the interpreter with superior vision vis-à-vis his subject.[3] From our point of view, again, this simply represents two differing constructions of the same situation, nothing more.

The dual nature of psychological interpretation

In our discussion of the nature of psychological interpretation thus far, we have been guilty of an elision that simplified discussion of some of the issues raised and yet did no harm. It is now time to correct this. Where we previously characterized psychological interpretation as bringing an alternate frame of reference, or language system, to bear upon a set of observations or behaviors, it is now necessary to be somewhat more precise in our characterization and to recognize that there are two aspects to the process rather than the one implied by this statement.

The first aspect of psychological interpretation is that of a translation of raw data into the terms of our theory or frame of reference. Where the client, for example, reports disturbed sleep, sweating palms, and dysrhythmic breathing, we may use the term anxiety; where the patient reports dreaming of climbing a telephone pole, for the pole we may read male sex organ; where the worker is described as always arguing with his boss, we may report this as his having difficulty in

[3] The question might arise as to whether, from this point of view, the patient himself can ever offer an interpretation which would be considered "deep" or revealing of unconscious motives. I believe that the answer is yes. In such a case the patient has adopted the interpreter's frame of reference and gives an explanation consistent with this frame of reference. If he refers to motives in his interpretation which he would not have been expected to refer to at the time the behavior being explained occurred, he would be making a "deep" interpretation or making the unconscious conscious. Similarly, if the patient's interpretation is one which would not be expected from a hypothetical, unsophisticated layman, it would be considered "deep." In both instances, it is still a discrepancy in construction that is crucial in deciding whether or not the interpretation is "deep."

authority relationships. It is clear that in each of these instances we are in effect using a different lexicon for the same referents. We add nothing to the situation other than this.

But there is frequently another aspect of psychological interpretation. Having translated the data into the language of our theory we then formulate propositions regarding the data. This is the second aspect of interpretation. It results in propositional statements that are at once consistent with our theory to the extent that the development of our theory permits such a judgment, and consistent with all the data at hand.

The propositional statements generated by the interpretive process are usually couched in theoretical terms and are not in and of themselves empirically verifiable. In order to achieve verification, a final translation back into the language of our data, the events, must be made. In practice the process is frequently short-circuited so that it appears that we go directly from observations to propositions regarding them. However, upon careful reflection it would become obvious that this is not possible. For it is only through theory, however rudimentary it might be, that we can find any basis for propositional statements. If nothing else, our theory provides us with a language and a set of rules for its use that permits us to abstract from situations and thereby note the various contingencies that are exemplified in a given propositional statement.

To illustrate the dual aspect of psychological interpretation more concretely, let us take the fellow who is continually arguing with his boss. We find that his entire work history is studded with such incidents, and furthermore that his school career was periodically interrupted by expulsions for misconduct in class. In translation, we might say that this individual seems to have a problem in his relations with authority figures, because by the rules of our theory the term "authority figures" can be applied to both teachers and bosses. It would be mistaken at this point to believe that we have discovered anything new or to regard our theoretical statement of the case as an explanation of his problem, as some are prone to do. To say that our patient doesn't get along with bosses because he has authority problems is tautological.

Depending upon our interests at this point, a number of different propositions might be formulated. For example, we might state that he has authority problems because he lacked an adequate father figure with whom to identify. After we specify in data language what we mean by "father figure" and "identify," the validity of this proposition is open to test. Such a proposition rests upon a theory that the father represents the prototype of authority and that all subsequent relations with authority figures will be conditioned by the nature of the relationship with him.

We might with equal ease advance the proposition that such a person will have difficulty developing an adequate relationship with his therapist in psychotherapy. Or again, that he is likely to show hostility toward members of minority groups. The latter proposition is based upon the additional concepts of repression and displacement. Because we have inferred an inadequate identification with his father, and because according to psychoanalytic theory this identification is crucial in the development of one's sex role, a further proposition might be offered regarding inadequate sexual identification. But again, before these propositions can be of much use or tested, they must be translated into the language of observation. However, had we not first had the theoretical concept of "authority figure" available to us, together with a number of theoretical statements regarding relations with authority figures, none of these propositions could have been legitimately formulated.

It is important to stress the point that the job of psychological interpretation can never stop at the stage of the formulation of theoretical propositions; there must always be the last step of returning to the language of observation. This must be stressed because failure to do this represents one of the major shortcomings of much that goes by the name of psychological interpretation today. Frequently this is termed "revealing the dynamics of the personality." I have no quarrel with one speaking of personality dynamics so long as he recognizes that this helps no one, least of all the patient, until these dynamics are spelled out in behavioral terms. For a patient to be described as having poor ego strength, negative goal expectancies, or a closed conceptual system may be gratifying to the person wielding these terms, but proves nothing about the adequacy or use of his theory nor tells us what to do for the patient, until the terms tell us what to look for. Unless we do this we are doing nothing more than engaging in "a mere exercise of wits."

As critics have been tireless in pointing out, it is the adequacy of the tie between the language of theory and the language of data that determines the ultimate meaning and utility of a theory. Where this tie is loose—that is, where the empirical referents for a given theoretical term are not clearly specified—the theory gains in viability at the expense of utility. It is less vulnerable to disproof, but it is also less useful in practical application. This does not mean, of course, that for each term of the theory there can be one and only one empirical referent. But it does imply that we should have some ultimate means of choosing between the referents to be applied in a given instance. Thus, for example, to say that an individual has poor impulse control, perhaps because of his performance on the Rorschach, is of little value until we know how this will manifest itself, whether in the expression of verbal, physical, or otherwise hostility, whether in frequent episodes of sexual promiscuity, or whether in gormandism. For purposes of testing a theory, it may be sufficient to treat all these referents as equivalent manifestations of inadequate impulse control. This is the case, for example, in studies of the construct validity of tests (Cronbach & Meehl, 1955). But in psychological interpretation in the practical clinical situation we cannot usually tolerate this luxury. For here the decisions we are likely to make about a patient will vary tremendously, depending upon which of the various ways we anticipate that the patient's inadequate impulse control will manifest itself.

Thus we see that between the clinician and the experimentalist there can be no distinction in terms of hardheadedness. The clinician, no less than the experimentalist, must have a sound appreciation for the importance of the tie between theory and data if he is to perform his job adequately.

Summary

Psychological interpretation was defined as "a redefining or restructuring of the situation through the presentation of an alternate description of some behavioral datum," and was therefore seen as an instance of pitting one language system, the interpreter's, against another, the patient's. Examination of those situations in which psychological interpretation occurs led to the conclusion that it is best understood as an activity—one of many—which we engage in when we are attempting to institute some change and believe that this change might be facilitated if the situation were viewed in some different perspective than that presently held.

Two aspects of interpretation were described. The first consists of simple translation in which the language of the interpreter is applied to the data under consideration, and the second consists of the formulation of propositions, usually derived from theory, whose consequences are potentially verifiable.

Rejected was the idea that psychological interpretation is a means of uncovering the truth or that it is meaningful to think of it in such terms as depth, insight, and the unconscious. The criteria by which we evaluate interpretations are their consistency with the theory from which they are derived as well as with the observations to which they are applied, and their effectiveness in bringing about the change intended.

CHAPTER 2

The Logic and Assumptions

of the Interpretive Process

I SHALL be concerned in this chapter with the logic and assumptions implicit in the interpretive process and shall leave for the next chapter a discussion of the principles followed. To borrow some terms from law, the logic I am to discuss is a *de facto* logic rather than a *de jure* one. It came into being in an evolutionary way and has rarely been made explicit. No one has ever explicitly given it assent. Nor has anyone expressed dissent. No one has asked what the alternatives are, if there are any. It is hoped that by explicating the rules which seem to be followed in practice, the stage will be set for others to consider such questions and take whatever action may seem necessary.

The distinction between assumptions and principles which I make is simply this: one could, as indeed many do, engage in the interpretation of material and never be concerned with the assumptions upon which this activity rests. One could teach a system of interpretation and never mention the assumptions implicit in the system. On the other hand, the principles of the process are always explicit; they are what are taught. They are the rules of transformation. Both the assumptions and principles involved have certain implications for the form which research should take, and this chapter and the next will discuss these implications.

Logically, another distinction may be made between assumptions and principles. This is one of priority of development and permanence. The assumptions of the interpretive process are both prior to the principles and more permanent. New principles may be developed; old principles may be discarded. But the assumptions remain the same, and all principles must satisfy them. Thus research, while governed by the assumptions of the interpretive process, poses no imminent threat to them; it is only the principles that are vulnerable. Of course, should a sufficient number of instances accumulate in which tests of principles of interpretation were negative, we would begin to call into question the validity of the underlying assumptions.

The Semantic and Propositional Aspects of Interpretation

In the previous chapter I observed that there were two aspects to the interpretive process, the bringing into play of a different language system in the description of events, and the formulation of propositional statements in the terms of this language system. It will be convenient to have terms for each of these two aspects, and so I shall refer to the first as the *semantic aspect* of interpretation and to the second as the *propositional aspect* of interpretation. Following Morris' (1938) definition of semantics as that aspect of his theory of signs dealing "with the relation of signs to their designata and so to the objects which they may or do denote," I shall understand the semantic aspect of interpretation to be concerned only with the relations between words and their referents. As such it is concerned with the application of rules that determine "under which conditions a sign is applicable to an object or situation," and that "correlate signs and situations denotable by the signs" (Morris, 1938). Therefore, to decide whether or not a particular act should be called hostile is a semantic problem, in that it depends upon whether or not the act meets the criteria for the application of this designation according to our rules.[1] Truth is in no sense an issue here; we may only question the acceptability of the rules and the correctness of their application. On the other hand, to state a proposition, for example, "He becomes hostile whenever his masculinity is questioned," is simply to formulate a sentence that may be judged as true or false (Cohen & Nagel, 1934); truth does become an issue for the propositional aspect of interpretation. If we remember that "true" and "false" are not being used in an absolute sense, but rather as judgments always conditional upon a given frame of reference and context, there need be no fear of misunderstanding when we speak of the semantic and propositional aspects of interpretation.

There are two additional ways in which the semantic and propositional aspects of psychological interpretation differ from each other. These might become more apparent if we consider some additional examples of each. A mother reports being extremely anxious about her child's health and cares for him in such a way that severe restrictions are put upon his play activity and independence. To say that this is an

1 It is evident that the processes involved in the semantic aspect of the interpretive process could be termed "perception," "classification," or "instantiation" (Sarbin, Taft, & Bailey, 1960). I prefer to use the term "semantic" over any of these to describe this aspect of interpretation, in order to emphasize the point that this is a problem in language usage and analysis.

instance of overprotection represents the semantic aspect of interpretation; to say that this mother fundamentally rejects her child represents the propositional aspect of interpretation. The former represents one way of describing certain phenomena and cannot as such be judged true or false except insofar as the rules of transformation were misapplied, while the latter represents an assertion that is presumably susceptible to empirical verification.

Let us consider one more example, this time in connection with dream interpretation, contrasting the semantic and propositional aspects of interpretation. A 27-year-old man, who was being seen in therapy because of his inability to derive sexual satisfaction from his relations with his wife, to whom he had been married for three years, reported the following dream: "I am in a florist's shop and looking for a bouquet. After searching for some time I find myself looking into the case where the flowers are kept. This case is very low so that I must get down on my knees to look into it. I find a light switch in the case and turn the light on and then stick my head in to look around. The case is cold, damp, and empty, except for one withered bouquet in a far corner. At this point I woke up."

I shall not discuss the principles involved in the interpretation of this dream since these are covered in the next chapter, but instead move right into interpretation, distinguishing between the semantic and propositional aspects as I do so. The bouquet for which the patient is searching represents sexual satisfaction (semantic aspect). The case which he finally turns to and investigates, describing it as cold, damp, and empty, represents his conception of his wife's genitalia and its ability to provide him with sexual gratification (semantic aspect). The whole dream suggests hostility toward his wife and a denial on the patient's part of any responsibility for his failure in deriving sexual gratification (propositional aspect). He sees the entire sexual problem as dependent upon some change in his wife (propositional aspect). If we were predisposed to considering persons' locations on the psycho-analytic scale of psychosexual development, we would say that this man is fixated at a pregenital level because of his refusal to accept any responsibility and because of his lack of concern with his wife's own sexual satisfaction. This last assertion also represents a proposition, since there are other behaviors that are presumed to be associated with fixation at the pregenital level, and so it is possible to judge this assertion as true or false depending upon whether these other behaviors are manifested by this individual.

It should be noted that in each example, the semantic aspect of interpretation was concerned with ways of describing events or behaviors, while the propositional aspect was concerned either with assertions of relationships between these events or with assessments of the personality of the person involved. Having subjected all the available data to the semantic aspect of interpretation, we find ourselves in a position to generate propositional statements, and these are of a relational nature generally having implications for the assessment of personality along some theoretical or practical dimensions.

The recognition of this difference in function between the semantic and propositional aspects of interpretation is important when we are engaging in the study of a particular individual. If our task is to provide an analysis of his personality—that is, to provide a series of statements about *him* —it becomes clear that we have not accomplished this until we have carried our interpretive analysis through the propositional stage. In many instances the proposition may be implicit in the statements arising at the semantic stage, but not in all. Thus, although we might characterize a mother's treatment of her child as overprotective, the implications of this for her own personality and attitudes toward her child still remain to be spelled out. Similarly, to describe certain behaviors of an individual as dependent is not equivalent to describing the individual as dependent, for dependent behavior may be manifested in many instances by persons who could not appropriately be described as dependent. Until the proposition has been stated, we have no indications of what to expect of the individual in the future or of how to rationalize his behavior of the past.

On the other hand, in therapy it may be sufficient for our purposes to remain at the semantic stage in many instances. To point out to our emotionally starved patient that her overeating represents a substitute for love and affection may be sufficient to make this behavior somewhat less accessible to her, while to inform her that she is fixated at the oral level may only provide her with an opening gambit at her next bridge party, leaving her as omnivorous as ever. However, this involves questions of how and when to interpret as well as how interpretation affects behavior, and these will be taken up in later chapters.

The second point to be made about the difference between the semantic and propositional aspects of interpretation involves the extent to which each is dependent upon theory; it is the propositional aspect that is the more dependent upon the structure of the theory in question. For it is the syntax of the theory, however loose it might be, that justifies the syntax of the proposition. The propositional statements we generate with regard to a particular case are only special instances of the propositions embodied by our theory. The propositional aspect always involves "going beyond the information given," to borrow an expression from Bruner (1957), while the semantic aspect simply involves a transformation of the data. In this leap from the data to the proposition our only guide is the theory, sometimes in the guise of "common sense," sometimes as elaborate (or simple) as a mathematical model, sometimes inchoate, but always the theory. It therefore becomes difficult to discuss in detail the propositional aspect of interpretation without recourse to the discussion of specific theories.

Since my concern is with an examination of the logic of psychological interpretation rather than with the espousal of any particular theory, I shall be most concerned with the assumptions and principles involved in the semantic aspect of psychological interpretation. The propositional aspect, being a particularization of the propositions of the theory, follows fairly readily once the events under consideration have been translated into the terms of the theory. I shall, however, have occasion to discuss cases where propositions seem to be more empirically than theoretically rooted.

To summarize the distinction that I see between the semantic and propositional aspects of interpretation, the former represents the substitution of one language system for another at the descriptive level and cannot be adjudged true or false, while the latter leads to assertions in this new language system that may be so adjudged. While the semantic aspect is concerned primarily with statements about events, the propositional aspect involves statements about relationships between events and about individuals. Whether one must carry psychological interpretation through both phases depends upon his purposes in a given instance. And finally, I have noted that while the semantic aspect utilizes the language of a given theory, it is the propositional aspect which is more dependent upon the structure of the theory.

It should be clear to the reader that I am not undertaking to lay down or endorse a set of dicta to be followed in psychological interpretation. Rather, I am attempting to explicate those rules that seem to be used in practice. In effect, what I propose to do in this chapter is to peer over the shoulder of a hypothetical psychologist as he engages in interpretation. I shall attempt here to make explicit those assumptions that seem to be implicit in practice without any judgment as to their validity or utility.

While I have previously described the semantic aspect of psychological interpretation as the substitution of one language system for another one, in understanding how this operates I shall need to distinguish between a class and the name of the class. For when we substitute one language system for another in describing an event we are in effect assigning that event to a particular class of events all bearing the same designation in the new language system.

The distinction between conjunctive and disjunctive classes

A class consists of a group of events all having at least one characteristic in common, which serves as the criterion for membership in it. Criteria for class membership may be stringent or lenient, complex or simple, depending upon the attributes and the possible relations between them which we set up as our definition of the class. While a single property is sufficient for the definition of a class, most significant classes in psychological interpretation involve several properties. Where this is the case, for an event to be assigned to a particular class, in some instances it is required that it possess all the properties contained in the definition of the class, while in others it may be sufficient that it possess only some of the properties contained in the definition of the class. The former, following Bruner, Goodnow, and Austin (1956), we may refer to as *conjunctive classes* (for example, both properties A *and* B must be present in order to qualify for class membership), while the latter may be referred to as *disjunctive classes* (the possession of either A *or* B is sufficient to satisfy the criterion for class membership). While Bruner, Goodnow, and Austin (1956), in a different context, define a third class, a *relational class,* where membership is based on the existence of some particular relationship between attributes, there seems to be no reason why, as Price (1953) suggests, relationships themselves cannot be treated as properties, either present or absent in any given instance, and thus handled under the conjunctive–disjunctive schema.

To illustrate what has been said with regard to classes, let me take a single item of behavior and see first how interpretation moves it from one class to another as we shift language systems, then consider the implications of the conjunctive–disjunctive distinction I have introduced. The behavior is that of requesting advice from others. When an individual engages in this behavior to a great extent, the layman might in characterizing it assign it to the class "never thinking for oneself," or, if he is more kindly disposed to the individual in question, to the class "respect for the opinions of others." Taking the latter class, this would include other behaviors also, such as, perhaps, wide reading of editorial opinion although not necessarily forming an opinion in sympathy with the leading editorial opinion, and engaging in discussion of controversial issues with people of divergent points of view. On the other hand, the psychologist who observes this item of behavior to be a frequently occurring one for the individual may assign it to the class "dependency." In this class it would in all probability part company from some of the other behaviors with which it had been lumped by the layman, and instead find itself treated similarly to such behaviors as vacillation in decision-making, conforming behavior, and refusal to volunteer to take responsibility. From an item of behavior to be fostered, it has become one to be coped with and controlled if possible. Clearly the classes we have available in our language system, and the classes to which events are assigned, make a difference.

It should also be obvious that there would be no point in arguing whether this item of behavior really represents an instance of "dependency" or "never thinking for oneself," or "respect for the opinions of others." These are matters of definition that can be resolved only by an enumeration of the attributes necessary for inclusion in each class. Where the criteria for two classes are coextensive, which is rarely the case, we have synonyms and it should make no difference which term is used; in all other instances one must ultimately choose the language system, or class within that system, that one feels will be most useful for one's purposes.

In some instances where two language systems are being compared, it will be found that the definition of a particular class in one language includes all the attributes required for membership in a certain class in the other language plus additional attributes that might serve to define yet another class in the latter language. Where this is found to be the case, we may say that the former language has greater generality or subsumptive power than the latter. This is frequently observed as we move from the language of the psychologist to that of the layman, and from the language of the genotype to that of the phenotype. It is the subsumptive power of a language that is responsible for its ability to describe phenomena economically. It is also this power that imposes whatever lawfulness we observe upon the universe.

The first task facing the interpreter of psychological material is that of analyzing the event into its component attributes. His theoretical language tells him what attributes are criteria for inclusion in each of the many classes covered by that language, and so it is only for the presence or absence of these attributes that any given event is searched. Some other theoretical language may include other attributes in its class definitions, but for all practical purposes, as we scan the universe we are blind to all attributes other than those considered significant by our own language system.

Having analyzed the to-be-interpreted event into its component attributes, the interpreter then scans the various theoretical classes available to him and attempts to match the event with one of these on the basis of class membership requirements. It is at this point that it becomes apparent that while conjunctive classes increase the stringency of their criteria for membership as the number of attributes required is increased, simplicity in application of the criteria also increases. For while it may be harder to satisfy the requirements for the presence of six attributes than for two, it also becomes relatively easier to recognize instances of failure to satisfy the criteria where six attributes must all be present than when two are required. On the other hand, in the case of a disjunctive class, as the number of attributes that might serve as alternative means of class entry increases the ease of gaining membership increases, but at the same time criterion complexity also increases—it becomes increasingly difficult to determine whether a given event is an exemplar of the class or not. For the absence of a single attribute is no longer a sufficient basis for exclusion from the class. Thus, as the number of disjunctive classes in a language system increases it appears to gain in flexibility but at the expense of increased probability of error of application due to increased complexity in application. That is, the rules the interpreter must use in working with disjunctive classes are considerably more complex than those for conjunctive classes. And as complexity increases, it is reasonable to expect error to increase as well. Consider, for example, the difference in rules by which an element may gain entry into either a conjunctive or a disjunctive class in which the three attributes *A, B,* and *C* serve to define the class. In the case of the conjunctive class there is a single rule: an element must possess all three attributes, *A, B,* and *C,* to gain membership. In the case of a disjunctive class, any one of the following conditions would serve to qualify an element for membership: *A, B, C, AB, BC,* and *ABC.*

I must confess now to that most ubiquitous of academic crimes, discussing the problem in terms of the abstract, ideal situation. The sad fact is that there is no theoretical language in use at this time which explicitly states all the attributes and their relations for each of the classes covered by that language. We have been describing a model of one part of the interpretive process. In most instances, it is only very poorly approximated in practice. One way of remedying this situation however, is that which we have here undertaken. For insofar as the model is accepted as reasonable, the disparity between it and the actual situation should serve as an incentive for those workers dependent upon it to work toward its improvement.

While it is difficult rigorously to define the criteria for class membership in any of the current theories of personality, it is possible to give examples of the two types of classes we have been discussing. It should, however, be apparent that we cannot in all cases be sure we are dealing with a disjunctive or conjunctive class if all of the elements entering into the criterion for membership are not made explicit. For what may appear to be a disjunctive class may in fact be a conjunctive class if it turns out that there is but a single attribute which must always be present before an event qualifies for membership. Where this becomes the case, all the other attributes become irrelevant from the standpoint of the criterion for membership.

The problem of disjunctive classes

Through the use of the concepts of reaction-formation and repression, psychoanalytic theory presents us with the prime example of a language system abounding with disjunctive classes. Let us take as an example the class that might be designated "hostility." What are its defining attributes? First we might note that they may be of a verbal or nonverbal nature. An insulting remark is an instance of hostility just as is a punch on the nose. Among the verbal attributes, it is not only culturally recognized abusive or insulting language that would qualify as a hostile event, but also any verbal response classified as such by the rules of some theory. We find, for example, that any percept in a Rorschach test protocol that contains a verb designating some form of destruction, or that involves the end product of the action of such a verb, would also be an instance of hostility (Elizur, 1949). Seeing a scowling face, an injured butterfly, an animal about to devour its prey, or even a pair of pliers, would all be instances of hostility by the rules of Rorschach content analysis. But the behavior may not contain any of these attributes and still qualify as hostility. The asking of a question of another individual that results in his discomfiture may qualify as hostility regardless of the content of the question. The expression of a dissenting opinion may qualify as hostility, and this again regardless of the content of the point under consideration. When we invoke the concept of reaction-formation, it then becomes possible for extreme concern for the well-being of another person, whether this is expressed verbally or otherwise, to be considered an expression of hostility. By an analogous process, inversion, dreams involving the expression of love or admiration may be considered hostile dreams. Finally, if we admit repression into the picture, a TAT protocol completely devoid of themes involving hostility (as we have thus far defined it) may be taken as an instance of repressed hostility. Obviously this class of events is not a very exclusive one. One might also wonder whether it is a very useful one.

It might be argued that I have chosen an unrepresentative concept or that the class is not actually as broad as I have presented it, but rather that there are a number of smaller concepts, such as verbal hostility, physical hostility, and repressed hostility. The question of representativeness is not crucial since the term was only chosen for illustration, not as a basis for evaluating the theory. In addition, I know of no way of selecting representative concepts from any theory. But the question of whether there are not actually distinguishable many subclasses of the more general class of hostility deserves more extended comment because the problem of subclasses is a general one and always begs the question of the meaningfulness of such breakdowns.

In ordinary discourse it is certainly true that we speak of various kinds of hostility. In many instances in practice we also distinguish between different types of hostility. Where this is the case we are certainly justified in maintaining that there are many kinds or classes of hostility. But in some instances, for many purposes, these classes are collapsed into a single class. And this is not, of course, confined to the concept of hostility. Thus, when we assert the proposition "This is a hostile person," or its contrary, as we frequently do, we act as though there is a single class, hostility, which we consult in some fashion in arriving at our conclusion.

Disjunctiveness of classes may be the price that we have to pay for increasing the range of applicability of a language system. That is, as we move from one medium to another we frequently find certain attributes which are by their very nature and that of the medium, impossible of occurrence. For example, as we move from the actual home situation of a patient to his TAT protocol the probability of his exhibiting a behavior which would result in physical injury or destruction decreases markedly. If we wish to use the term hostility in both media, we must be prepared to accept a disjunctive criterion.

The question arises, however, of whether a term retains the same meaning as it is applied alternately to material from different media. Although disjunctive classes are a logically meaningful type of class, are they psychologically meaningful as well? Does hostility, for example, mean the same thing when we use it to designate a verbal event occurring in the context of a TAT protocol as it does when it is used to designate a behavioral event between a parent and child? While this question has been raised in connection with our discussion of disjunctive classes as a type of class, it must also be asked in the case of individual conjunctive classes as well.

For while the conjunctive class appears to have a much more stringent criterion for membership, we must remember that this criterion, as in the case of disjunctive classes, is an analytical one, and the question we have posed about meaning is an empirical one.

It is here that logic must make its obeisance to reality. And it is also at this point of our discussion that we begin to glimpse the first broad outlines of a research program which must be undertaken if our language system is ever to achieve the univocality required by the canons of science and the demands of the clinic. For, while logic requires only that our definition of a class be such that it can be applied without exception and without ambiguity within some realm of discourse, unless we are interested in the development of classes as a purely intellectual exercise, we must make additional demands upon the classes we have defined. These demands are dictated by the assumptions and purposes of the interpretive process. We have discussed the purposes of interpretation previously; let us now turn to its major assumptions.

ASSUMPTIONS OF THE INTERPRETIVE PROCESS

The equivalence of events within a given class

This assumption states that all members of a given class are in some way, other than their having satisfied the criterion for admission, equivalent with each other. This may be through a common cause or source, or it may be through a common implication or effect. This assumption is a broad and crucial one in the operation of the interpretive process.

It is this assumption that is made, for example, when the seeing of eyes on the Rorschach is taken as equivalent to complaints of being watched, and used as a basis for inferring suspiciousness and paranoid tendencies. Indeed, it is this assumption that underlies the entire rationale for subjecting a projective test protocol to interpretation and deriving inferences about the nontest behavior of the individual. For in all such cases, as we shall see later, the events of the test in question are assigned to the same classes as nontest events. For all intents and purposes, the test situation is treated as a miniature life situation.

It is this same assumption that justifies the search for a frustrating agent when hostility is observed, whether it be in the form of physical aggression on the part of a child or verbal vituperation from an adult. If our theory contains the proposition that frustration leads to aggression, then according to this assumption, it matters not what form this aggression takes; we expect to be able to trace it back to some event interpreted as frustrating. Of course the theory may contain other propositions relating hostility or aggression to other classes of events as well as frustrating ones, and in this case should no frustrating event be found the search would be continued for events falling into these other categories.

Examples of the operation of this assumption could be easily multiplied. The point is that this assumption lies at the very basis of the entire interpretive enterprise and that unless the classes contained in our language system satisfy it—that is, unless the events contained in them behave in accordance with this assumption—interpretation will lead to nothing but confusion and dismay. The problem is that of determining when the equivalence assumption is satisfied and when it is not. In some instances the answer to this question will lead to a change in our language system, in others the language may remain essentially the same but the assumption will be applied less broadly. This latter result would, of course, be tantamount to a modification of our language also. But this would be in the direction of greater precision of application rather than radical revision of classes and at most would result in a multiplication of classes.

Research implications. The form a research program would take is easy to specify; the content of it less so, since this would depend upon the theory involved and the experimenter's ingenuity. Fundamentally, such a program would consist of formulating hypotheses concerning the relations between certain classes of events. These hypotheses represent deductions from theory, however crude such a theory might be. Following the formulation of the hypotheses, we would test their validity in terms of various exemplars of the classes that form their terms. If our hypothesis were that frustration leads to aggression, we would test this hypothesis in terms of specific events which we take as exemplars of frustration and aggression. If the hypothesis gained support in the experiment, we would accept these events as members of the classes to which we had assigned them. If not, we would question their claim to such membership.

The difference between the type of research program we are suggesting here and that commonly found in the literature should be obvious. For our purposes we do not question the theory. We accept this as given and question only the legitimacy of assignment of specific events to given classes, or the definition of the classes. Theories do not stand or fall with this research, but definitions do. Although hypotheses are formulated, it is not their validity that is at stake. They merely provide the means of testing the validity of our use of a particular language system. Clearly, if over a period of time it became apparent that it was impossible to find sets of events to fill the classes of the theory so as to yield valid hypotheses, we would begin to suspect the theory.

In form, the research undertaken to evaluate a set of definitions may not differ from that undertaken to evaluate a theory. The difference occurs only in what we take for granted and how we use our results. In all research one must begin at some point that one does not question. For those who are testing a theory, it is the form of the data that is unquestioned. For those who would test the legitimacy of certain events as claimants to the role of data in the theory, it is the theory that must remain unquestioned. I am not suggesting that theories go untested. It is simply that one cannot ask both questions at the same time.

I do not propose to review research bearing on the questions that I have raised regarding the definition of classes. This is best done within the context of the particular theory or language system that one is interested in evaluating. But we might consider two examples as illustrations of my conception of the form of research required and how it differs from that done to test a theory. The first is by Wertheimer (1953) and is concerned with the legitimacy of the "eye" content response on the Rorschach as a member of the class that might be termed "suspiciousness" or perhaps more precisely, "delusions of surveillance." Usual Rorschach practice takes the eye percept as an indication of suspiciousness on the grounds that the individual's percepts reveal, among other things, his major preoccupations and that anyone who sees eyes must be preoccupied with being watched by eyes. Because suspiciousness —or more accurately, events taken as exemplars of this class —is frequently found associated with paranoia and paranoid schizophrenia, themselves class names, a number of eye percepts occurring in a Rorschach protocol is regarded as an indication of paranoid trends at the very minimum. Wertheimer's research was an attempt to determine whether this was justified.

Wertheimer examined 230 Rorschach protocols of mental hospital patients for the occurrence of the word "eyes" and the number of eye responses. Comparing paranoids and paranoid schizophrenics with seven other diagnostic groups, he did not find that the paranoid patients produced significantly more eye content responses, as one would expect from the usual criterion for the diagnosis of paranoia and paranoid schizophrenia. Wertheimer concluded that there does not appear to be a one-to-one correspondence between behavior and Rorschach signs—another way of saying that it is questionable whether all Rorschach signs fit into the classes to which they have been assigned. He did not, however, question the belief that suspiciousness is a characteristic of paranoid individuals, nor did he, as he might have, question the definitions of his diagnostic groups. These points he rightly took as given for the purposes of his research. The hypothesis was not supported, but this had no relevance for any theory of paranoia or paranoid schizophrenia, only for the interpretation or classification of one item of behavior.

On the other hand, in the work of Blum (1949) we have an example of research in which the form of the data, and their interpretation, is unquestioned, and it is a theory that is at stake. In attempting to investigate the validity of the psychoanalytic theory of psychosexual development, Blum made use of a series of cartoon drawings of a dog, Blacky, in a number of situations assumed to represent various critical stages and significant aspects of psychosexual development, for which individuals were asked to make up stories and answer a series of questions. There was no questioning as to whether a given cartoon and the response associated with it represented oral sadism or not; this was taken as given. The question was simply whether responses to this particular card conformed or did not conform to an hypothesis derived from psychoanalytic theory. Blum's conclusions were that according to his reading of Fenichel (1945), the research using the data obtained via the Blacky cartoons supported the psychoanalytic theory of psychosexual development. Should the data not have conformed to expectations, presumably it would have been the theory which would come out the loser, not Blacky. Thus, in the original investigation by Blum it was not a language system and its usage which was at stake; it was assumed that the language system was developed to the point that an event classified as "castration anxiety" was equivalent to any other event that might also be so classified. The only question was whether a correlation existed between, let us say, castration anxiety and masturbatory guilt among males.

So encouraged apparently was Blum and some of his followers by the outcome of his original investigation, that the instrument developed to investigate the theory was accorded the status of a "test." From this point on research on the Blacky Pictures was no longer concerned with the theory of psychosexual development; this was now inviolate. Instead, subsequent studies of the validity of the Blacky Pictures represented, in certain instances at least, questions about their interpretation. A good example of this kind of research, which quite clearly is concerned with determining whether the assumption of the equivalence of all members of a given class was satisfied, was one in which amount of ice cream consumed was correlated with "oral eroticism" as inferred from the test (Blum & Miller, 1952). Here the question was whether variance in consumption of ice cream could be accounted for by variance in response on a particular dimension of the test. If the correlation exists this is presumptive evidence that the language system is being used appropriately vis-à-vis the Blacky Pictures. In this instance it is taken for granted that consumption of ice cream is correctly classified as indicative of oral eroticism. The question is, have responses to Cartoon #1 also been correctly identified. Here, should the correlation fail to materialize, it is not the theory which is in danger, but membership of this particular event in a given class of the theory. Thus, in the Adventures of Blacky, Blum has provided us not only with an excursion through the nether world of psychoanalytic theory, but also with an interesting example of theory and instrument alternately occupying the roles of agent and reagent vis-à-vis each other!

The non-independence of members within a class

The assumption that events belonging to a given class are not independent of each other has far-reaching implications for the interpretive process. It is this assumption, whether or not stated in the form of a principle, that underlies many of the predictions made from projective material, interviews, and observational material. Frequently it is stated in terms of one of its major implications: that the probability that an event in a given class will occur increases as the number of events already observed in that class increases. Thus the more events we have classified as hostile occurring in the case of a given individual, the more certain we are that when placed in a given situation he will contribute another event belonging to that class. The more "signs" we have of "dependency" the more certain we feel in calling an individual "dependent." The more F- responses on the Rorschach, which we might interpret as instances of perceptual distortion, the more instances of perceptual distortion we expect of the individual in his non-Rorschach behavior. These expectations all depend upon the assumption that instances which we label "hostile," "dependent," and "perceptual distortion," are, in each case, not independent of each other, so that with the observation of each instance there is an increment in the probabilities that another and similar instance will be observed under suitable circumstances.[2]

We find this assumption explicitly stated by Lindzey (1952) in connection with the interpretation of the TAT, when he states as one of the assumptions made in determining revealing portions of stories: "Themes that are recurrent in a series of stories are particularly apt to mirror the impulses and conflicts of the story-teller." Obviously one would not be interested in the frequency of occurrence of themes unless this could be used in some way in the predictive venture we call psychodiagnosis. The non-independence assumption per-

2 This assumption is also involved in the so-called "gambler's fallacy," although its implications for the gambler are just the reverse: that as a sequence of occurrences of a particular event (such as heads on a coin, or losses in a game of chance) increases in length, the probability of another event of the same type occurring diminishes. This, of course, could hold true only if the events were not independent of each other.

mits the prediction to be made that x need will manifest itself in the subsequent behavior of an individual to the extent that it has manifested itself in his previously observed behavior. Thus, since—according to the assumption of equivalence of members of a class—we make no distinction between the need as manifested in TAT themes and as manifested in other situations, we may predict the operation (or probability of operation), of a given need or disposition from its frequency of occurrence in a TAT protocol.

There would seem to be some support for this assumption from the vast amount of research in learning theory, whereby it is generally found that the frequency of occurrence of a response increases (or alternatively, its probability of occurrence increases) with increased training and reinforcement. Thus if one wished to predict whether responses A_1 or A_2 would occur on trial $(n + 1)$, and if he did not have available to him the history of reinforcements for each of these responses, his best bet would be to observe the relative frequency of the occurrence of each during the n preceding trials and predict the occurrence of that response which had occurred most frequently in the past. This is precisely what the clinician does, albeit in a looser fashion. His tests, interviews, or other sources of information constitute the "n trials" from which he will make his prediction for the "$(n + 1)$st trial."

Of course, the language of interpretation does not always sound like the language of the learning theorist. In many instances the pronouncement of the clinician will not sound like a prediction. Frequently, in fact, it sounds more like an indictment! But we should understand that when he says that this man is dependent and that man hostile, this one suffering from unresolved infantile dependency needs and that one overcompensating for feelings of inferiority, he is in each instance making an implicit statement about the future behavior of these hapless individuals. As Sarbin (1941) has pointed out, a diagnostic statement has meaning only when it has a referent in the future—when it provides a prediction. To call a man dependent is to say that there is a higher probability that in a given situation he will manifest behavior which we will classify as dependent rather than independent. To say that he is compensating for feelings of inferiority is, likewise, to say that we predict the occurrence of more instances of behavior on his part which can be characterized as compensatory for feelings of inferiority than as noncompensatory.

It may be noted that the equivalence assumption and the present one are not entirely independent of each other. Their relationship is an asymmetrical one, whereby an event that satisfied the nonindependence assumption would also satisfy the equivalence assumption, but the equivalence assumption could be satisfied without any implication for the assumption of nonindependence. Recognition of the nature of this relationship is of primary importance in the formulation, design, and interpretation of research, since it means that in some cases the data would have implications for how well both assumptions are satisfied, while in other instances only for how well the equivalence assumption is satisfied.

Research implications. Let us now consider the research implications of the nonindependence assumption. We might note at the outset that this assumption, like the equivalence assumption, is theoretically neutral. We find it reflected in interpretations made from the most diverse points of view. However, unlike the equivalence assumption, which was dependent to a certain extent upon theory for hypotheses that would provide the tests for the legitimacy of assignment of events to a given class, the assumption of nonindependence requires no such theoretical substrate for its testing. Theory again provides the language or classes to which events are assigned, but that is all. To determine whether the assumption has been satisfied, we proceed in a straightforward empirical fashion.

The form which research here takes may be schematically illustrated by the following list of steps, which begin with the establishment of a class or term of the language:

1. Establishment of a class k, with criteria for membership in it.
2. For each of N individuals, the assignment of $(n - x)$ events occurring in situations $s_1, s_2, \ldots s_n$, to this class k where x represents those events observed which do not meet the membership criteria.
3. For each of the above N individuals then placed in situation s_{n+1}, the observation of the frequency of occurrence or nonoccurrence of an event e meeting criteria for membership in class k.
4. The correlation over N cases of $(n - x)$ with the frequency of occurrence or nonoccurrence of e.

Where the obtained correlation is statistically significant it may be asserted that the assignment of events to the class in question has been such as to satisfy the nonindependence assumption. Where the correlation fails to reach significance this may imply one of two things: (a) That although the criteria are applied correctly, the events classified by them simply do not form a class which satisfies the nonindependence assumption, or, (b) that the criteria have been incorrectly applied so that the number of events assigned to the class for each individual is incorrect. In the latter instance further explication of the criteria is all that is called for, while in the former, a re-evaluation of the language system would seem indicated.

Deciding between these two alternatives is not an easy matter and is not wisely done on the basis of a single investigation. To a large extent, the decision must be based on a review of the findings utilizing a given language system in a large number of studies. Where the weight of the evidence is positive this would suggest that in a particular study such as that outlined above where negative findings occurred it was the application of the criterion which was at fault rather than the language system. If the results of a given study should be another in a long series yielding negative results, it would seem time to call into question the utility of the language system. Unfortunately, in choosing between these alternatives, there are no statistical guideposts as there are in hypothesis testing. In the final analysis, the temperament of the individual researcher undoubtedly has some influence—indeterminate, but nonetheless there—on his treatment of negative results.

In stating that the nonindependence assumption implies that the probability of observing the occurrence of an event belonging to a given class is an increasing function of the number of events already belonging to that class, we have said nothing about the nature of this function. And it is to this that much basic research must eventually be devoted. The problems here are exceedingly complex, although they have been for the most part ignored. It is quite likely that one reason they have not been given their due is that interpretive systems, such as they are, have not been concerned with the basic logic of the process, but more with the particular theoretical language and the rules for its use.

There are two interrelated problems here. The first is that given a number of events all fitting the criterion for membership in a particular class, they may vary in their potency as contributors to the probability that the next event observed will also belong to that class. For example, given a mildly derisive comment upon someone's ability and an instance of physical assault, it seems reasonable that the pugnacious individual would be more likely, on the next occasion where aggressive behavior is a possibility, to exhibit such behavior than the derisive commentator, other things being equal. The theoretical and research problem here is the development of a system of weighting events for what might be termed their "incremental probability implication."

No system has explicitly addressed itself to the problem of the differential incremental probability implications of events falling within the realm of discourse by that system, but we might point to one case as an illustration of what might be considered a limited attempt in this direction. This is the work by Watkins and Stauffacher (1952) and those following them (Powers & Hamlin, 1955) in the development of a measure of deviant verbalization for the Rorschach. Beginning with Rapaport's (1946) listing of illustrations of deviant thinking on the Rorschach, Watkins and Stauffacher developed a system of weighting such instances so that the "more deviant" instances were given higher weights, and so that by summing all the weighted instances of deviant verbalization in a given protocol one obtained a "delta score." This score has been found (Watkins & Stauffacher, 1952; Powers & Hamlin, 1955) to vary with the judged severity of psychopathology.

Interpreted within the present framework, the delta score represents in essence an estimate of the probability that the next verbalization of a given individual will also be classed as deviant. That this score has been found to vary with judged psychopathology argues for the validity of this means of estimation and also possibly for the weight given to deviant verbalization in judging severity of psychopathology. But this work is limited in two ways. The first is that the delta weights for each type of deviant verbalization were arrived at in an a priori fashion, and the second is that the system is fairly well restricted to the verbalization which occurs in the Rorschach testing situation.

While the positive results obtained thus far testify to the good judgment of Watkins and Stauffacher in their assignment of weights, it is highly unlikely that their system contains the optimum weighting of the events they are concerned with. Ultimately, some refinement, empirically based, must be made.

That the deviant verbalization scoring system is restricted to the Rorschach testing situation may represent a temporary limitation. If deviant verbalization represents a psychologically meaningful classification, then it should be possible to extend the Watkins and Stauffacher system ultimately to the entire gamut of situations involving verbal behavior. This, in a sense, is analogous to the concept of validity generalization in psychometrics. Such an attempt at extension is necessary in the final analysis to answer the question of the range of applicability of the concept.

It may be possible to solve the problem of weighting so that each event may be given a score reflecting its incremental probability implication when considered in isolation, but this still poses problems concerning the shape of the curve relating the number of such events to the probability that the next event will also be similarly classified. This constitutes the second problem, namely, the possible interactions between events as they begin to accumulate. Such interactions may affect the probabilities and this effect may vary from class to class.

It is entirely possible that at different stages in the accumulation of events in a class, the addition of another event of a given incremental probability implication affects the total probability differently. In effect, what this means is that while we have spoken of events as possibly differing in their incremental probability implications (implying that these could be ascertained for each event), it is quite likely that these implications are modified by the point in event-accumulation where the new event occurs. Thus it becomes impossible to derive the probability of the occurrence of an event of a given class simply from a knowledge of the incremental probability implications of each of the events already belonging to the class; it becomes necessary to also know the influence of sheer number of events as well as the serial nature of the events. Knowing this, however, it should be possible to plot the curve relating number of events in a class to the probability of observing the occurrence of another event belonging to that class. We might refer to such a curve as an "event-occurrence probability function."

That the shape of event-occurrence probability functions may vary from one class of behavior to another poses yet another problem in this area. Broadly speaking, there are some classes of events which are socially acceptable, condoned, fought-for, and encouraged, while there are other classes for which the opposite is true. It would seem reasonable that such factors would play a significant role in determining the shapes of event-occurrence probability functions. There are, of course, other ways in which classes of events also differ, and a thorough program of research in this area would have to consider each of these in turn for their effects on the shape of the function.

Finally, there is some evidence already accumulating to suggest that the event-occurrence probability function for one class may be affected by that of another class. The most clear-cut evidence for this comes in recent work with the TAT and the relation between hostility and aggression as expressed in the TAT and as expressed overtly. Here, work by Mussen and Naylor (1954), by Purcell (1956), and by Lesser (1957), indicates that expectancy of punishment and the nature of this punishment are important factors determining whether or not the aggression found in the TAT proctocol will be predictive of aggression found in nontest situations.

It will have become obvious to the reader by this time that most of the research cited has been concerned with test interpretation. No apology need be offered for this; it simply reflects the rudimentary stage of research and conceptualization in this area. The most highly refined systems of interpretation to date have been constructed in connection with particular tests. It may be that this is where we must start, if for no other reason than that the test provides us with a somewhat restricted and simplified sample of behavior thereby permitting us to work out some of the problems which any interpretive system dealing with the still more complex events of the nontest situation must ultimately resolve. For it must be recognized that before the kind of research we have been discussing can be carried out, the language system to be used must have reached a fairly high degree of rigor.

The lawfulness of all behavior

This is the third and last assumption which we make in the interpretive process. Although it is the most fundamental of the three, and one not limited to the semantic aspect of interpretation, I have chosen to discuss it last since our major concerns have been with the research implications of our assumptions, and this assumption leads to no particular implication for research other than that it is a meaningful enterprise. For if we did not make this assumption there would be no point in performing any research; the results of any given study would have to be considered fortuitous and no generalizations would be possible. Indeed, if we did not make this assumption there would be no point in engaging in the interpretation of behavior, since it would be impossible to construct any language system having applicability beyond the specific case.

Freud's concept of psychic determinism represents but a special case of this more general assumption, an assumption which, in fact, is one of the foundation stones of the entire scientific enterprise. It should be clear that when the assertion is made that all behavior is motivated, this is an analytic statement, not an empirical one. It says in effect, that we will accept as one of the rules of the game that no behavior is completely fortuitous in its occurrence, that we will always look for an explanation of the behavior in terms of its antecedents and context of occurrence. The one explanation that is ruled out by this assumption is chance.

It is the assumption of lawfulness that justifies the serious investigation of such diverse forms of behavior as slips of the tongue, dreams, responses to ink blots, handwriting, and interpersonal relationships. Unfortunately, many workers in this area have confused—or at least failed to distinguish between—the assumption of lawfulness of behavior and the question of the *relevance* of the event for the problem at hand. As we pointed out earlier, the assumption of lawfulness is an analytic proposition which states that we will not write off any behavior as pure happenstance. It implies nothing about the relevance of the behavior for any particular problem. The matter of relevance can only be determined empirically.

Thus it becomes possible to accept the assumption of lawfulness of behavior and still write off some behavior as unworthy of our interest if we have reason to believe that this behavior is irrelevant for our purposes. It also becomes possible to rank-order behaviors in terms of their probability of relevance for our purposes. Therefore, while we may agree, for example, that behavior in a Rorschach testing situation, a TAT testing situation, a role-playing situation, and a parent-child interaction situation is all lawful we may see these as varying in their relevance for our treatment of a patient complaining of feelings of inadequacy as a parent. In this particular instance, from our knowledge and theory regarding stimulus generalization gradients, we would have some basis for ranking these behaviors for relevance, probably in the order in which they have just been presented, from least to most relevant. Of course, it becomes necessary to determine whether this ranking is correct in this particular case. But rather than making this determination for each case, an obviously inexpedient procedure, we would rely upon research findings in connection with similar cases.

The assumption of lawfulness of behavior plays a somewhat different role in connection with the semantic and propositional aspects of the interpretive process. With regard to the former, this assumption provides the justification for the expectation that the assumptions of equivalence and non-independence may be fulfilled given the proper set of classes, criteria, etc. With regard to the propositional aspect, it simply permits us to assert a given proposition with some assurance that we will be able to make a determination as to its truth or falsity. Without this assumption there would be no point in stating propositions since they represent assertions about the form which the lawfulness of behavior will take in a given case.

THE PROPOSITIONAL ASPECT AS ASSERTION OF RELATIONS

Once we go beyond the mere assignment of events to classes and make any statement bearing upon the implications of such assignments we are, in effect, making assertions regarding the relation between one set of events and another, i.e., we are formulating propositions. Sometimes these assertions deal only with the relations themselves, as when we say that John Jones becomes hostile with authority figures. Sometimes they deal instead with the implications of these relations or with the variables believed to account for them, as when we say that John Jones' hostility toward authority is responsible for his inability to successfully complete graduate school, or that it is due to his unhappy relationship with his father when he was a child. In either case, it is obvious that each of the assumptions (with the exception of the last) automatically leads to the formulation of propositions. And insofar as these propositions are determined only by the assumptions underlying the classification system, and not by any theoretical postulate, we may think of them as empirically rooted. Where, however, it is the postulates of our theory that lead us to expect a relationship to exist between one class of events and another, the proposition is theoretically rooted. But in either event, to state a proposition is to make an assertion concerning relations.

As an assertion of relations, propositions may have yet another source. This is in the direct observation or reporting of an event sequence. Having observed a sequence of events, and assuming that all behavior is lawful, it is reasonable to expect that this observed sequence represents a lawful relation between the events in question. This may in some instances lead to an assertion of a causal relationship and in others to a covariant one, such that given an event of one class we expect some event of the other class to occur. These are also empirically rooted propositions. The paradigm here might be taken as the correlational study in psychometrics where we attempt to determine the best set of signs or weighting of scores to predict a given criterion. Theory plays an exceedingly minor role.

Let us consider another example of what may be considered an empirically rooted proposition more closely related to the process of psychological interpretation and one, again, where the assertion is based upon the observing or reporting of a particular event sequence. A patient comes to the psychological clinic and reports that he is exceedingly anxious, has difficulty concentrating, sees what seem to be lights occasionally darting across his field of vision, and believes that his head jerks at times so that he is afraid of sitting in a barber chair for fear of being cut. These are all events which we might reasonably classify as anxiety reactions. The clinician obtains an elaboration of the complaint. When did it first occur? What seems to make it worse? And so on. The patient reports that his trouble seemed to start during the summer when he was taking an art course. He did not like the instructor; he felt uncomfortable in his presence. One day the instructor played music rather loudly as a kind of inspirational context for the class to paint in. The client began noticing that he had trouble breathing, his heart beat harder, he felt ill, left the classroom, and withdrew from the course the next day. Again, these are all events that would fit the rubric of anxiety reaction.

The clinician interpreted this event sequence as representing a near homosexual panic. What he was doing by this was making the assertion that given an event with homosexual connotations or homosexually evocative qualities, this patient reacts with extreme anxiety. In formulating this proposition the clinician was taking the art instructor as the antecedent event and classifying him as having homosexually evocative qualities for the patient. Although the clinician was not characterizing the art instructor as a homosexual, he did have some reason to believe that he was effeminate. Given this reported sequence in the context of the client's having reported difficulties in dating girls, the proposition seemed to be one worth investigating further. Such a proposition would fit our conception of an empirically based one.

Theory, however, does enter into even this proposition in two ways. The first, which we have pointed out before, is that of supplying the language system employed. The second is in sensitizing the clinician to certain event sequences. The theory we subscribe to acts as a perceptual tuning device. Had this clinician not been cognizant of theories in which homosexuality is treated as a source of threat and anxiety and in which various kinds of symptomatology are accounted for as reactions to, or attempts to cope with, this threat, it is doubtful that he would have been as quick to recognize the event sequence which led to his interpretation. It is, however, a telling commentary upon the inarticulate state of our current theories of personality and psychopathology that many clinicians believe that the event sequences he observes arise *sui generis*.

It should be evident that theoretically based propositions

do not stem only from explicitly, rigorously formulated networks of postulates: in many instances to say that a proposition is theoretically derived is only to distinguish it from one which is clearly empirically derived. In this connection, it might be well to note that Sarbin, Taft, and Bailey (1960) distinguish between four different sources of postulates: induction, construction, analogy, and authority. Their inductively derived postulates correspond to what I would prefer to label empirically rooted postulates, while their remaining three origins would produce what I have referred to as theoretically derived postulates. For our purposes I cannot find the justification for making as fine a distinction between the origins of nonempirically based propositions as they do.

The distinction between empirically and theoretically rooted propositions, although not always a clear-cut one, does have important implications for our evaluation of instances of their confirmation and disconfirmation. Leaving aside the problems discussed in connection with the semantic aspect of the interpretive process—all of which would need to be considered in any instance of disconfirmation—when a theoretically rooted proposition fails to be confirmed the failure redounds to the validity of the theory from which it stems. As instances of such disconfirmation accumulate the validity of the theory becomes increasingly suspect. On the other hand, when an empirically rooted proposition is disconfirmed the implications of this are specific to the clinician responsible for its formulation and the material he used in its formulation. As instances of disconfirmation of empirically rooted propositions build up for a given clinician, the only thing that suffers is his reputation as a clinician. Theory remains untouched.

Thus, the proposition asserting a relationship between paranoid tendencies and homosexuality—a theoretical proposition stemming from psychoanalytic theory—led our clinician to interpret the patient's difficulty in getting along with his same-sex peers as a defense against his latent homosexual impulses. Should this be disconfirmed we would be likely to suggest that the clinician consider some other theoretical position in analyzing personality dynamics. On the other hand, should his other interpretation (proposition) be disconfirmed we would suggest, among other things, that he consider more carefully the evidence he had for the event sequence he claimed to have isolated from the anamnesis. Were there not other factors in the case that might equally well have served as antecedents for the patient's anxiety attacks? Was he correct in his characterization of the art instructor? In his classification of the client's symptoms? Does this reflect some personal difficulty of his own?

For these reasons, it is worth making the distinction between empirically and theoretically based propositions, although it is, of course, recognized that a pure case of either does not exist in nature. Similarly, it is important to recognize that all propositions represent assertions of a relationship, although in many instances the members of the relationship as well as its nature are not easily determined. For it is only by making such distinctions that we are able to isolate those aspects of the verbal behavior of the clinician which are interpretive and propositional from those which may be only semantic, and from those which, properly considered, are not interpretive at all.

We began this chapter by characterizing the logic of psychological interpretation as *de facto*. By this I meant to imply simply that it had never been formalized and stated explicitly, but rather that its claim to consideration rests in the fact that it is implicit in the behavior of the psychologist when he begins to interpret content. One of the difficulties in presenting such a logic is that one's accuracy and comprehensiveness depends entirely upon the range of behavior he has observed and his skill in abstracting from these observations. With no attempts at modesty, I make no special claims for the completeness of the foregoing presentation. In fact, depending as it does upon the practice of the interpreter, it must of necessity be incomplete. For so long as the rules of the game are not formalized and stated explicitly, every player may write his own. Thus the logic of the interpretive process grows and changes to some extent as each new worker enters the field. Nevertheless, it may be hoped that the present enterprise will have some salutary influence upon the quality of this plasticity in the future.

SUMMARY

Psychological interpretation, which we have conceived of as a process involving the bringing to bear of an alternate frame of reference or language system upon a set of observations or behaviors, was seen in this chapter as consisting of two aspects that we have labeled *semantic* and *propositional*. The semantic aspect of the interpretive process is concerned with the assignment of events to classes contained in the language system of the interpreter and as such is only concerned with the means by which these classes are defined and assignments are made. As such, theory plays a very minor role in this aspect of the interpretive process. On the other hand, the propositional aspect of the interpretive process deals with the assertion of relationships between events and classes of events. Propositions may be mainly inductively (or empirically) derived or mainly theoretically derived, although it is recognized that here theory is often of the sketchiest sort. The outcome of the propositional aspect was seen as subject to judgments of true or false within the language system being used, while that of the semantic aspect could only be judged as correct or incorrect with reference to the appropriateness of usage of the classes defined by the system.

A distinction between conjunctive and disjunctive classes was made, the former term referring to classes in which elements claiming membership must all possess the same set of attributes in common, while in the latter all elements need not possess all the attributes defining the class. Problems involved in using disjunctive classes in psychological interpretation derive from the greater complexity in the rules by which events are assigned to these classes, with the likelihood of greater error in application, and the question of whether events gaining membership by alternative means have identical psychological value.

Three assumptions were presented as being implicit in the interpretive process. These were: (1) The equivalence of events within a given class, in other words, the assumption that events within a particular class are interchangeable with each other so far as their psychological implications are concerned; (2) The nonindependence of members within a class; the assumption that the probability of an additional event occurring which may be assigned to a given class increases as the number of events already assigned to that class increases; and (3) the lawfulness of all behavior. The third assumption is common to all scientific endeavor and is one without which psychological interpretation would be a meaningless activity. The first two assumptions, on the other hand, have particular implications for the interpretive process and these were described, together with the forms that research would take to determine if they were being met by a particular interpretive system.

CHAPTER 3.

The Process and Principles

of Interpretation at the Semantic Stage

In the previous chapter the assumptions implicit in the processs of psychological interpretation were considered. These are the assumptions that must be made if one is to make sense out of the process of psychological interpretation and that must be satisfied if any order is to be observed in the outcomes of this process. The principles now to be considered are those that guide the interpreter as he actually takes his raw material —dreams, verbalizations of all sorts, expressive movements, and so on—and places a new construction upon them, an interpretation in the terms of a language different from that of the source of this raw material. Some of these principles have been stated explicitly in various forms in handbooks concerned with the interpretation of dreams or projective test material. The present plan is to state these principles in somewhat more general terms so that it will be obvious that their application is not that limited, and that, in fact, their application is seen wherever psychological interpretation is undertaken. The psychological interpretation of events, be they dreams, Rorschach responses, remarks in an interview, or relations between two people, has been seen in the previous chapters to be logically separable into two parts, which have been designated the semantic and propositional aspects. This chapter will be devoted to the semantic aspect of interpretation, since it is here where most of the principles lie; the principles involved in the formulation of propositions will be considered in Chapter 4.

THE PROCESS OF INTERPRETATION: SEMANTIC ASPECT

The semantic aspect of interpretation has been characterized as the assignment of events to classes as defined by one's theoretical language. Before considering the principles guiding this, it is necessary to consider the process involved in its accomplishment. Each class of a language system has a criterion for admission involving the presence or absence of certain attributes that an event must satisfy. Thus, in the semantic phase, the interpreter attempts to determine what the attributes of the event under consideration are and then attempts to find that class which requires just these attributes for membership in it. When he has accomplished this he pins a new label on the event, the label pinned on all events belonging to that class, and is ready, if he wishes, to move into the propositional aspect of interpretation.

The problem is complicated, however, by the fact that most events are multidimensional in nature and that, considering each dimension in turn, one could, on the basis of attributes associated with that dimension, place the event in any one of several classes. There are few events for which there is only one possible interpretation in any language system. For example, a frankly sexual dream may be interpreted as sexual, aggressive, competitive, ego enhancing, and so on, depending upon which aspects of the dream one focused upon. It may, of course, in many instances be the wisest course to place more than one interpretation upon the event. The psycho-analytic principle of overdetermination is a recognition of this fact. The first step, at any rate, in the process of inter-pretation is the analysis of the event into its component dimensions and its attributes with respect to each. But having considered the various attributes of the event, which ones shall the interpreter select as the basis for his classification if it turns out that different interpretations may be made, de-pending upon the choice made here? Logically, this is equiva-lent to asking which dimension of the event shall be de-pended upon as the source of attributes to be used for purposes of classification. This involves the interpreter in the act of abstraction; deciding what to focus upon and what to ignore. Having made this decision, he is then ready to move forward with the assignment of the event to a particular class and to take whatever action implied by this assignment that seems appropriate at that point.

The interpretive process at this stage is therefore best con-ceptualized as involving a three-step sequence: analysis, ab-straction, and action. Each of these makes different demands upon the interpreter, and it may be well to consider each briefly before considering the principles that guide this process.

Analysis

As we move from events whose forms are fairly well cir-cumscribed by the nature of the situation, as for instance in the case of responses to the Rorschach, to those where morphology is more likely to reflect idiosyncrasies of context, experience, and learning, as in the case of interpersonal re-lations and dreams, the possibility of producing a compendium of such events with all of their possible interpretations decreases. It therefore falls to the interpreter to introduce a structure that will permit him to treat any event that falls within his ken. This structure consists of the many dimensions that may be passed through the event, thereby generating the attributes that will serve as the ultimate basis for the final step in this process: action. What these various dimensions are will be taken up in the elaboration of the principles guiding this process. At this point it is sufficient to recognize that in any one instance they are likely to be several and that they cannot all be applied to every event. Thus, the demands placed upon the interpreter at this point are two: to be aware of all of the dimensions of analysis that might be relevant to a given event, and to be able and willing to consider each in turn. Biases of perception or narrowness of conception will severely limit the interpreter in the variety and scope of his interpretations. The problem is not unlike that of a concept-formation task where the items to be classified are multi-dimensional. The individual who is unable to marshall all of the applicable dimensions will fail at the task. It can therefore be said with reasonable assurance that the brain-injured will not find psychological interpretation their forte! What other characteristics are likely to act as impediments here is not as clear, but certainly the intellectual demands of this task are of the highest order.

Abstraction

Having before him the array of attributes characteristic of the event in question, these attributes stemming from various dimensions, the interpreter is likely to find that they are far from univocal in pointing to the class to which that event shall be assigned. Thus he must abstract those attributes that, in this particular instance, lead to the most reasonable interpretation. These become figure; the rest ground. The paying of a compliment may in one case be best interpreted in terms of its nurturant effects upon its recipient, while in another the very same event may better be placed among the class of behaviors labeled self-abasing. Different attributes of the same event are marshaled to support the one or the other interpretation.

Three factors characteristically determine the direction that abstraction takes: theory, context, and bias. The theory to which one subscribes determines in a gross but frequently subtle way what attributes one will favor by hypostasizing certain factors and not others in accounting for personality development and functioning. Consequently it is to attributes associated with these factors that one will be most acutely tuned in analyzing a given event. For example, if one subscribes to a theory that places great emphasis upon the early experience a child has with his parents as determining the quality of his interpersonal relations in later life, then one will more likely abstract those attributes of a situation that permit an interpretation in these terms than in others. More concretely, a student reports being unable to get along with his economics instructor. The economics instructor is a male, older than the student, a husband and father, a graduate of a well-known eastern school, ectomorphic, a Democrat, pedantic, and pipe-smoking, to list just some of his attributes. Given the aforementioned theoretical predilections, one is most likely to fasten onto or abstract from these attributes the age differential and sex of the instructor and consequently interpret this event as an instance of the student's hostility toward his father being transferred to the instructor. It would be just as reasonable, other things being equal, to interpret the antagonism as an instance of envy of the instructor's connubial achievements, prejudice against graduates of eastern schools, previous unhappy encounters with ectomorphs, political zeal, the annoying characteristics of pedants as pedagogues, or allergy to tobacco smoke. One could, of course, also consider all the attributes of this particular type of relationship as well. It may be, for example, that this student uses antagonism as a way of rationalizing his lack of interest in economics. But the theory chosen may be mute on these points or lead to these being considered superficial interpretations at best. Thus the attributes which would support them are ignored.

The second source of determination of the direction of abstraction is the context in which the event occurs. This context includes all that is known about the personality of the individual involved as well as the situation of which the event is a part. Where more than one interpretation is possible, that interpretation is selected which is most consistent with this context. In turn, only those attributes are abstracted that are consistent with the interpretation believed most appropriate.

In a similar way, the personal biases of the interpreter will affect what he abstracts regarding a particular event. That certain clinicians are more prone to see anxiety where others see hostility and that all are to some extent pawns of the forces and conflicts operating in their own personalities has become one of the truisms of clinical psychology and mainstays of many a psychoanalyst's practice. There is, no doubt, an element of truth here although the wisdom of the solutions offered may be doubted. One probably always operates with some bias, even when he is presumably aware of his biases and therefore compensating for them. At best, it may only be possible to trade one set of biases for another, albeit in many instances subtler and more sophisticated ones. The point is that in understanding the process of interpretation and that of abstraction in particular, it is important to recognize personal bias as another important source of variance; beware the "unbiased" interpreter!

Here it becomes obvious, perhaps for the first time, that psychological interpretation cannot depend upon some mechanical process based upon actuarial tables (Meehl, 1956). Because of the multiplex nature of the material dealt with, such tables would be completely unwieldy if they were to include all the forms of content or events that might belong to a given class together with data concerning all the qualifications contingent upon the context that would further affect interpretation. This is not to say that such tables may have no place in the entire interpretive process or in clinical psychology. Their most likely and most economical point of application in the interpretive process would seem to be in connection with the propositional aspect. The semantic aspect represents, in effect, a coding of the raw data into a form which may be used in the construction of experience tables. Such tables could generate propositions of stated probabilities for various relations between events as regards a given individual. But before this is possible, a very large accumulation of propositions "made by hand" will be needed. There need be no fear of "technological unemployment."

In view of this, it is clear that there can be no substitute for adequate training of the clinician in personality theory and dynamics, and that individual differences in intelligence and skill are as likely to be felt in psychological interpretation as in any other endeavor which has not been completely routinized. Thus it can be seen that the assurance issued in the first chapter that an explication of the logic of the interpretive process would not deprive it of its potential as a source of satisfaction of needs for achievement, or prestige and status, was not an idle one.

The interpreter who views his task as the discovery of truth will have a particularly difficult time of it at this step of the interpretive process. For here he comes face to face with the essentially arbitrary element of the process. What is to be abstracted and what not rests solely upon his discretion and neither has greater claim to reality than the other. Unless the process of interpretation is clearly seen and accepted simply as the application of an alternate construction for a given event, the interpreter either remains unaware that he engages in abstraction at this point and hence proceeds in a blithe manner to discover the "truth" through interpretation, or is aware, and suffers from fears that he has not done justice to the true complexity of the event. In either case such a person will lack the flexibility of approach needed in treating the multiform events that parade themselves before him. Therefore, another demand which is made upon the interpreter at this point is considerable sophistication regarding the nature of his task.

Because a decision is required, because the interpreter is aware that he is making a decision, and because this decision involves the disregarding of certain attributes in favor of others, the interpreter faces risk. His abstraction may be incorrect; his interpretation is determined by what he does at this point; his professional reputation is placed in jeopardy. To the personally or professionally insecure, this may pose such a threat that they can proceed no farther, or if they do it is only by first distorting the nature of the task. They may complain that the event in question is too complex and perhaps mention several of the interpretations which are possible but never commit themselves to one of them; they may adopt a naive realism and deny that the interpretation they present involves abstraction at all: for them the facts speak for themselves; or they may scurry to some "expert" for his opinion on "an extremely interesting case." But whatever course is taken, such a person's effectiveness is limited. Thus, abstraction requires somewhat more than a modicum of personal and professional security of those who would engage in psychological interpretation.

Action

Abstraction fixes the class membership of the event but does not complete the sequence involved in the semantic aspect of interpretation. For it does not indicate what is to be done about it; it does not involve any action. This represents the final step in the sequence and again involves the clinician in decision-making and risk-taking.

The courses of action open to the interpreter are many, with any one situation barring certain courses by its very nature but always leaving more than one course open for consideration. It remains for the interpreter to make the choice.

What are the choices open to the interpreter? His first choice is whether to record or make known in one form or another a particular interpretation. Certain interpretations are irrelevant or trivial for a given case and so do not merit consideration at all. The clinician therefore disregards them. Other interpretations may seem to rest upon such tenuous bases that the clinician may decide to hold off granting them recognition until more evidence is accumulated. To record the interpretation at this time might bias subsequent observations to which he looks for confirmation or denial. But the clinician may decide that his interpretation is essentially correct and should be accorded some form of recognition. What form should this take?

If the interpreter is acting in an ancillary role as a diagnostician the form his interpretation should take is fairly well decided for him. It is usually some oral or written report to the professional person having primary responsibility for the case. But even here, in the formulation of the report, the clinician may in many instances remain at the semantic stage of interpretation, or he may go on from this and attempt to present propositions regarding the patient and his behavior. This is a decision that may well hinge upon the security of the clinician and his knowledge and experience in psychodynamics. He risks less at the semantic stage but he may contribute more at the propositional.

When interpretation occurs in the context of psychotherapy other decisions present themselves to the clinician. Not every interpretation that is believed to be correct should be communicated to the patient. One must at least always consider appropriateness and timing of interpretations before making them. In many instances the clinician may let the interpretation govern the course of psychotherapy but decide not to share the interpretation with the patient. This is strikingly illustrated in Margaret Sechehaye's (1952) symbolic approach to the treatment of schizophrenics. The factors that enter into these considerations have not been thoroughly investigated and so the individual clinician is thrown back upon his training and experience. Similarly, if it is decided that a given interpretation should be communicated to the patient, the form this should take confronts the clinician with still further choices. Shall it be stated tentatively? As an assertion? A question? It is quite likely that the form in which the interpretation is given is of consequence for its acceptance and effectiveness (see Chapter 9), but the factors which should be taken into consideration here also have not been studied systematically. Consequently, again the clinician must rely upon his training and experience, however inchoate these may be. If it is true that fools rush in where wise men fear to tread, then interpretation in psychotherapy should prove itself a very sensitive diagnostic device in this regard!

The demands that action makes upon the interpreter are the most exhaustive. For it is here that he actually, publicly commits himself. Depending upon his training and security, each clinician will set for himself a particular level of certainty that an interpretation must reach before he will translate it into action. Again, the form that this action will take, as well as its quality—whether it be some form of verbal or nonverbal communication of the interpretation or a decision regarding therapeutic strategy or case disposition—depends upon the interpreter's knowledge and skill. Interpretation is therefore clearly not an endeavor for the faint of heart, nor for those lacking in training and experience. But training and experience are only of value if they are guided by solid knowledge, and so we come back once again to the critical need for research.

Research implications. Throughout the process of interpretation at the semantic stage, the interpreter is continually being faced with decisions. The ultimate objective of research here should be to provide hard facts that will reduce such decision-making to a minimum. Such an objective is not contrary to the earlier observation that an actuarial approach at this stage is not likely to be feasible. Reducing decision-making to a minimum is not the same as eliminating it. And it may well be that ultimately many of the decisions which the clinician will face will involve choices *between* actuarial tables.

The interpreter must first consider all the possible sources of attributes that an event may contain. How he does this will be the subject of the next section in this chapter. Next, where these various sources yield attributes leading to differing classifications, he must abstract or focus only on those which yield that interpretation which seems most appropriate in a given instance. Finally, he must decide what action to take in connection with this interpretation. The first step in reducing the subjective aspect of these decisions is the development and explication of conceptual systems of considerably more power than those in use at present.

At least four such systems are needed. One would be concerned with the conceptualization of the individual and a second with the conceptualization of the situation in which he is involved. The first has been the major concern of personality theorists and is at present represented by nosological systems of varying reliability and a plethora of terminology of varying ambiguity (Rotter, 1954). The need for an adequate conceptualization of the environment has been receiving increasing recognition (Rotter, 1960), but systems here are of the most rudimentary type. Attempts to conceptualize the therapeutic situation are also of relevance here and likewise must be counted as inadequate at present.

It should be noted that the development of such systems and the research thereby entailed, while not properly a part of research on the interpretive process, is a necessary precondition for such research. An adequate conceptual system of the first type would be applicable to any individual and, from the standpoint of interpretation, would permit the answering of such questions as: Given interpretive alternatives *a, b,* and *c* for a given event, which is the most appropriate one for a person with *x* characteristics? For a person with *x* characteristics, what form should interpretation take? At present there are suggestions, such as that by Fromm-Reichmann (1950) that whereas with neurotics one should interpret content, with schizophrenics the emphasis should be on dynamics. As a conceptualization of the patient, however, the neurotic-psychotic dichotomy is much too broad to be of much value. And the case is much the same with the distinction between content and dynamics.

Psychotherapy, as indeed life itself, is a series of continually changing situations for the person involved in it. Should a conceptual system be developed that could capture the significant aspects of such situations it would then be possible to investigate the questions of timing and appropriateness of various forms of interpretation. At present there exists a broad spectrum, bounded at one end by the early nondirective approach to psychotherapy that eschewed interpretation of all kinds at any point in the process and at the other by the therapy of such persons as Klein (1933) and Rosen (1953), who let little escape interpretation at any point in therapy. This should not be a matter settled by testimonials or the development of schools of psychotherapy. But until a conceptual system has been developed of such analytic power that it can encompass the therapeutic situation with all of its vicissitudes as well as the nontherapeutic situation, an empirical approach to these questions is barred.

The need for the other two conceptual systems required is implicit in what has just been discussed. One would provide a means of characterizing the nature of the interpretation, such as Fromm-Reichmann's content–dynamics distinction, and the other would be concerned with the form that interpretations take, whether communicated or not, and how communicated. Interpretations vary not only with regard to the content–dynamics dimension, but also with regard to the nature of the content, threat value, plausibility to the individual, extensiveness of import for his life, and so on (see Chapter 8). It seems more than likely that a conceptual system containing these dimensions as well as others would reveal that the appropriateness of interpretations so conceptualized would vary with the type of individual involved and his current situation. A similar finding would no doubt result if the question of the form of interpretation, whether declarative, interrogatory, tentative, and so on, were included.

Ideally, research concerned with these matters should make use of a four-way classification design consisting of: persons × situations × nature of interpretation × form of interpretation; the nature of the dependent variable being determined by the specific purposes of the study as well as available criterion measures. For purposes of illustration, and using conventional, gross, and sometimes overlapping categories, Table I lists some of the conditions that might be included in an investigation of the effect of interpretation on movement in psychotherapy. The various interactions in such a design would be of particular interest and significance. Unfortunately, it is in the nature of the problem and material being dealt with that this ideal is unlikely ever to be completely obtained.

The major barrier to the realization of this ideal is the fact that research concerned with this aspect of the interpretive

TABLE 1

CONDITIONS VARIED IN STUDY OF EFFECT OF INTERPRETATION ON MOVEMENT IN PSYCHOTHERAPY

Persons	Situations	Nature of interpretation	Form of interpretation
Schizophrenics	Early therapy	Reflection	Question
Neurotics (mixed)	Middle therapy	Moderately dissonant[a]	Analogy
Depressives	Late therapy	Strongly dissonant[a]	Tentative assertion
Anxiety disorders	or	or	Strong assertion
Sociopaths	Negative transference	Content	Nonverbal
	Positive transference	Dynamics	

[a] In conventional terminology this would refer to moderate and very "deep" interpretations. The value for a theory of psychological interpretation of the concept of dissonance is discussed in Chapter 8.

process would seem to be only possible *in situ*. By definition, one cannot duplicate a given stage of psychotherapy in the laboratory. At best one might come up with an experimental analogue. Likewise, it would be unlikely that the cooperation of individuals representing the entire gamut of types of interest could be secured outside of the therapeutic situation. Much therefore depends upon the clinician and his interest and willingness to participate in such an endeavor. It is equally clear that no one clinician could undertake such a program of research—if for no other reason than that he could not possibly, within a reasonable time, accumulate a sufficiently large number of cases to fill all the cells of the projected design. This would have to be a collaborative endeavor of considerable magnitude.

However, by executing less ambitious designs and by replicating them, except for changes in one of the classifications it may be possible over time to accumulate sufficient data so as to approach the ideal research design called for here. But in the final analysis this entire enterprise will stand or fall with the comprehensiveness and rigor of the conceptual systems employed. The more comprehensive and rigorous they are the more confidence we can have as we move from the confines of the laboratory to those of the consulting room. Thus it is to the development of such systems that attention should be given first.

Psychodiagnostic interpretation, in contrast to therapeutic interpretation, can be investigated essentially by a two-way classification design. The problem here is to determine for each type of person described by the conceptual system the most effective or useful interpretation for a given class of event. The diagnostician is not usually called upon to make decisions as to the form which interpretation should take with the client or its appropriateness in a given situation. While the research design here is simpler than that above, the significance of results obtained depend no less heavily upon adequate conceptualization of the variables involved.

It might seem that the interpreter has been neglected as a source of variance to be investigated. This was not unintentional. There are two good reasons for this neglect. First, including the interpreter as a variable would so encumber an already complex design that it would seem all the more unlikely that anyone would ever attack the problem in a comprehensive fashion. The addition of the interpreter would markedly increase the number of cases needed in any study in this area and also contribute additional error through the additional conceptual system that would need to be introduced. Second, although there is good evidence to suspect that the interpreter does contribute some variance, adopting a representative design (Brunswik, 1947) with regard to the interpreter variable should result in more stable and significant relationships between the other variables. If this is done, with therapists or interpreters varying randomly, any significant relationships obtained between the person, situation, nature of interpretation, and form of interpretation variables should be all the more stable and useful in a practical sense.

In this section an attempt was made to outline the implications for research that the interpretive process at the semantic stage involves; *mutatis mutandis,* this can also be read as a discussion of all of the potential sources of error one must consider whenever he embarks upon this process. For the research-minded this should serve as a source of stimulation and direction; for the practitioner, as a source of caution.

THE PRINCIPLES OF INTERPRETATION: SEMANTIC ASPECT

The principles guiding the interpretive process at this stage may be grouped into two major classes, those that define what is permissible and those that indicate the possible sources of attributes or dimensions to be considered in the classification or interpretation of an event. The main function of the former is to provide the interpreter with the greatest possible amount of freedom as he approaches the task of transforming his data from one language system to another, while the latter may be seen as providing guideposts in the use of this freedom.

Principles defining what is permissible

It might appear to many that all is permissible in psychological interpretation and that no principles are involved here. This, however, is not very helpful in understanding the process, first because there are certain constraints to which all interpreters assent, and second because "all is permissible" means different things to different people and must be defined denotatively. Five principles seem to apply to this question.

1. *The principle of dissonance.* When the interpreter is presented with an item of behavior he is faced with the question of what to accept at face value, so to speak, and what to transform through interpretation into other terms. Frequently this question is only implicit, but nevertheless it exists. How does he make this decision? The principle of dissonance is one guide for the interpreter at this point. In effect, this states that anything which, within the context of its occurrence, strikes a dissonant note to the observer is properly subject to interpretation. This is a highly subjective matter to be sure, and what will appear as dissonant will vary with the training, personality, and theoretical orientation of the interpreter, but it is one of the major determining factors in the selection of material for interpretation.

Almost any event causing the interpreter to ask the question "Why?" would be dissonant within that context. Thus, for example, emotional reactions that seem to be inappropriate, either because of their nature or because they are excessive or less than one would expect, would be candidates for interpretation. Any content or behavior that appears to be unrealistic, illogical, or inconsistent would also be grist for the interpreter's mill. Behaviors or relationships that from the standpoint of the biography of the individual involved represent deviations would similarly be taken as material for interpretation. The point here may be grasped most simply if it is remembered that the purposes of interpretation include that of reducing inconsistency. In other words, dissonance is reduced to the extent that interpretation has been successful.

This principle applies no less to fantasy behavior than it does to other forms of behavior. The importance placed upon unusual stories, or unusual aspects of stories in the TAT, represents the application of this principle. A similar application is the interest shown in the interpretation of the more bizarre or unusual aspects of dreams.

Recognizing the dissonant elements of a situation probably represents one of the major problems of the beginner in this field. Typically, the beginning student tends to be too tolerant of patient behavior. The fact that a 45-year-old patient who had been an accountant for all his adult life decides to take courses in philosophy and art may be seen by the student as simply an attempt to "broaden" himself and something all to the good at any rate, rather than possibly reflecting an abrupt change in orientation that may well merit some reflection concerning its "meaning" for the patient and its possible implications for his adjustment. In attempting to compensate for these permissive tendencies it is not unusual for the student to swing all the way over to the other direction and take nothing as understandable on its own terms, over-interpreting every act of the client. Much of what represents the "art of interpretation" involves stabilizing the clinician at some point between these two extremes. To the extent that the rules for the application of this principle are not made entirely explicit, interpretation does remain an art; to that same extent it is fraught with error and confusion.

2. *The principle of congruence.*   For the clinician wearing the hat of the interpreter, it is not only that which is dissonant which stands out as figure for him. For tucked somewhere under this same hat is a theory of personality, which usually includes in one form or another postulates regarding defense mechanisms, types of relationships between various classes of people, and assorted other behavioral phenomena. Given a set of events, the clinician scans these for those events or event sequences that are congruent with postulates of this theory. When such congruences are found, the interpretation is made. In this case it consists of recasting the observed phenomenon in the terms of the prototype postulated by the theory.

There may be no dissonance involved here. To the casual observer, as to the clinician entertaining some other theoretical position, the events being interpreted may seem perfectly reasonable on their own terms and not warrant any transformation. For example, the fact that a man becomes a very skilled surgeon and had, as a child, frequently dissected insects may not seem at all worthy of interpretation. This may be seen by many simply as the outcome of a longstanding scientific interest. However, to the clinician equipped with the concepts of sublimation and sadism there exists here a congruence that he is not likely to let escape recognition. He "sees" this professional man as having successfully sublimated his sadistic tendencies, and probably as still having stronger sadistic impulses than his colleague who is an anesthetist!

It is through the principle of congruence that the various theories of symbolism find their expression directly in the interpretive process. The process itself need not logically be concerned with how symbolism operates, nor need it be concerned with the validity of any of the theories concerned with symbolism. However, if the interpreter holds a theory which maintains, for example, that long, pointed objects are likely to be symbols of the male genitalia, he will interpret a drawing involving such an object as representing, by the principle of congruence, the male genitalia. The process of interpretation is not contingent upon the validity of this theory, but its product is.

Similarly, the various mental mechanisms postulated by psychoanalysis and accepted widely by clinicians of other theoretical persuasions enter into the interpretive process through the principle of congruence. From reaction formation through undoing, from projection through displacement, the mechanisms postulated to account for the individual's reactions to threat, anxiety, and frustration serve both as the sensitizers and the rationale for the clinician acting as interpreter. In no other way could the clinician possibly take some behavioral datum, which seems perfectly reasonable in its context and about which he necessarily knows little as regards its unique determinants, and claim that it is better understood in some other terms.

It is perfectly possible to speak of various mental mechanisms—rationalization, repression, reaction formation, and so on—in connection with the interpretive process and still not accept the notion that the aim of this process is the uncovering of the "real truth" which these mechanisms have only served to distort. By means of the principle of congruence these mechanisms serve only as logical operators that aid in the transformation of the datum from one system to another. Whereas the realist sees these mechanisms as transforming the original datum into another, which must then be interpreted so as to reveal the original datum again, one who adopts the present position need make no assumptions as to the nature of the original datum. There simply exists an event and several mechanisms that would justify some transformation of the labeling of this event. One makes that transformation (interpretation) which is most congruent with the event and the particular mechanism he has decided to invoke.

To take reaction formation as an example, this mechanism is most frequently invoked with events containing affective components. More specifically, it is invoked when one wishes to justify a transformation of some instance of positive affect into one of negative affect. When the child makes much of his worry about the welfare of his parents, through the use of the concept of reaction formation this is interpreted as representing hostility toward his parents. When the reformer wages a militant crusade against sin, one justifies interpreting this behavior as a reflection of his sinful impulses by invoking the concept of reaction formation.

To justify other interpretations one would invoke other mechanisms. But all these can be viewed as simply serving the interpretive process through justifying the transformations involved. Reaction formation justifies one type of transformation with one class of events, projection another with a different class of events, denial still another, and so on. Because the mechanisms one uses are bound up with one's theoretical position, there will be no attempt to spell out the uses to which each of these might be put. The point of this discussion is only to show how these fit into the logic of the interpretive process.

In many instances more than one mechanism may be invoked in connection with a given event. In some of these the resulting interpretations will be convergent and in others divergent. For example, giving a great many "hostile" percepts on the Rorschach may, if one invokes the mechanism of supplementary projection, lead to the interpretation that the respondent possesses a great many hostile tendencies. On the other hand, one could just as legitimately invoke the concept of complementary projection to justify interpreting the same Rorschach protocol as indicating the presence of a great deal of anxiety. Here the interpretations are quite obviously divergent and which one is accepted would presumably make a difference. It is here again that we reach the frontiers of knowledge. In certain situations this creates no problems; the constraints of the context rule out one interpretation or the other. But this is not always the case. It would therefore seem that an important research problem resides in attempting to determine the conditions under which one mechanism or another would be most appropriately invoked.

3. *The principle of interchangeability of genus.* This is one of the primary principles involved in all interpretation of symbolism. It permits animate objects to be interpreted as referents for inanimate ones; humans for animals; males for females; physical posture for attitudes. This principle also underlies the treatment of aspects of the Rorschach inkblots as aspects of the real world, that is to say, the socially significant world. Another way of putting this might be that genus is not one of the attributes to be considered in determining class membership. A building may be classed as phallic just as would the male sex organ, a twitch of the nose as rejection just as would the denial of entrance to a house, and a business organization as nurturant just as would a mother, all according to the principle of interchangeability of genus.

Marked differences may be observed here among adherents of different theoretical positions in the extent to which they follow or exploit this principle in practice. But there can be no a priori basis for asserting which expressions of it will lead to sense and which to nonsense. This judgment can be rendered only within a particular theoretical framework and context.

While this principle finds its most frequent application in the interpretation of autistic and fantasy materials, it is not limited to these and may also be found applied to the formal and substantive aspects of behavior. Its application is governed only by the other four principles making up this set.

4. *The principle of analysis and synthesis in the relationship between symbols and referents.* Again, this is a principle that finds its widest scope of application in the analysis of autistic

and fantasy materials from the standpoint of their symbolism. According to this principle, any referent may be represented by more than one symbol and one symbol may have more than one referent.

The representation of the referent by more than one symbol may be spoken of as analysis. Here the various symbols represent different aspects or attributes of the referent. The referent is in a sense broken up into its components and a different symbol is used to represent each of these. An individual may dream of a contest between a male and female athlete, and this may be taken to represent the conflict he feels within himself between his own masculine and feminine inclinations. Here the two athletes have the single referent, the individual, but they represent different aspects of him. Similarly, in TAT analysis it is not uncommon to conceive of the various characters in a story as representing different aspects of the story-teller's personality.

It is likewise possible for one symbol to have several referents. Where this is the case, the symbol usually synthesizes or embodies the characteristics that are unique to each of the referents in question. An example of this would be the dream of climbing a mountain by a patient during therapy. He reported that the mountain was a treacherous one, the climb difficult and at times frightening, but that as he climbed he felt a certain exhilaration. It became apparent that the mountain could be interpreted as having two referents. One was therapy itself, which was seen as somewhat overwhelming and arduous, sometimes fraught with anxiety, but nevertheless holding out hope for a better way of life than he had known before. The other referent for the mountain appeared to be the patient's father, who had been a rather domineering person. The patient's climbing up the mountain represented his gradually overpowering his father or at least liberating himself from his power. Hence the exhilaration as he climbed.

This principle is not limited to the interpretation of symbol.

ism in dreams and similar materials. It finds broad application in the interpretation of transference relationships, where, for example, the therapist may be interpreted as representing both mother and father, as well as in the interpretation of various behaviors that may serve more than one end. As these broader applications of the principle are considered, it should be borne in mind that the terms "symbol" and "referent" bear the same logical relationship to each other as do "event" and "class." In the former instance it is more frequently the case that the referent defines and is the only member of the class, but this is not always the case. Thus, a person has only one mother and this may be conceived of as an instance of a class defined and occupied by a single member. But in many instances it is more productive for our purposes to conceive of a class of "mother figures." The identification of referents for symbols regardless of their source may be conceived of as simply another instance of the semantic aspect of interpretation. The problem is still that of finding the "best" class for the event from the standpoint of our purposes and of the particular context in which the event occurs.

5. *The principle of contextual consistency.* Interpretation never occurs in a vacuum. The event being interpreted is part of a context that consists of other events upon which some interpretation has already been placed, the individuals involved, who have already been characterized in some fashion, and the particular language system or theory of the interpreter. This context sets the limits within which an interpretation must fit. It must be consistent with this context. For example, a fear of knives in a female already known to have conflicts involving heterosexual relations would more likely be interpreted in terms of the phallic connotations of the knives than their possible uses as instruments of aggression, whereas the reverse would be true for a person already characterized as having difficulty controlling hostile impulses.

This principle has already been alluded to in the discussion of abstraction and so need not be gone into further at this point. The way in which it is followed will depend to a great extent upon the knowledge of psychodynamics of the interpreter and the theory to which he subscribes, since consistency or inconsistency will only be apparent to him to the extent that these equip him to make such judgments.

There is, however, one point which should be made with regard to this principle. This is that insofar as it serves as the basis for choosing between competing interpretations it may also serve to blind the interpreter to what might be the more valuable interpretation in particular instances. Man abhors inconsistency no less than does nature a vacuum; yet it is frequently from inconsistencies that we stand to learn the most and this may be no less true of psychological interpretation than of any other intellectual endeavor. Ultimately, it is true, our judgment of the value of a theory rests upon a consistency criterion—it must if the lawfulness of behavior is one of our assumptions—but the problem is at what level or point in the data gathering and conceptualization process one should invoke this criterion. Invoked too early it serves only to confirm our prejudices and insure our ignorance; invoked too late, we have only chaos and confusion. This is a dilemma with which we are always faced, and it would be well if the interpreter were aware of it.

Interpretive perspectives

If the semantic aspect of interpretation consists of assigning events to certain classes defined by the language system of the interpreter, where does one look for the basis for deciding to what class the event shall be assigned? How is the translation effected from one language, that of the patient for example, to another, that of the interpreter? How are events to be viewed? This is the crux of the problem of interpretation at this stage. Events may be viewed from many perspectives and each may suggest a different interpretation or class membership for the event. These various perspectives will be described in this section. It will be seen that each perspective yields up a particular set of attributes or dimensions which will permit the event to satisfy criteria for membership in one class or another. It will also be noticed that not all perspectives are equally applicable to all events. Some seem most applicable to dream content, others to interpersonal relationships, and still others to verbal material only.

From another standpoint, that of the psychology of the interpreter, these interpretive perspectives may be viewed as havens of refuge from accusations of irrationality, mysticism, or arbitrariness. That is, having made a given interpretation, the interpreter, if challenged, can point to the perspective he adopted as a point of reference and thus provide a semblance of order and rationality to his endeavor. The question thus becomes one of the validity of the system used by the interpreter rather than one of his own personal merit or sanity. The attack becomes one upon the system, impersonal, and not upon the individual. And this is a comfort.

Unless the challenge is made, the interpretive perspectives upon which an interpretation is based are seldom made explicit. Frequently however, because the interpretation is a common one, with a long history, these perspectives are well known and the validity of their use appears obvious once they are stated. Unfortunately, as will become obvious as these perspectives are described in this section, the validity of their use has never been established by any empirical procedure. Their validity is face validity, frequently very compelling but nevertheless still face validity. In an era of rationalism this may have been sufficient; today, we demand more.

Associated with and supporting the face validity of the interpretive perspectives is the belief that the interpretive enterprise is essentially a reversal of the process engaged in by the patient in the production of the to-be-interpreted material. At least since Freud first posited the existence of a censor monitoring traffic between the conscious and unconscious, it has been assumed that the individual distorts many expressions of his feelings, thoughts, and actions so as to gain some end which might otherwise be denied him. From this assertion stems the further belief that the interpretive perspectives about to be described actually represent the well-worn footpaths trodden by these feelings, thoughts, and actions in their journey to the land of inscrutability and impunity. Thus, from this point of view, interpretation consists of taking events in tow up each path until they "come clean" as to their origin, that is, their true meaning.

Since this is an analysis of the logic and process of interpretation, there is no need to take any stand on the mechanisms preceding the occurrence of the events to be interpreted. For our purposes they can be treated as simply existing; in fact, this seems desirable. Since there can be no empirical means of determining the mental processes of a particular individual prior to his presentation of the events with which we are concerned, these processes should not be referred to in justifying the interpretations made. To do this would quickly and inevitably involve one in a circularity from which there could be no escape. To repeat a point made previously, we are dealing here with an analytical system that requires no empirical justification for its existence. The only *empirical* question involved in the evaluation of any analytical system is whether it serves the purposes for which it is being used. In this case, the question is whether or not the interpretive perspectives lead to interpretations which accomplish for the interpreter that which he had intended by engaging in the enterprise in the first place.

The order in which the perspectives are discussed is not intended to have any significance. It may appear that some are prior to others, that some may be subsumed by others, and this is quite likely. However, these questions frequently involve the making of nice distinctions, which, for our purposes, would not repay the effort.

    1. *Structure.* This perspective, perhaps the best known, finds its most frequent application in dream interpretation and the analysis of objects of art. Any object, when viewed from the structural standpoint, yields a set of attributes, some of which will permit its assignment to a larger class of objects having at least one of these same structural attributes. It is obvious, of course, that when this is done other attributes stemming from other perspectives are largely, if not totally, ignored.

    The major attributes stemming from this perspective are those of length, width, height, angularity, complexity of structure, symmetry, texture or composition, and color. Thus, it is on the basis of the structural dimension that long, narrow, and angular objects are assigned to the class of masculine objects, frequently the class of phallic objects. Similarly, finger paints and clay being soft, pliable, and frequently dark in color, are considered symbolic equivalents of excrement, so that the reactions of the child or adult when presented with this type of material are interpreted as those one would observe if he were presented with any other member of this class, including presumably, his own feces.

    Much of the formal interpretation of the Rorschach test stems from the application of this perspective. Here it becomes clear that interpretations need not be of an object–object type—that is, that this object stands for such and such an object. The bright colored blots are therefore taken as representing emotionally laden situations and the parts (details) of blots, as compared with the whole blots, are taken as representing parts in problem-solving situations or interpersonal situations, or any other situation to which the detail–whole distinction might be applied. Similarly, the textural attributes of the blots are assigned to the same class as a caress, or any other form of human "contact." "Shades of gray" and concern with them are taken as belonging to the same class as "shades of gray" in interpersonal situations and concern with them. To be sure, interpretations vary from one authority to the next, as does the complexity of the reasoning behind them, but the fact remains that these are all based upon attributes of the blots obtained by viewing them structurally. While this might appear to represent a play on words, the Rorschach analyst is not disturbed by such allegations, and perhaps need not be. That is to say, while concern with details in ink blots is only very loosely analogous to concern with details in interpersonal situations, the question of whether or not this kind of interpretation yields useful predictions is an empirical one. Whether the analogy is justified or not is an analytical problem; whether it is useful or not is an empirical problem.

2. *Function.* There are actually two perspectives involved here. The one is that which is usually applied to inanimate objects and refers to the action of their various parts, and the second is usually applied to animate objects, most often humans, and refers to the role played by them. However, these two uses are occasionally interchanged. For example, Stein's suggestion (1955) that a description of the figure in TAT card #17BM as climbing up and down the rope should be interpreted as masturbation represents an application of the mechanical action perspective to a human, while the interpretation of an automatic food vending machine as a mother symbol, because it performs a nurturant function, would be an application of the role perspective to an inanimate object. For this reason it seems that no harm is done in speaking of a single perspective of function.

To apply the perspective of function the interpreter asks either or both of the following questions concerning the object of analysis: (1) "What are the characteristics of the activity of its various parts—how can its action be described?" and (2) "What role does it play in the situation—what is its relationship to other aspects of the situation?" Attributes resulting from answering the first question would include the following: reciprocating action as found in a steam engine as well as in coitus; expulsion as found in a volcano as well as in elimination, ejaculation, and vomiting; incorporation as found in whirlpools as well as in eating, digesting, and loss of personal identity; falling; balancing or resisting gravitational forces; enlargement; shrinkage; and drifting. Each of these attributes, as was demonstrated with the first three, may be used to define a class of object or a concept, and any object possessing the attribute becomes a member of the class and may represent some other member or be an exemplar of the concept.

Representative of the attributes yielded by the second question include age, dependency, authority, hostility, nurturance, dominance, and submission. Again, each of these attributes defines a class in which, for purposes of interpretation, any member may be taken as representing any other. On this basis, it is possible to speak of mother figures, father figures, authority figures, etc.

This perspective finds very broad application in the interpretation of dream content and thematic material, as well as in the analysis of behavior in interpersonal situations. While interpretations based upon it frequently seem much more plausible than those based upon the structural perspective, it must still be realized that their basis too is an analogical one, not an empirical one.

3. *Effect.* Closely related to function is the perspective of effect. Events, whether they be instances of human behavior or natural occurrences such as rain, fire, floods, and earthquakes, can be viewed from the standpoint of their effect upon some particular individual or situation. The interpretation of an event may therefore take the form of ascribing to it membership in a class of other events which have similar effects. The

event may then either be taken as representative of the class or as a substitute for some other member of the class.

For example, a mother forcing a bad tasting "tonic" upon her youngster may be said to be expressing hostility toward him since the medication has the effect of producing a very unpleasant experience for him, just as would any other instance of hostility directed toward him. Flattering another person to the point where he becomes embarrassed and uncomfortable may, upon the basis of this effect, again be interpreted as an expression of hostility. The interpretation of the classic dream of losing one's teeth as representing a desire to return to a state of infancy and dependency, is based on the fact that the effect of such an occurrence would be to require special food preparation just as is required for an infant (also without teeth—a structural similarity) who is also very dependent and accepted as such.

A problem which becomes more apparent in connection with this perspective than with either of the two previous ones, but which is present to varying degrees for almost all, is that a given interpretive perspective may yield several quite different attributes and interpretations. Sometimes some of these may be ruled out by the context, but not always. For example, a dream in which rain figures prominently may be interpreted variously as being concerned with fertility, depression, menstruation, enuresis, nurturance, or guilt, in which latter case the rain is symbolic of the cleansing of past sins. The choice is not always easy, as for example in the case of a 38-year-old woman who had been promiscuous in her youth, had one abortion, is now contemplating marriage, and in therapy reports a dream in which she is caught in a downpour of rain and drenched to the skin. Further elaboration of the dream and accompanying emotions may help, but again, not always. The point is, that ultimately, the interpreter must take a gamble. And it would be well if he were aware that this is what he is doing.

The gamble, of course, is not that he has guessed the true meaning of rain in this instance, but rather that he has guessed the appropriate interpretation, the one which satisfies the patient's expectations and purposes in telling the dream and the one which furthers the process of therapy. Sometimes, of course, these two criteria may be incompatible, and, always, they are not readily discernible.

4. *Affect.* Events frequently have a particular affect associated with them, and this may therefore serve as another interpretive perspective. Included in the concept of affect is that of connotation. Two events which share the same connotation or produce the same affect may therefore be interchangeable for purposes of interpretation, the one serving as the symbol for the other, or the one serving as a surrogate for the other. Again, this perspective cannot in all cases be separated from that of effect, for events producing similar effects, frequently also give rise to similar affective experiences, or have similar connotations.

Systems of content analysis for the Rorschach such as Elizur's (1949) are for the most part examples of the application of this perspective. Thus, reports of percepts that might be frightening or threatening are all scored for anxiety or hostility. Some of these scorings would seem to be based as much upon effect as upon affect, and the problem of distinguishing between them is not an easy one.

In some cases, however, it is clear that the analysis can be based only upon affect or connotation. For example, if, in the case of the dream of being drenched by rain, the patient reported that she felt cleaner afterward and enjoyed the experience, the interpretation of the dream as representing a concern with guilt and its removal would gain in plausibility on the basis of the affective component of the report.

The form of interpretation may be of either of two types, as exemplified in Elizur's content analysis and the cited interpretation of the dream. In the first case, the event was taken simply as representative of a class and the interpretation took the form of asserting that this is an instance of anxiety or hostility, whereas in the second case the interpretation was specific with regard to the "meaning" of the event in terms of some other event in the person's life. That is to say, one is of the form event = affect; while the other is of the form event = affect = event. In the latter case the affect serves a mediating function, while in the former it constitutes an end in itself. Depending upon the purposes of the interpreter, he may make use of one form or the other, and frequently will make use of both, as in the case where he is concerned with evaluating the emotional status of the individual and at the same time determining the nature of his conflicts and pre-occupations.

5. *Metaphor.* As an interpretive perspective, the principle of interchangeability of genus (page 88) permits metaphor to be logically subsumed under the dimensions of structure, function, effect, and affect. However, viewing events as potential metaphors for other events is frequently presented as an approach to interpretation in its own right. While on the basis of our analysis this may be seen to be not strictly the case, it must be admitted that many interpretations are made most expediently in this fashion. This is particularly true where the metaphor is a culturally common one. For example, it seems most simple to interpret, on the basis of meta-phorical analysis, a pain in the neck as an expression of dis-like for someone whose presence always seems to be associated with the complaint, although it might just as well be achieved through the application of the perspective of affect.

The more acquainted the interpreter is with the cultural context of the event he is interpreting, and the more facile he is with the language of that culture, the more easily will he be able to approach the problem directly on the basis of metaphor. While this may be taken as a good argument for a sound liberal education along with the professional training of the interpreter, it must be recognized that relying solely on a repertoire of culturally common metaphors would soon leave the interpreter at sea. The language of the schizophrenic, just as the every-day behavior of the normal individual, provides many instances where knowledge of common metaphors would be of little help, and it is only by the painstaking application of each of the dimensions of analysis thus far discussed that the interpreter can achieve some transformation which makes sense in terms of his objectives.

6. *Phonetic analysis.* What may appear as a bad pun to the uninitiated, may be a "shrewd interpretation" to the cognoscenti. This interpretive perspective, which can obviously only be applied to language, is frequently applied to reports of dreams, as well as to the analysis of some literary productions. Interpretation here simply consists of substituting the meaning of a phonetically similar word or homonym for the one originally given. At times this is even done across languages, so that the interpreter with a polylingual background has a much broader range of material to draw upon and will certainly have the edge on his less fortunate colleagues.

Theodore Reik (1948) provides us with a classic example of the application of the phonetic perspective across languages in his account of the interpretation of a dream by an American in which Metternich figured prominently and for which no apparent explanation could be given until he and the patient dissected the name and got "met her *nicht*"—an Anglo-German sentence meaning "I did not meet her."

As a dimension of analysis, phonetics is of limited importance since it is both limited to verbal material and can only be used to establish equivalences between particular words. The results of its application range from the farfetched to the astounding, frequently depending upon the authority with which the interpretation is made.

One interesting offshoot of this dimension of analysis, however, has been the development of word association tests and sentence completion tests making use of homonyms. From the association of the examinee, it is possible to determine which meaning of the word he has responded to and this, in turn, provides the basis for a variety of inferences about his personality and preoccupations. In one use of this approach, Secord (1953) used associations to such words as *colon, arch, graft,* and *tablet* as a means of measuring concerns with bodily functioning. Like so much else in this area, the validity of these instruments is yet to be established, but on the surface they appear very convincing.

7. *Logical extension and reversal.* This perspective is usually applied in the interpretive treatment of reported feelings and attitudes as well as in the ascription of attributes to certain events, people, or objects. The mechanism of reaction formation is often employed to justify the application of this perspective, as, for example, when demonstrations of filial devotion are interpreted as representing filial hatred and the concern of the super-moralist with the routing out of all immorality in the community is seen as an attempt to control his own immoral impulses. In applying this perspective, the interpreter does one or both of two things. He either takes the report of some feeling or attitude or behavior, asks what would be its polar opposite, and interprets the report in these terms, or he asks to what other events might these terms or their opposites have been applied and then proceeds to formulate his interpretation on the basis of his answer to this question. For example, a patient in a mental hospital continually reports in therapy that the personnel of the hospital are just wonderful, that they are kind and considerate, and that he attributes all his improvement to their treatment of him. The therapist employing this perspective might take this to mean that there are other people in this patient's life who he feels are not kind and considerate and who he believes are responsible for his illness. The therapist assumes that the

patient cannot make this indictment in any other way, perhaps because of the anxiety which such an overt expression of hostility would evoke in him, perhaps because of fears of counter-aggression, and so on. But these assumptions are all by way of justifying the interpretation that stems from this perspective; they are not part of the perspective per se.

As an interpretive perspective logical extension and reversal demonstrates perhaps better than any other the extremely flexible or fluid attitude one assumes toward events when one decides to subject them to interpretive analysis. Also, perhaps more than any other perspective, it points up the problem of deciding when to take material at face value and when to interpret it. For in most instances the material viewed from this perspective makes perfectly good sense in its original form. What are the cues the interpreter relies on in making his decision? Here we see most clearly the need for explicit formulation of principles guiding these decisions, and perhaps also of the working of these principles.

8. *Sequence.* When an interview, or a dream, or a behavioral segment is viewed from the standpoint of what led to what—the sequence of events—interpretations for certain events will be suggested by virtue of the nature of the events that precede and follow them. Sequence as an interpretive perspective has been formalized to some extent in analytic procedures suggested for word association tests and Rorschach and TAT protocols. Of all of the perspectives discussed thus far, it comes closest to approximating the behavior of the scientist himself in the process of theory construction and testing. The assumption involved here is simply that if A follows B, this is due to something other than chance, and so the investigator begins to muse about the possible meanings of A and B which could account for this sequential relationship.

While this perspective is easiest to recognize and apply in connection with diagnostic tests and discrete items of behavior, it also finds application in the analysis of the content of interviews. This, however, requires somewhat more detachment than some clinicians can muster. To apply sequential analysis to the interview, it is necessary to step back from the situation and view the entire interview as a whole, to disengage oneself from concerns about the meaning of discrete aspects of the interview and about how one should have responded to such and such a remark by the interviewee. Only when this is done, do patterns begin to emerge. Only then does the clinician begin to wonder why such and such a topic followed such and such a topic and why this in turn led to such and such reaction by the client. And wondering, as we have observed before, is the first step in the interpretive process.

The application of this perspective takes two forms. The first involves the assignment of one event to a class and then, on the basis of its sequential relationship to some other event, deciding upon the appropriate classification of this latter event. For example, having observed that a patient, after speaking for some time about the problems of getting a promotion on his job, begins speaking about his wife and his concern that she had never completed her formal education, the clinician, having first interpreted the discussion of getting a promotion as a discussion of something which the client felt was virtually unattainable for him, is led, by observation of the sequence of events, to interpret the patient's concern about his wife's educational background as a concern about her as a possible barrier to his attainment of success.

The second form of application actually shades into the propositional aspect of interpretation and may be illustrated by taking the above example one step further. On the basis of his interpretation of the client's concern about his wife's educational deficiency as a concern about her as a barrier to his own advancement, the clinician infers the presence of hostility on the part of the patient toward his wife. In doing this the clinician is, of course, making use of the frustration-aggression hypothesis, having had no other indications that the patient does harbor any hostile feelings toward his wife. Note that in the absence of any other evidence the validity of this inference depends upon the validity of the theory upon which it is based as well as its correct application in this specific instance. This is always the case with propositional statements.

Frequently, applications of the sequence perspective will appear to be only of the second form. Logically, however, this always presupposes classifications of the events involved on the basis either of their sequential relationship or of some other interpretive perspective. In contrast to the other perspectives, sequence is thus applied in both the semantic and propositional aspects of interpretation and may build upon the outcomes of analyses using these other perspectives.

9. *Associations.* Word association procedures as well as free association represent attempts to develop interpretations of events on the basis of their associations. Since these associations are frequently highly personal and idiosyncratic, they usually lead to interpretations that could not be made from any other perspective, and in many instances associations are used when plausible interpretations by means of other perspectives are not forthcoming. While the associations usually used are those of the patient, one occasionally finds the use of the interpreter's own associations to the event being advocated. Although this latter procedure is obviously fraught with danger, it must be recognized that with uncooperative patients it may be the only way open to the application of this perspective. How useful the interpreter's associations are will certainly vary from case to case and from interpreter to interpreter and it might be generally agreed that such a technique should only be employed as a last resort.

In applying this perspective to an event, the basic procedure is to ask the patient to think of the event and then to verbalize whatever comes to his mind after that. There are, to be sure, many variations on this procedure, but their net product is the same: the elicitation of a sequence of events with the to-be-interpreted event as the first step in the sequence. With this material in his possession, the interpreter proceeds to employ a sequential rationale and perspective. The associative perspective might therefore be more properly considered as an adjunct of the sequential perspective. However, its claim to consideration as a separate perspective rests on the fact that, in contrast to the sequential perspective, its application depends upon the interpreter's deciding to apply it and upon his treatment of the patient, in the form of special instructions, so that he produces the sequence or set of associations. Thus the associative perspective depends upon the cooperation of the patient and the modification of his natural behavior by special instructions, while the sequential perspective does not require the explicit cooperation of the patient or any special instructions from the clinician. From this point of view, the difference between the associative and sequential perspective is analogous to that between the experimental and correlational approaches to research; the former depends upon some manipulation of nature while the latter lets nature take its course and works with the outcome.

10. *Reactions of the interpreter.* The adoption of this perspective, advocated by such diverse authorities as H. A. Murray (1938), who referred to it as "recipathy," and Frieda Fromm-Reichmann (1950), requires the assumptions that (a) the interpreter's reactions are essentially similar to those of the significant others in the patient's life, (b) the interpreter is an accurate observer of his own reactions, and (c) those reactions elicited by the patient's behavior were the ones intended by the patient. If one is willing to make these assumptions, he can make use of his own reactions to the behavior of the patient as the basis for an interpretation of this behavior. This is a large order and there are few who openly

advocate the employment of this perspective, although there are undoubtedly many more who are unwittingly influenced by it. Most recently, this perspective has been represented in the growing interest in countertransference and its analysis as a technique in psychoanalysis (Orr, 1954).

While to some this interpretive perspective, like the use of the interpreter's own associations to events, may seem to be just this side of madness, if one is going to engage in psychological interpretation at all it cannot be gainsaid on this basis alone. Again, the only criterion is the fruitfulness of its application. Nevertheless, this is not a perspective likely to be employed by the faint of heart. For in employing it there is always the question of whether one is revealing more about oneself than he is about the patient. For example, does the erotic response the clinician experiences suggest that the patient's behavior should be interpreted as sexually provocative, or does it reflect upon his own needs and possible deficiencies? Obviously, for many, such questions would be intolerable, and for some, best if never raised!

But if one is willing to conceive of the clinician as the most sensitive instrument in our armamentarium of psychodiagnostic techniques, this perspective must be accepted as no less worthy of consideration than any other we have discussed. However, this points to a problem which has yet to be adequately resolved in psychology and psychiatry, that of the "calibration" of the clinician. The ease with which interpretation from this perspective could be used as rationalizations for the clinician's own inadequacies and idiosyncrasies is too obvious to need further elaboration. It is yet to be demonstrated that psychoanalysis of the clinician does very much to reduce the "error" introduced into interpretations by the clinician's own needs, and so on, although it must be admitted that it remains the only systematic attempt to cope with this problem.

Perhaps this perspective, more than any other, points up

the two alternatives between which clinical psychology must choose. It can either institute training and research that will reduce the "error variance" of interpretations based upon the reactions of the interpreter—or, more generally, the operations of the interpreter—to a minimum, or it can move, as it has for some time, in the direction of developing diagnostic and therapeutic techniques that will obviate the need for the use of these perspectives. While the latter would seem the more economical, there are many who would maintain that we will never be able to do without the former. At this point, it seems sufficient that we are cognizant of the problem and the choices open to us; the evidence upon which to base a choice is obviously not at hand.

11. *Frequency.* We come now to several perspectives that are not employed in interpretation per se, but rather in providing some basis for assertions or evaluations of the significance for a particular case of the material already interpreted. The most important of these is frequency.

The relative frequency of occurrence of a thought, a theme, or an action has gained almost universal acceptance as a basis for evaluating its significance relative to other events. This perspective is incorporated in the interpretive systems developed for both the Rorschach test and the Thematic Apperception Test. It can be equally well applied to interview content and interpersonal behavior.

An analogue to this perspective may be found in learning theory whereby the habit strength of a response is measured, in part, by its frequency of occurrence. On the face of it, this perspective seems so eminently reasonable that it would seem that little more need be said about it. However, there is one point that must be made. While the perspective is easy to grasp, one assumption underlying its calculus is open to question in many instances. This is that there is a linear relationship between the frequency of occurrence of an event and its significance, or to put it in other terms, that all occurrences of an event count equally in the tabulation of frequency.

While there has been no reason to call this assumption into question in the utilization of such simple responses as bar presses or eye blinks, there is good reason to believe that all expressions of hostility, for example, cannot be simply added up to determine the amount of hostility felt by an individual. The reason for this discrepancy is not hard to find. It is simply that the events dealt with in psychological interpretation are seldom unidimensional, as is more likely to be the case with the responses of interest to the learning theorist. Hence they are likely to be subject to interactions between their various dimensions and therefore cannot simply be summated. Since this problem was discussed at some length in connection with the assumptions of the interpretative process (pages 54–57), we shall not go into it further at this point. As a rule of thumb in evaluating significance of material, this perspective has done yeoman service. The problem is not to discard it, but to refine its application.

12. *Intensity.* Judgments of the significance of events that recur can be made on the basis of their frequency of occurrence; however, there are many events that are either non-recurring or of very limited frequency, at least within the period of observation, but that nevertheless must be evaluated from the standpoint of their significance in the understanding of a particular individual. Intensity, pervasiveness, and uniqueness are perspectives that the clinician applies in such situations.

Intensity may be applied in either a relative or an absolute sense, as when the clinician is either making a judgment of the significance of each of several conflict themes given by a particular patient in his TAT protocol, or when the clinician is simply trying to arrive at an estimate of the degree of hostility expressed toward another person in a dream. These judgments are based upon such semantic considerations as the kinds of adjectives and adverbs used, the use of expletives, and the degree of deterioration of syntax, and such behavioral and physiological observations as the presence of tremors, alterations in speech rhythm, pitch, loudness, and rate, perseveration, and vasomotor changes.

Intensity presumably reflects the amount of energy, emotion, or ego invested in the behavioral event and it therefore seems a very reasonable dimension to apply. The problem here resides in the fact that we have no norms by which to order our observations, so that judgments of intensity, in the final analysis, reflect to some unknown degree the experience or adaptation level (Helson, 1948) of the clinician. While the obvious solution might appear to be the development of such norms, this does not seem to be a practical one, at least not until we have refined descriptive language to the point that we can reliably describe those subtle nuances in the individual's functioning upon which intensity judgments seem to rest. The alternative, and one that does seem feasible, is, first the investigation of those factors responsible for individual variations in the clinician's judgments of intensity for standard sets of material and then the development of training programs and experience requirements that will reduce individual differences in these factors to a minimum. Undoubtedly, whatever reliability intensity judgments now possess reflects the rough equivalence in clinical training and experience of the clinicians involved.

13. *Pervasiveness.* Having assigned an event to a particular class of events, the clinician then searches all the other information available about the patient for other instances of the occurrence of members of this event class. The more pervasive their incidence, either from the standpoint of the variety of situations in which they are observed or from the temporal standpoint as in the life history of the individual, the greater the significance that will be attributed to the class in question.

Let us, for example, suppose that the event to be interpreted is a student's having failed an examination, which there was every reason to believe that he would have passed, because he had gotten drunk the night before and therefore took the exam under less than optimal conditions. The clinician decides to assign this event to the class "self-defeating behaviors." But should the clinician be very concerned with this event? Is it important in understanding the student's main complaint of feeling inadequate?

In order to answer this question, the clinician reviews the student's life history and searches for other instances of self-defeating behaviors. He also looks closely into the student's current life situation, his interpersonal relations, his performance on a part-time job, his functioning as vice-president of his fraternity, and so on, for the occurrence of self-defeating behaviors.

If the clinician finds no other such instances he may come to one of two conclusions: (a) this event is noncontributory in understanding the patient; it is, in effect, an accident, or (b) the event has been misclassified. Conclusion (a) does not mean that the clinician believes the event to be truly a chance occurrence, merely that for his present purposes he does not believe that it merits further consideration. Before placing all of his money on conclusion (a) however, the clinician may wish to entertain the possibility of the validity of conclusion (b). For because of the assumption of nonindependence of members within a class (see pages 49–58) he does not expect to find many classes filled with only one member. Therefore the clinician may initiate a search for other attributes of the event and scan the available event classes for another possible interpretation. Should this be unavailing, he may then return to conclusion (a) with a bit more comfort.

Where the clinician does find other members of the event class in the life history or current functioning of the patient, he then is once again faced with the normative problem: How pervasive is n occurrences of the event class in question? And as in the closely related dimensions of frequency and intensity, the problems and issues raised by this question have yet to be systematically investigated. Thus again, the norms applied are the implicit ones developed by the clinician out of his own personal training and experience.

14. *Uniqueness.* For any event we can ask either how common it is in the life of an individual or how common it is in the situation in which it was observed. Whereas frequency and pervasiveness took the individual as the frame of reference in appraising the significance of an event, uniqueness takes the context of occurrence of the event as its frame of reference. Thus an event could be considered unique but still be judged to be a member of a class of quite frequent or pervasive events. Events judged to be unique or approaching uniqueness are generally accorded greater significance than those not so judged.

Quite obviously, uniqueness is a judgment that can only be made of events occurring in situations for which we have some normative expectations. For this reason we find this perspective being applied primarily in the interpretation of responses to tests such as the word association technique, TAT, and the Rorschach, where we have informal, if not formal, means of identifying unique responses. Its application in connection with events found in interpersonal, or less standardized, situations depends upon the extent to which the interpreter feels confident that he knows what the common response or set of responses would be in such situations.

The fact that interpreters will accord special significance to unique events can be easily accounted for by the Gestalt principle of figure-ground relationships, but the claim to validity of this perspective must rest upon other grounds. One possible rationale for this perspective is that the unique event, in contrast to the common event, is more likely to derive from some unique aspect of the individual which sets him apart from others. Hence, insofar as we are interested in the ways in which one individual differs from another, we accord special importance to the behaviors they manifest that we regard as unique. This line of reasoning finds one form of expression in Berg's (1955) statement that "deviant response patterns tend to be general; hence those deviant behavior patterns which are significant for abnormality and thus regarded as symptoms, are associated with other deviant response patterns which are in noncritical areas of behavior and which are not regarded as symptoms of personality aberration" (p. 70). This, of course, still leaves us with the question of how this comes about, if it does, but we shall not pursue this matter further here.

Although my purpose throughout this chapter has been to describe and not to evaluate the logic of the interpretive process, in view of my frequent caveats concerning the distinction between face validity and empirical validity, it might be instructive to consider one study that attempted to test directly the validity of the perspective of uniqueness in evaluating the significance of interpretive material. It is widely held (Rotter, 1946; Lindzey, 1952) that TAT stories which are in any way unusual are particularly revealing of the storyteller's personality. Miller and Scodel (1955), however, found that, when for thirty-five therapy cases they selected one "usual" and one "unusual" story, and asked judges to match each of these stories with the thirty-five psychotherapy protocols, there was no difference in the level of accuracy with which these two types of stories could be matched, and that in both instances matching was at a better than chance level. True, this is but one study concerned with but one perspective and dealing with a very limited segment of the material to which it might be applied, but still it should give one pause. In how many other instances does nature show such careless disregard for the cogency of our reasoning?

With this chapter we have begun our analysis of the interpretive process, treating it as a cognitive activity, and have attempted to make explicit those operations and principles that seem to guide it at the semantic stage.

The interpretive process at this stage consists of three steps: analysis, abstraction, and action. The first step involves the viewing of the event to be interpreted from a variety of perspectives, each of which produces a certain number of different attributes for consideration in deciding upon the class membership of the event in the language system of the interpreter. Those attributes leading to the class assignment most consistent with the context and theory and bias of the interpreter are abstracted and used as the basis for assignment, while the rest are ignored in the next step. In the final step, action, the interpreter makes a decision as to how the resulting interpretation should be treated: whether it should be communicated verbally or not; if communicated the form which the communication should take, and so on. Viewed in this manner, the general form of research suggested for dealing with the semantic aspect of the interpretive process becomes one in which questions involving relationships between types of persons, types of situation, content of interpretation, and forms of interpretation, can be investigated. At present, however, programs of research following this format are severely hampered by our inadequate conceptualization of each of the variables involved.

Interpretive activity at the semantic stage appears to be guided by five principles: The principles of dissonance and congruence each serve as criteria for deciding what material shall be subjected to interpretation. Any event or observation that is dissonant within its context in the eyes of the observer is eligible for interpretation, just as is any event that is congruent with some aspect of the theory of behavior subscribed to be the interpreter. The principle of interchangeability of genus, which finds its primary application in the interpretation of symbolism, states that genus is not a criterial attribute in determining class membership. This permits persons to be represented by animals, animate qualities by inanimate ones, and so on. The fourth principle, analysis and synthesis in the relationship between symbols and referents, serves together with the principle of interchangeability of genus to define the broad limits of freedom within which the interpreter might operate upon the material he has selected for interpretation. According to the fourth principle any referent may be represented by more than one symbol, and one symbol may have more than one referent. This principle is found most frequently in the interpretation of fantasy and autistic material. The fifth principle, contextual consistency, indicates the final criterion by which interpretations are evaluated and choices made between alternative interpretations. The interpretation must fit within the context of pertinent observations and already interpreted material.

Each event chosen for interpretation is viewed by the interpreter from a number of different perspectives in the first step, analysis, of the semantic stage of interpretation. Viewed from each perspective the event manifests different sets of attributes that in turn may qualify it for membership in different classes within the language system of the interpreter. The most frequently applied perspectives were described in some detail. These were: Structure, function, effect, affect, metaphor, phonetic analysis, logical extension and reversal, sequence, associations (of subject), reactions of the interpreter, frequency, intensity, pervasiveness, and uniqueness. The first ten serve to provide the attributes upon which interpretation will be based, while the last four function as criteria for evaluating the significance of the event or interpretation. Problems likely to arise in the application of each of these perspectives were also considered.

Accepting psychological interpretation as merely one of

several ways in which an event might be treated (it might, for example, also be taken at face value or it might be treated as a sign in an empirical or psychometric sense), it was seen in this chapter that its principles could be made explicit and that these do not in any way commit one to any particular personality theory or position regarding the nature of mental mechanisms or the unconscious.

CHAPTER 4

The Propositional Aspect

of Interpretation

STATEMENTS about "personality dynamics," personality or character traits, conflicts, expectancies, or simple behavioral tendencies that are generated by the psychological interpretation of content, arise out of the propositional aspect of this process. It is here that assertions are made which are either in themselves predictions of behavior or which figure in the making of such predictions. Similarly, it is here that assertions are made which are said to lead to the "understanding" of a particular personality, episode, or item of behavior, assertions which are essentially postdictive rather than predictive. With the propositional aspect of interpretation we therefore come to that aspect of the interpretive process which gives rise to assertions whose truth value may be determined empirically, in principle if not in fact.

Relationships between events begin to emerge following the

semantic stage of interpretation. These relationships are, of course, the result of the particular perspectives finally chosen from which to view the events in question. The choice of perspectives determines the relationships we observe. But, faced with patternings resulting from his efforts at the semantic stage of interpretation, many a clinician is inclined to believe that he has stumbled upon, or divined (depending upon his nature) some elemental truth about the meaning of the material. While no great harm comes of such naive realism generally, it is to be hoped that the clinician of the future will be sophisticated enough to realize from whence these relationships spring. For as charming as we might find naivete, we must recognize that it is also the seed bed of dogmatism and fatuity and therefore a condition which we can ill afford to nourish from either a professional or a scientific standpoint. In this chapter we shall examine in detail the process of interpretation at the propositional stage, with particular attention to the problems and sources of error encountered and to the attempts of the interpreter to cope with these.

The process engaged in by the clinician at the propositional stage is in all aspects equivalent to that of the scientist who has made a series of observations and is now pondering their meaning. He has essentially two choices or strategies that he may follow at this point. He can make an assertion of the order "If A, then B," in which A and B are names of classes to which observed events have been assigned, and in which he is asserting that some specified relationship exists between these two classes of events; or he can make an assertion of the order "If A and B, then x," where A and B are again names of classes of events, and x is a condition, state, or hypothetical entity, not observed but either implied by the observed relationship between A and B or invoked to account for it. In discussing these two strategies in more detail, it will be convenient to refer to the first as generalization, and to the second as construction.[1]

For purposes of illustration, I have presented a set of hypothetical interpretations in Table 2. While we can in no way determine the representativeness of this set of interpretations, there should be general agreement that they are of the type generally produced by interpreters when they are discussing "the dynamics of a case," "the latent content of a dream," or the "psychological meaning of some behavior." Whether the generalizations do, in fact, follow from the raw material to which they have been applied is beside the point here, and must be taken for granted. We shall use these examples as the basis for an analysis of the characteristics of generalizations and constructions as well as of the relationships between them. Each, in some sense, is a product of the propositional aspect of interpretation.

It will be noted, to begin with, that the generalizations vary in the extent to which they reflect the efforts of the interpreter at the semantic stage, ranging from numbers 3, 6, and 7, in which no interpretation was made at that stage, to numbers 9 and 10, where the events dealt with have all been subjected to interpretation. That is, in no instance in numbers 3, 6, and 7 were individual events, the choice of occupation, the "terms," and the persons involved assigned to broader classes of events, while the percepts and Rorschach cards in number 9 and the TAT stories in number 10 have

1 The reader may note some similarity between the processes referred to as generalization and construction and those usually referred to as induction and deduction. While this similarity is not denied, it seems desirable for our purposes to use the terms generalization and construction in order to avoid becoming encumbered by the historical, logical, and philosophical freight accumulated by the terms induction and deduction.

TABLE 2

Examples of Two Types of Propositions

Generalizations	Constructions
1. He reacts with hostility whenever he is criticized	1a. He is insecure
	1b. He has an authority problem
2. He reacts with hostility only when criticized by X and Y, but not by Z	2. He sees X and Y as competing with him, but not so, Z
3. Her mother was a nurse and she has also decided to be a nurse	3. She identifies with her mother
4. He feels anxious whenever any woman shows him any affection	4a. He fears domination, with which affection has been associated in his past
	4b. He is suffering from an unresolved Oedipus complex
5. When subject to public observation, he becomes anxious	5. He has guilt feelings and fears detection
6. She uses the same terms to describe her minister as she does to describe her father	6. The minister is a father figure to her
7. She uses the same terms to criticize her therapist as she does her father	7. She is manifesting transference
8. His drawings of females are masculine while his drawings of males are feminine	8. He has not established a clear-cut sexual identification
9. The mood quality of his percepts on Card IV, the father card, is much more dysphoric than it is for his percepts on Card VII, the mother card	9. He fears his father due to an unresolved Oedipus complex
10. In all his TAT stories involving authority relationships, the hero rebels or thwarts the demands of the authority figure in some passive way	10a. He has an authority problem
	10b. He is a passive-aggressive individual
	10c. He grew up in an authoritarian home
	10d. He fears expressing his own individuality

all been treated simply as exemplars of some more general class in each instance.

Thus, it is apparent, the justification for referring to the statements in the first column of Table 2 as generalizations cannot rest upon the fact that their elements represent generalizations. Rather, this term is justified because the statement of relationship itself represents a generalization, in that it implies that the relationship asserted is a recurring one, or that it is enduring in its implications if not in its identity. Even in the case of number 3, implied here is the idea that the daughter's choice of occupation similar to that of her mother's will be found, not only today, but tomorrow, and tomorrow, and whenever we choose to examine it. Similarly, although the patient referred to in number 10 may never take the TAT again, implied in the generalization is a manner in which he would react in an authority situation whenever he would be involved in one. In this sense, each of these statements are generalizations and go beyond the data, even where it appears that no interpretation of a semantic type has been undertaken. And while sharing with all such extrapolative ventures the risks of error, it must be recognized that they also serve to expand, potentially at least, the utility of our observations.

Assuming that they are not in error, generalizations serve the very useful function of providing us with a basis for anticipation with regard to the events or classes of events referred to in them. These anticipations, in turn, guide our subsequent decision-making, treatment plans, or behavior with respect to the individual in question. If, for example, the first generalization in Table 2 were applied to a particular patient we would be able to tell those dealing with him that they should be prepared for a show of hostility if they should attempt to criticize or correct him in any fashion. They may alter their behavior accordingly. Similarly, the individual to whom we offer the fourth or fifth generalizations will, as a result, be better able to anticipate when he is going to be anxious and either avoid such situations, or, more hopefully, become somewhat less overwhelmed by what had previously been perceived by him as "free-floating," and consequently be in a better position to deal cognitively with his entire problem.

But the interpreter may not be satisfied with having stated what appears to be a valid generalization. He may want to know why the relationship he has just described exists. He may want an explanation. Or he may be interested not so much in the anticipation of events about the patient as he is in describing the personality of the patient. He may be looking for the answers to such questions as: What kind of a person would behave that way? What kind of a person would make such a drawing? Have such a dream? If these are his concerns, the clinician offers an interpretation of the type we have chosen to refer to as construction.

Three points should be apparent from Table 2 about the relationship between generalizations and constructions. The first is that there are always generalizations prior to constructions. Although in practice the generalization may be implicit, without it there can be no justification for the construction. The existence of the generalization serves not only as the impetus for the construction, but is its *raison d'être* as well.

However, any one generalization may give rise to several equally plausible constructions, as we have illustrated in the case of generalizations 1, 4, and 10. While it is obvious that even in these cases we have not exhausted the realm of possible and plausible constructions, they serve to illustrate the second point to be made about the relationship between generalizations and constructions. This is that with regard to the question of the validity of the construction, the validity of the generalization to which it has been applied represents a necessary, but not a sufficient, condition. Consequently the choice between competing constructions cannot be made by recourse to the original generalization, but requires an appeal to other data. For example, whether an individual's hatred of his father and love of his mother is adequately accounted for as the operation of an Oedipus complex, or as a rebellion against authority, or as a realistic reflection of his parents' treatment of him can be decided only on the basis of additional evidence. One can only wonder at how much controversy psychology would be spared if this point were fully recognized and appreciated.

Finally, it should be recognized that despite the fact that generalizations do go beyond the data, they stay closer to the data than do constructions. Even where the generalization has had the benefit of full treatment at the semantic stage of interpretation, this is true. For this reason, constructions are inherently more subject to error than are generalizations, and clinicians working at this stage of interpretation should treat them accordingly. Whether the interpreter wishes to expose himself to the additional hazards of formulating constructions or to rest his labors with generalizations should depend upon his best estimate of what is to be gained by the adventure. Undoubtedly, however, this decision has been more often determined by the temperament of the clinician and what he has been taught represents interpretation than it has been by any rational consideration of the gains and losses likely to be entailed. We may hope, however, that the distinction between generalizations and constructions suggested here will be a first step in making clinicians aware of this problem and in fostering a search for a better basis for its solution.

Constructions owe their paternity in approximately equal measure to the generalizations for which they are supposed to account and to the theoretical system of the interpreter. However, as a glance at the constructions we have presented in Table 2 will indicate, we must be prepared to view with extreme generosity one of the agents in this tableau if we are to refer to it as a theoretical system. For involved here we find in some instances a true theoretical system, as in the cases of constructions numbers 4b, 7, and 9; in some instances what we might refer to as general purpose constructs, not the exclusive property of any single system, as in constructions 1a, 1b, 3 and 6; and in yet other instances, simply an appeal to the phenomenal field of the subject to account for the generalization as in constructions 2, 4a, and 5.

Where the clinician fails to recognize these diverse qualities of the sources from which his constructions spring we find him sanguinely formulating and juxtaposing assertions that either represent theoretically divergent points of view, or that are in some sense redundant with each other, either because the one subsumes the other or because they are, in effect, synonymous with each other. While this makes for bulk in interpretive analyses; it makes for little else besides weariness and confusion. For example, it is not at all unusual to find within the same report on the same individual both constructions number 1a and 1b or 10a, 10b, and 10c, presented as though each construction were conveying new information.

Although in a sense each construction does say something different about the person in question, there is a very real question as to whether it is sufficiently different in import from the others to warrant utterance along with them. There is obviously overlap in the examples just cited and there is even more overlap in cases that occur regularly but that would be too painful to cite. The remedy for this situation, as for so much else that we have examined in the interpretive process, is further conceptual development and empirical research. For to a large extent this situation arises because of a paucity of adequate concepts that would serve to integrate and subsume the partially redundant constructions now competing with each other. In addition, research focused upon the decision-making process in psychodiagnosis and psychotherapy and how it uses information fed into it would serve to indicate how much redundancy is necessary or tolerable. Ideally, constructions should serve to make the individual's behavior predictable and understandable over a wider range of situations than would be true of generalizations. This belief, common to such divergent enterprises as the factor analytic description of personality exemplified by the work of Cattell (1946, 1957) and the psychoanalytic study of character types, is part of the incentive for the interpreter's going beyond generalizations and formulating constructions at the propositional stage.

Another characteristic of constructions which makes their formulation particularly alluring to many interpreters is that they appear to be saying something much more personal than do generalizations. While generalizations deal with events, constructions usually have as their referent the individual, either his character structure, some trait or internal state, or his perception or experience. To make these latter types of statements in the interpretation of content seems to be much more gratifying, especially to those who hold to a substantive view of personality: here at last, they believe, they are able to get below the surface manifestations (generalizations?) of personality to its structure and content.

The promise, whether theoretical or intuitive, held out by constructions that they will permit more meaningful statements to be made about the individual, is yet to be realized. For where they have not generated tautologies, as is often the case in psychoanalysis where the construct is used to predict one of its own criterial attributes—for example, where, from having said that the son identifies with his father the analyst then goes on to predict those very behaviors that are necessary to justify his having applied the concept of identification in the first place—constructions have not provided very impressive results by way of predicting the future course of behavior of individuals.

The evidence for this contention is admittedly sparse and

comes from those studies that have been summarized and discussed by Meehl (1954), in which the clinician was pitted against the actuary in predicting behavior. In at least some of these studies, the clinician was free to interpret content and use it as the basis for his predictions, and could chalk up no better record than could a clerk working from a regression equation and a very limited number of variables. Although it is quite possible that where the clinicians involved did use interpretation they resorted to both generalizations and constructions, from our knowledge of the general predilections of clinicians it would seem safe to assume that most of their ill-starred ventures rested more heavily upon constructions than they did upon generalizations. It might be argued with some justification that these contests were unfair to the clinician in that he was being asked to make predictions of a type which were not ideally suited to his skills, but it must be recognized that we have no other comparable research evidence to go by at present in evaluating the clinician or the utility of interpretation, constructive or otherwise, in the prediction of behavior.

Let us now turn from the examination of the characteristics of generalizations and constructions to an analysis of the process by which these come into being. The questions with which we shall be concerned in the ensuing discussion are those of how generalizations and constructions are formed, how they are justified logically, and the potential sources of error to which the clinician must be ever alert and respectful at this stage of the interpretive process.

GENERALIZATION

The process involved here appears to be essentially similar to that described by Bartlett (1932) and aptly designated by him as "effort after meaning." For it seems likely that every clinician approaching the task of interpretation at the propositional stage by way of generalization begins with a schema consisting of all of the possible and plausible relationships between events postulated by the theories to which he subscribes or which are exemplified in his past experience. Theory and experience therefore enter in varying degrees in the formation of generalizations.

Apart from supplying the language of interpretation, theory provides the clinician with a schema which helps him in organizing his observations in such a way that he frequently begins his approach to generalization with a number of different theoretically hypothesized relationships and scans sets of events he has just interpreted semantically for instances of these relationships. For example, if the clinician subscribes to Bruch's (1957) theory of the causation of obesity he will scan the anamnesis provided him by an obese person for instances where an event, interpreted as frustration or deprivation of affection, was followed by eating, which in turn was interpreted as symbolic gratification of love and affection needs. In like manner, the therapist who accepts Freud's theory of the relationship between homosexuality and paranoia would be likely to have this as one of the relationships in his schema which would guide his scanning of the material presented him by a patient, and consequently might interpret the suspiciousness and hostility of his patient toward some other individual as being related to the homosexual impulses aroused in him by that person.

The schema with which the clinician approaches his material might just as well have been built out of his previous experience, although it is probably rarely, if ever, that schemata are exclusively either experientially or theoretically based. For the purposes of our analysis, however, it is important to recognize, or, more accurately, postulate, the existence of schemata, whether they be experimentally or theoretically derived, for they play an important role in understanding how the interpreter either justifies or assigns some confidence level to the generalization he has made.

When the interpreter asserts the existence of a relationship between two classes of events, we assume that this is based upon his observation of one or more instances where exemplars of these classes had the relationship he asserts to exist. But how is he to be sure that he is "correct" in this assertion? What are the criteria by which, in practice, such an evaluation is made?

This problem is not unlike that faced by the scientist in evaluating the significance of some relationship he has observed between one or more variables under study. However, the clinician solves it in a considerably less rigorous fashion, and with certain differences as well. Let us begin by considering all the possible sources of error, or reasons why the generalization may be incorrect.

"Correct" and "incorrect," in the sense in which we are using these terms, here should be understood as implying the existence of a language system adopted by the interpreter and his colleagues, which contains rules of interpretation by means of which these judgments may be rendered. Thus, within a given system of interpretation, a generalization would be considered correct, or not in error, if its derivation was consistent with the rules of the system, and if other observations, either concurrently or subsequently interpreted within the same system, did not yield contrary findings. Reality is always filtered through some coding system, and statements about it can be evaluated only in terms of that system.

Sources of error in generalizations

Because we never deal with universes, only samples, all generalizations are essentially probabilistic in nature, and so are inherently subject to error. For to say that event A is in some fashion related to event B is to say that out of a universe of events possessing all possible relationships with each other, a sample of events was drawn or observed which clearly revealed the relationship asserted to exist between A and B. And while samples may vary in the extent to which they approximate all the characteristics of the universe, as well as in the extent to which they approach the universe in size, our interest is always in the universe and our interpretations are universal in intent. Since this is the case, the question arises as to how large a sample of events containing instances of the asserted relationship between A and B should be demanded before we accord significance or confidence to the generalization in question.

In a well-designed experiment this question can easily be answered by referring to the variance in the data under investigation: generally, the greater the variance, the larger the sample we would require. The clinician can only crudely approximate this in an impressionistic fashion. But by recognizing his predicament and trying for an approximation he is in a better position than he would be by not recognizing that the content he is subjecting to interpretation is a sample, not a universe, and hence that any assertion he makes based upon this content must be viewed probabilistically, with the consequence that he is likely to encounter some negative instances as well as positive ones.

The first major source of potential error therefore lies in the magnitude of the ratio between the size of the content sample and the size of the universe from which it was drawn. The higher the ratio, all other things being equal, the less likely that the generalization will be in error. It must be recognized, however, that we are speaking here in ideal terms, since, in point of fact, we have no way of estimating the sizes of either the samples or the universes with which we deal in psychological interpretation. But this does not, analytically, alter in any way the fact that this problem does exist and must be considered.

Failure by the interpreter to recognize the probabilistic

nature of his enterprise leaves him vulnerable to either or both of two conditions that we find endemic among practitioners in this field. The first of these is that of ignoring or denying the relevance of negative instances for the generalization he has made. This is not difficult to do in as freewheeling an activity as psychological interpretation, where events are subject to multiple interpretations and the ground rules for choosing between them are not clearly formulated. The second consequence, in some ways perhaps more devastating (to the clinician at least) than the first, is that the interpreter may yield too readily at the first approach of a negative instance of the proposition he has asserted. If the clinician has not made the distinction between sample and universe, and therefore believes that his observations represented the universe of possible observations for which he has formulated his generalization, his discarding of an interpretation with the appearance of the first discordant datum is perfectly understandable and rational. Unfortunately, it would also be paralyzing.

However, the clinician who does recognize that his assertions are of a probabilistic nature, even when not stated so explicitly, and who reminds us that we must have some tolerance for ambiguity if we are to work in this field, is also prey to mischief: he may be too tolerant of negative instances or ambiguity.

Although we may look longingly at the researcher for whom there seems to exist ever-faithful 5 percent and 1 percent levels of significance for either accepting or rejecting a given hypothesis, our envy is unwarranted. For although lacking the quantitative statement, the clinician is actually in no poorer position than the researcher, since for both there exists an ultimate point where each must make a personal decision—although this is less obvious in the case of the researcher. The fact is, however, that the researcher must *choose* the level of significance which his data must satisfy, and this choice, unless relegated to convention or conformity, is no more easily made and usually no more objective than is the clinician's decision as to how much discordance he should tolerate before abandoning an interpretation. The clinician must make this decision on the basis of the possible effects of either discarding or retaining the interpretation should it be incorrect, and in many instances may legitimately not even be concerned with error in interpretation, if it appears that the interpretation will have its desired effect. But in all instances, the clinician must guard against the claims of his own vested interests in his ultimate decision vis-à-vis the interpretation he has made and the events that appear to be discordant with it. Tolerance for ambiguity must not become a shield for the inept or self-serving.

If sample size is one problem that the interpreter has in common with the researcher, the manner in which the sample was drawn is another, and, in psychological interpretation, is a source of error that has never been given sufficient weight. The generalizations that are made are in some instances based upon the clinician's personal observations of behavior, in some instances based upon reports of behavior by the patient or some collateral source, and in still others upon dreams, projective tests, and autobiographical material. As we have seen earlier, the logic of psychological interpretation at the semantic stage makes it possible to take events from any of these sources and treat them similarly. Although this represents a great gain in analytic power at the semantic stage of interpretation, there is—because there is no means of distinguishing between the sources of our observations at the propositional stage—a very strong temptation to treat them all as of equal credibility. And so what we gain at one stage is in danger of being offset at the other, unless the clinician is sufficiently sophisticated and disciplined in his thinking to recognize and avoid this snare. For although we have as yet no firm basis in research upon which to rank the various sources of our observations for credibility, it would certainly appear that failure to distinguish between them is just as likely to lead to embarrassments for the clinician as it is for the laboratory researcher.

Failure to make the distinction between sources of observation leads to the clinician treating as of equal reliability his observations of one patient's blanching and demonstrating an increasing number of speech disturbances whenever the patient discusses sexual matters, with the report of another patient that he becomes "upset" every time he thinks about sex, and with yet another case where the patient, after an unusually long latency, gives sexual content in his responses to Card VI of the Rorschach. Although it has been customary to consider this problem under the heading of validity, it should be recognized that it is just as legitimate, and perhaps even salutary, to consider it as one of reliability and sample-to-universe ratio.

I am therefore suggesting that it may be helpful from both a clinical and a research standpoint to pose the question about sources of samples in a different form than is usual: for a desired level of confidence in a given generalization, how large a sample of events from a given source consistent with that generalization is necessary? The answer to this question would result in an ordering of sources of content, not in terms of validity but in terms of relative magnitudes of samples that they must yield consistent with a generalization held at some specified level of confidence.

Putting the question in this form undercuts the whole question of the validity of depth versus nondepth observations (a question made meaningless if we have rejected the concept of depth in the first place) and substitutes the requirement of a quantitative answer for the categorical one of valid or invalid with respect to a given source of content. And this should be a gain. For while the categorical answer, if accepted, closes off an area of research and if not opens up an area of controversy, the quantitative answer, by its very nature, discourages polarization of opinion and, therefore, can only serve to encourage further research.

To the extent that his observations and generalizations therefrom fit easily into some theoretical framework, the interpreter feels comfortable about them; he would, if he could, assign a high confidence level to them. In this way, schemata enter in two ways into the interpretative process: first, as we have seen, in helping to organize observational data as the bases for generalizations, and second, as a basis for assigning some confidence level to the generalizations so formed. While this second function of schemata, despite the apparent circularity involved, has much to recommend it, we must recognize that it too is fraught with danger for the unwary.

Whenever the relationship between events observed by the clinician jibes with the relationship contained in his schema appropriate to these events, he is likely to feel a sense of familiarity with the observed relationship and confident in his assertions about it. The real world seems to be behaving as it should, according to past experience, according to Freud, or according to Dollard and Miller, or even according to Mowrer. There are no surprises; everything is in its place.

But more than a sense of complacency is likely to be fostered by this state of affairs; there is often also a profound sense of gratification if not triumph. For as the clinician finds that events do relate to each other as his mentors said they would, as he finds that his map really fits the world that he is dealing with, he is quite likely to congratulate himself on having placed his bets on the right theory, for having gone to the right school, for having chosen the right professors, and so on. In a sense, he is likely to experience vindication for all of his past choices and doubts. And herein lies the danger that we shall refer to as "schematic pull."

Schematic pull is a phenomenon closely related to premature closure and intolerance for ambiguity (Frenkel-Bruns-wik, 1949), but I prefer to coin this new term because of the pathological connotations that have accrued to these latter ones. Specifically, what I intend by this term is the tendency for the interpreter to assign a higher confidence level to his generalization than is warranted on the basis of the amount of evidence available to him because of the fit that seems to exist between the structure of the events he has observed and the schema he brings into the situation. Had the schema not been available, or had his observations not been so neatly in accord with his schema, the interpreter would have required a larger sample of data either before making the generalization, or before according it the confidence he did.

This is not to be confused with perceptual distortion, nor is it to be considered a pathological phenomenon. We perceive meaning only as a result of the schemata available to us, and it is simply a matter of recognizing that, through the reinforcing effects of finding meaning in events by means of these schemata, we are in danger of being too lenient in our demands of the sample with which we are dealing. Doubtless there are individual differences in susceptibility to schematic pull, but these are best not emphasized here lest the reader conclude that it is only "others" who are likely to be so affected. It is probable, however, that the best immunity against excess susceptibility to schematic pull is a recognition of its existence plus a sound grounding in the scientific method as applied in psychology.

The role of the personality of the clinician in determining the kind of content obtained from patients and how this is interpreted is too well documented (Masling, 1960) to require extended comment. The clinician's personality may enter as a source of error in either or both of the following ways: first, through its contribution to the total stimulus context in which the patient is behaving and which therefore exerts some influence on the kind of content produced, and second, through the operation of certain needs that may, for various reasons, predispose the clinician toward one interpretation rather than another. Unfortunately, research to date has only demonstrated that an interaction exists between the clinician's and the patient's personality as manifested in various kinds of projective test protocols; similarly it has only demonstrated that there are individual differences in the interpretations made of test material. Research has yet to focus upon the major problem here of describing the nature of the interaction in terms of what characteristics of the clinician are likely to interact in what fashion with what characteristics of the patient (Levy, 1956). Until this is done, we can only acknowledge that the clinician's personality contributes some unknown amount of error variance to his interpretations.

CONSTRUCTION

If the generalization formulated by the interpreter is one dealt with by the theory of personality or behavior to which he subscribes, the construction follows as a matter of course. The interpreter has merely to assert the explanation contained in the theory for the relationship he has described in his generalization. Providing that his theory is comprehensive enough and he is sufficiently familiar with it, the interpreter is unlikely to experience any difficulty in formulating constructions. This is likely to be all the more true in those instances in which it was the interpreter's strong allegiance to his theory that predisposed him toward the search for certain relationships between particular classes of events in the first place, or where schematic pull has caused him to assert one generalization rather than another.

There is no personality theory today that approaches the claim to comprehensiveness made by psychoanalysis. That this comprehensiveness is purchased at the price of looseness and ambiguity at many points does not diminish its attractiveness to many who are faced with the task of interpretation and particularly with the formulation of constructions; psychoanalytic theory remains the only theory to which the clinician can expect to turn for an appropriate construction without disappointment. Thus, beyond registering this mild caveat, there is little more that we can say about the process involved in constructive interpretation by the true believer.

In contrast to the orthodox psychoanalytic interpreter who operates with the smooth efficiency of an electronic computer and the calm assurance of a master craftsman, his heterodox colleague is likely to appear, and at times to be, clumsy, unsure, and nonplused as he approaches constructive interpretation. Our inconoclast may congratulate himself on having made the break with dogma, on having been shrewd enough to recognize psychoanalytic theory as unscientific, on enjoying the blessings of philosophy of science, and on being a member of the new wave in psychology, but let us see what he has set in its stead. Is he truly a harbinger of the millenium? Sober and dispassionate reflection suggests that the time for rejoicing is not yet upon us, and that, quite possibly, the nature of the efforts of the uncommitted or emancipated, as they undertake psychological interpretation, is likely to hinder its approach rather than hasten it.

To appreciate this point it is necessary to recognize that in addition to its pragmatic function of helping both the interpreter and his patient or public recast content in different terms, with all of the benefits likely to accrue therefrom, interpretation, particularly constructive interpretation, serves as one of the proving grounds of theory. In drawing upon any theory for its constructions, it is also testing the adequacy of that theory. Each instance where a given theory provides a satisfactory explanation for a generalization adds an increment to its stature; each instance where that theory fails to provide a construction, or where the construction is ambiguous or equivocal, counts as a decrement. It is in this sense that psychological interpretation no less than rigorous experimentation provides a touchstone for theory. And it is here that we question the extent of the contribution to our knowledge of personality by those who have adopted an eclectic approach to interpretation over a systematic one. And this not because the system they have rejected necessarily counts as a major loss, but because ultimately psychology must have a single comprehensive system for the understanding of behavior, and the current form eclecticism has taken in psychological interpretation is very likely to impede its development.

The route by which those less enchanted by psychoanalytic theory arrive at constructions is a complex and often tortuous one, which usually involves borrowings from several theories (psychoanalysis included), *ad hoc* theorizing, and appeals to the supposed phenomenal field of the patient or agent responsible for the content being subjected to interpretation. In this way they have replaced the obvious weaknesses of psychoanalytic theory with the obscure ones that inhere in eclecticism. They have set in the place of a theory of dubious quality an amalgam of essentially unknown quality. While this does not in any way reduce the pragmatic value of the interpreter's efforts, it does serve to vitiate his contribution to the development and testing of theories in psychology.

For to the extent that he shifts his bases for constructive interpretations he fails to give any single approach the thorough trial by fire it deserves, and he also sees no incentive or need for further theory construction; his needs are served. And so long as he thinks only in terms of his practical needs, those of his day-to-day clinical work, this is true. But if he feels any identification with the quest for knowledge, he should recognize that this is not true. So long as the interpreter employs the tactic of selecting the theory or approach to fit his problem at the moment he helps to maintain the present fragmentary and patchwork status of psychological theory.

Since constructions are theoretical in intent and are intended to account for sets of observations in terms that will not only make them understandable but will also provide a basis for the anticipation of subsequent events, it is meaningful to speak of error in construction under one of three conditions: (1) The construction does not follow logically from the generalization according to the rules of the theory being applied; in other words, the interpreter has departed from the structure of the system he has invoked. Obviously, the less well defined the system being used, the less this condition will count as a criterion in evaluating constructions. (2) The past history of the individual producing the content for which the construction was intended contains one or more incidents not consistent with the construction. (3) Predictions mediated by the construction are not confirmed. The latter two conditions, failure in postdiction and failure in prediction, again require sufficient univocality in the system so that the failure can be directly attributed to the construction in question and not to the way in which it is combined with other constructions or other data. Thus error can be attributed to a construction from either a dialectical or an empirical standpoint or from both. In addition, of course, constructions must satisfy the pragmatic criteria of the interpreter, and these may not, as we have seen, necessarily involve either postdiction or prediction.

Setting aside the possibility of faulty logical derivation as a source of error, constructions are subject to various other sources of error. Despite the tenuousness of the tie between constructions and theories in many cases, one source of error that must be recognized is the theories themselves. Although it has been customary to think of theories as being tested by well-designed experiments, interpretation, no less than experimentation, serves to test theory. While the experiment renders its verdict on the basis of the confirmation or discon-firmation of some hypothesis derived from the theory, inter-pretation does so on the basis of how well constructions derived from the theory survive the tests of postdiction and prediction in each case. In this sense, faults in theories con-tribute to errors in construction.

Another major source of error in constructions, of course, is contained in the generalizations for which they are asked to account. Should these be in error, the construction would also be in error. Because we have discussed the sources of error in generalizations at some length we shall not elaborate on them here again. However, it will be helpful at this point to have available a concrete example to illustrate some of the points at which the interpreter may fall into error in constructive interpretation.

A nine-year-old girl was referred to a clinician for dif-ferential diagnosis with regard to the specific question of the extent to which her behavior was due to brain damage as opposed to emotional factors. Her parents reported, when asked by the clinician whether she showed much affection, that she showed and demanded a great deal of affection, but that it was often difficult to respond to her as she desired. This was because of a pattern her parents observed, in which the child would first torment or physically hurt the person, not only her parents, and then throw her arms around him, ask if he loved her, and demand some show of affection. The child's parents reported that this was a frequently recurring pattern and that they were at a loss to explain it.

Clearly, this episode cries out for interpretation. But just as clearly, it permits of several interpretations. To illustrate the various interpretational problems involved, Table 3 pre-sents the two events, labeled *A* and *B,* as described by the parents, corresponding sets of interpretations that might be made at the semantic level, and finally, a set of constructions that might be asserted to account for the generalizations. We have not included the generalizations themselves, which would consist of various combinations of the interpretations of events *A* and *B*, leaving this as an exercise for the reader. The order in which the semantic interpretations appear in the two columns is not intended to suggest any particular generalization and the reader will readily observe that with any single interpretation of event *A* it is possible to pair two or more interpretations of event *B*, and that as these pairings change so do the constructions in most instances.

TABLE 3

An Illustration of Alternative Interpretations of Two Events

	Event A	*Event B*
Parents' description	Child inflicts pain or torments person	Child expresses affection toward same person and demands reciprocation
Semantic interpretations of events	1. An act which makes her unlovable 2. A hostile act 3. A means of communicating with person 4. A means of relating to person	1. Demands that which she cannot have 2. An expression of love 3. A demand for love 4. A demand for attention or for interaction
Constructions	1. Child is acting out ambivalence she feels toward others 2. Child is extremely hostile and fears rejection or counteraggression 3. Child is testing, trying to determine whether she is really loved—trial by ordeal 4. Child is trying to prove that she is rejected or not loved 5. Child does not know of any other way of relating (or communicating) with others 6. A vicious circle in which frustration of her desire for love leads to expression of hostility which only makes more likely further frustrations and further hostility	

We may hope that additional information about the case, a full description of the context in which the events occur, as well as clinical observations of the child herself, would help to reduce the degrees of freedom which the interpreter encounters as he tries to move from anamnesis to construction. But this is not likely to reduce all the slippage; we have so many alternatives at each of the stages of interpretation partially because we have not restricted ourselves to any single personality theory. In this sense the alternatives are not mutually exclusive and it would not be at all unusual to find the interpreter opting for more than one, perhaps each reflecting a different systematic position, at each stage of interpretation. Unfortunately, each degree of freedom remaining to the clinician is an invitation to error from a variety of sources, as we have pointed out in connection with both the semantic stage of interpretation and the formulation of generalizations; where the formulation is not completely determined by the data and the theory it will also be determined by extraneous factors; where the interpreter is free to swing from theory to theory, or perhaps to embrace a clutch of theories at the same time, we are inviting expediency as well as other irrelevant factors to act as major determinants of interpretation. And this is courting error.

Lest this discussion be taken as an excoriation of the interpreter, we should hasten to point out that in the absence of any single, comprehensive, well-articulated theory of personality, he has little choice. He is in a sense covering his bets, much as the gambler does in a risky situation, and he is at least trying to cope with the problem before him rather than retreating into the sanctuary of an intellectual nihilism. Furthermore, if he has managed by his interpretation to move his client off dead center, if he has suggested some new perspective from which to understand the problem posed by the content with which he is dealing, he has performed a real service: his interpretation was justified and appropriate.

SUBSUMPTION, PREDICTION, POSTDICTION, AND UNDERSTANDING

Just as at the semantic stage many events are found to be susceptible to more than one interpretation, so too at the propositional stage, as illustrated in Table 3, we frequently find that several generalizations are vying with each other for application to a particular relationship or episode, and that each of these generalizations, in turn, may be accounted for by more than one construction. The interpreter is therefore again faced with the problem of choice. Assuming that the alternative interpretations hold equal strategic and tactical promise, how does the clinician decide between them at the propositional stage?

We shall not distinguish between generalizations and constructions in the following discussion, since the criteria that are likely to be applied, as well as their method of application, do not differ for these two types of propositional interpretations. We find the interpreter relying upon these criteria, singly or in combination, whenever he is faced with a choice either between generalizations or between constructions.

Subsumption

The intellectual history of man from ancient Greece to the present can largely be read as an odyssey in search of universal principles. To find a principle or concept which will account for many seemingly diverse phenomena is both esthetically and intellectually satisfying as well as potentially enlarging of man's control over the universe. This point is so obvious that any documentation would represent sheer pedantry. It is therefore understandable that the interpreter should measure competing interpretations against a criterion of subsumption, giving preference to those interpretations that will subsume the largest portion of the material with which he has to deal. Both within the single case and over a series of cases, where

two or more interpretations present themselves for consideration, some ordering is usually possible between them in the
extent to which they approach the universal principle that
sets everything in order, that makes every phenomenon appear
reasonable and orderly. By this criteria the interpreter makes
his choice between interpretations in a particular case; the one
selected handles more of the case material. In this way the
interpreter develops predilections for certain interpretations
in his general practice; he has seen them work so well in so
many cases.

Subsumption is a reasonable criterion to apply in this
situation. But it must be applied with care for two reasons.
The first is that as we approach universality in a principle
we find that its power to account for the unique aspects of the
particular case diminishes. For this reason the interpreter must
always recognize that in applying this criterion he must strike
some bargain between the subsumptive power of his interpretation and what he is willing to give up, or overlook, in
the particular case. It is his decision as to how much he is
willing to pay by way of ambiguity in the particular instance
for an interpretation which will encompass not only that instance but many others as well. That this decision may be
determined by the interpreter's personal needs and training
should come as no surprise; that his decision should hinge
upon his purposes in the particular case should be apparent.
There can be no categorical decision here between the universal and the particularistic except as fits the problem at
hand.

The second point of which the interpreter must be aware in
applying this criterion is that many interpretations gain in
apparent subsumptive power by vagueness of terminology and
looseness of reasoning—a point not to be confused with the
inverse relationship between universality and particularity of
explanatory power just noted. This danger becomes increasingly serious as we search for our interpretations amidst the

lower depths of the unconscious and use as our guides loosely developed theoretical systems. Interpretations, like theories, gain in viability and generality the less well defined their terms and so the interpreter must constantly guard against specious claims to subsumptive power whenever he invokes this criterion.

Prediction

This is the most universally accepted criterion of knowledge (Reichenbach, 1951), although its applicability in any given area may be open to question. With regard to the evaluation of interpretations its application seems forthright enough; if our interpretation of behavior is correct, regardless of its source, we should be able to predict its future course. To be sure, the area in which prediction is possible may have to be circumscribed by a variety of considerations, such as the relevance of the to-be-interpreted sample to the to-be-predicted, but nevertheless prediction remains the final arbiter in any question of validity in interpretation.

While we would grant the validity of demurrers entered to the effect that success rate in predicting behavior hinges upon many circumstances over which we have no control and can have no prior knowledge, we interpret this only to mean that predictions, like the interpretations upon which they are based, must be viewed probabilistically, not that prediction is an unrealistic criterion. The interpreter must decide upon what he will accept as an acceptable success *rate*.

But to apply this criterion the interpretation must have been made, must have been recorded, the interpreter must have already made his choice between competing interpretations. In this sense prediction is only of value retrospectively; it tells us how well we *have done*, it is of much less value in aiding us in the job before us, in telling us what we *should do*.

Only to the extent that the interpreter can attach prediction success rates to the alternatives before him on the basis of previous experience with them, is he likely to have recourse to this criterion *while in the act of interpretation.* Like any reinforced response, that interpretation among a set of available interpretations which has most often led to the successful prediction of behavior in the comparable past is the one most likely to be chosen in the future. But while in the absence of any other basis for choice this is a very reasonable one, it should be recognized that each situation differs from all previous ones and that, like any other reinforced response, it is always in danger of being found inappropriate, particularly if history of prior reinforcement becomes the sole basis for its selection.

We might therefore say with regard to prediction that as a basis for evaluation of past performance the interpreter has no choice but to accept it fully; as a guide or criterion for present performance he must be alert to its dangers lest a helpful guide becomes an alluring snare. The only protection here is an alert and inquiring attitude.

Postdiction

Prediction backwards in time, postdiction, is often cited as of equal status with prediction as a criterion of knowledge. The logic justifying the one is identical with that justifying the other. The problem in connection with postdiction is to insure against the contamination of the predictor variables by the events to be postdicted, and if there is any difference in degree of rigor between postdiction and prediction it resides here. It is not only a matter of depriving the predictor of direct knowledge of the to-be-postdicted events, it is also one of controlling the possible effects these events may have had on the variables to be used in postdiction. This latter is a problem that does not exist in connection with prediction.

Suppose, for example, that we are asked to postdict the quality of a patient's relationship with his commanding officer in the service. This relationship has already conditioned in some fashion much of the behavior we are likely to subject to interpretation; in a sense the answer is already contained in this behavior. We should, therefore, expect greater success at this task than if we had been asked to predict the kind of relationship the patient will have in the future with his commanding officer, an event that has not occurred and that therefore has not had any chance to etch its message upon the behavior available to us.

Since it is impossible either to control or to estimate the effects of the to-be-postdicted events upon the content we use in our interpretation and postdiction, it must be recognized that postdiction will always pose an easier hurdle for the interpretation and theory than will prediction. This is not to impugn the logic behind its use as a criterion; rather, it is simply to recognize the difference in demands between it and prediction. Thus it might be expected that many theories, tests, and other instruments will do a better job of postdiction than they will of prediction.

In contrast to prediction, postdiction holds out the prospect of aid to the embattled clinician faced with a choice between interpretations. But this is a promise not to be taken lightly. For in selecting the interpretation which proves most accurate in postdiction the clinician must recognize that he has of necessity violated the rule of independence between predictor and criterion; he was not completely innocent of knowledge of the events postdicted at the time he made his choice between interpretations. If he had been he would not have been able to resort to postdiction to begin with.

Criterion contamination is impossible to avoid in clinical practice and needs no apology. The clinician must recognize this so that if he should desire to appeal to postdiction he will be prepared to make the effort necessary to make its use at all meaningful; he must, in other words, strive in his thinking to approximate the independence between criterion and predictor that we demand in fact in clinical research. How well he will be able to do this will depend upon his intellectual discipline and so will certainly vary from clinician to clinician. But unless he makes this effort, to speak of postdiction here is pointless.

Understanding

When the interpreter is not willing to commit himself as to his use of any of the three preceding criteria in guiding his interpretive efforts, he is likely to subscribe to something called understanding. Although it is likely that careful analysis of the referent here would reveal that it is composed in varying proportions of subsumption, prediction, and postdiction, the interpreter who claims to use understanding as his guide would find such an analysis repugnant. It would be akin to factor-analyzing a religious experience.

Deriving in part from the German *Verstehendepsychologie* (Allport, 1937) and receiving recent infusions from the emphasis on empathy by Rogers (1961) and his followers as well as from Existentialism (May, Angel, & Ellenberger, 1958) and Zen Buddhism (Fromm, 1960) the concept of understanding when used as a criterion in interpretation seems to imply an experience of closeness to the subject, a feeling that all of the parts in the puzzle fit together, a feeling of empathy, insight, and enlightenment that cannot be analyzed further. The interpretation that yields this understanding is the one accepted and we can say little more.

As a personal guide one could ask for nothing better. That interpretation which is satisfying to the interpreter is the one selected and certainly the interpreter should be satisfied with his labors. But as a basis for communication, for teaching, for science building, the analysis cannot stop here; we want to know why one interpretation leads to understanding and another does not; we want to know if our understanding of understanding is the same as our colleagues'. Without answers to these questions we have art, not science; we enhance our own egos, not our patients'; we impress, but we do not enlighten.

Thus we find understanding, when meant to imply something beyond subsumption, prediction, and postdiction, of very dubious merit as a guide to the interpreter caught between conflicting interpretations. To continue to embrace it, unanalyzed, is to come dangerously close to mysticism.

The interpreter is always wearing two hats whether he desires to or not: that of the clinician or pragmatist who uses interpretation as a tool in working in the world of perplexity and troubled people, and that of the scientist or theorist whose use of interpretation provides a potent stimulant to knowledge as a test of existing theories and as a guide in the development of new theories. This latter function of interpretation was stressed more heavily in the present chapter because I believe that it has not received the recognition which it deserves, that too many clinicians in their zeal to help others are not aware of their ability and responsibility to contribute to the body of knowledge in psychology. In the following chapters we shall be concerned with the role of interpretation in psychodiagnosis and psychotherapy, with illustrations of the process in each of these endeavors and with questions of how interpretations are made, how they should be made, and how they effect changes in the behavior of the patient.

SUMMARY

The propositional, in contrast to the semantic, aspect of the interpretive process is concerned with assertions that have one of two qualities: they are in themselves empirically verifiable or they permit deductions that can be empirically verified. These assertions may be of one of two forms: generalizations or constructions. The former consists of statements of relationships between events or classes of events, such as "She engages in self-defeating behaviors whenever in an achievement situation," while the latter involves attempts to account for these relationships, such as "Achievement is inconsistent with her concept of femininity." Although generalizations appear to stay closer to observations than do constructions, it is important to recognize that they too go beyond the data. The role of the interpreter's schemata in determining the kinds of generalizations he makes or relationships he "observes" cannot be too strongly emphasized. In particular, the concept of "schematic pull" was developed to describe those situations in which the interpreter is led to make a generalization on the basis of what might be considered insufficient evidence simply because of the consistency between his observations and some relationship contained in his schemata or postulated by the theory to which he subscribes.

Constructions always derive from theory, although in many instances the theory may not be far beyond the level of crude analogy. While generalizations have as their focus relationships between events, constructions most often refer to characteristics of the individual that are believed to account for the relationships observed. Thus, although generalizations are usually sufficient to permit behavioral prediction, if the interpreter is interested in providing a personality assessment he will usually proceed beyond these to constructions. Sources of error in both generalization and construction were reviewed in this chapter, and it was concluded that, because constructions are somewhat further removed from the data than are generalizations, and because any one generalization will usually permit more than one construction, constructions are more susceptible to error than are generalizations. For this reason, the interpreter should always weigh carefully the question of whether his purposes require that he proceed to construction, or whether they will not be as well, or perhaps better, served if he sets generalization as his objective.

The criteria by which the interpreter decides between interpretations at the propositional stage are in no way different from those applied by science in the evaluation of any theory. These are subsumption, the amount of material accounted for by the interpretation; prediction, our ability to use the interpretation in the prediction of the future course of events; and postdiction, the extent to which the interpretation would have permitted prediction of events that have already occurred. Each of these criteria were seen to entail certain difficulties in their application: in subsumption it was observed that there is an inverse relationship between the subsumptive power of an interpretation and its ability to account for the unique aspects of the individual case, and that this power is often purchased at the price of vagueness of language; prediction, while indispensible in the confirmation of an interpretation, is of limited utility in helping the interpreter in the act of choosing between interpretations; postdiction, while logically identical with prediction except for temporal direction, may be of greater value to the interpreter in the act of deciding between interpretations or in evaluation of a particular interpretation but is highly vulnerable to criterion contamination. Nevertheless, it is to these three criteria that the interpreter must appeal in evaluating his efforts at the propositional stage of interpretation. Understanding, which is often cited as a criterion, appears to refer to an emotional response on the part of the interpreter. It was concluded that except where it actually refers to either subsumption, prediction, or postdiction, understanding cannot be accepted as a criterion in the evaluation of interpretations.

The fact that we have, in this and the preceding chapters, pointed up all the various sources of error in the interpretive enterprise and indicated the large extent to which the personality, training, and experience of the interpreter enter into its final product, should not be taken as grounds for setting psychological interpretation beyond the pale. Far from it. It means simply that psychological interpretation is a human enterprise, of a piece with science and technology no less than with the arts, and that in striving toward its perfection our first step must be that of taking its true dimensions.

CHAPTER 5.

A Brief Schematic Reprise

IN much the same manner as will viewing a highly enlarged photograph at nose-length distance, the analysis of the interpretive process in which we have just been engaged has undoubtedly produced many unfamiliar images. The reader may be wondering how the pieces fit together—if indeed they do—into anything resembling the activity that he knows as interpretation. In the present chapter I hope to provide the perspective necessary to see psychological interpretation as a whole, as an ongoing activity comprised of several integrally related parts.

In order to examine psychological interpretation in all its aspects it was necessary to slow down the process analytically to the point where the impression could easily have been gained that it was an extremely ponderous and cumbersome activity presided over by only the most ruminative of individuals, that because of its complexity the interpreter must constantly be at least ten steps behind the march of reality, or that we have consigned the interpreter to interment together with Tolman's rats, still buried in thought at some choice point. Nothing could be further from the truth.

With but few exceptions, interpretation presents itself phenomenally as a deft, smoothly operating process, possessed of a unity that defies analysis. The patient yawns and the therapist immediately sees this as resistance; a dream involving a flaming gasoline truck is taken as indicating a patient's fear of his sexual impulses; a painting of an individual looking out at an empty expanse of ocean is unhesitatingly interpreted as an expression of feelings of personal insignificance. Interpretation appears as one of the truly human and exciting accomplishments of man's intellect.

This is the way interpretation appears when we encounter it in the clinic, the textbook, or the lecture hall. But if we are to incorporate it into the realm of science, exploit its potentialities to the fullest, and assess its limitations objectively, we must be willing to exchange this view for one that will be more productive of these purposes. As we shift our vantage point from that of the practitioner or spectator to that of the scientist we enter a new world where familiar objects and events take on very unfamiliar appearances. So long as we recognize that this comes about only as a result of a shift in perspective, that we are not setting one view of reality over against some other as the more valid, we should have no difficulty. The last four chapters have indeed set forth a view —let us call it a model—of the interpretive process quite different from that customarily held, but it is one that appears particularly suited to describe its logical and psychological nature in such a way as to promote further research and development.

This model is schematically represented in Figure 1. It is a six-step communication system with content as its input and with outputs possible after the semantic stage, or after either generalization or construction at the propositional stage. Each step performs some transformation on the message passing

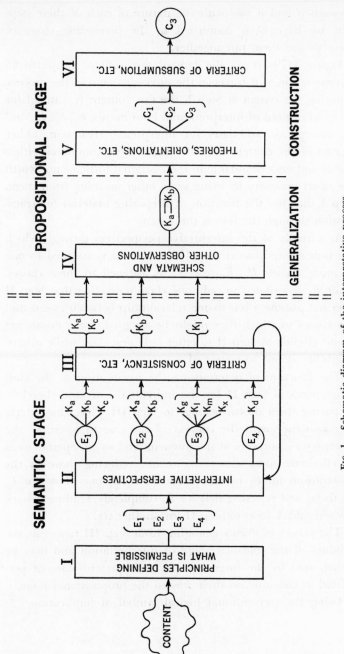

Fig. 1. Schematic diagram of the interpretative process

through it and it was with the nature of each of these steps that we have been concerned in the preceeding chapters. Here we see them put together.

Figure 1 illustrates the fate of any content subjected to interpretation as it traverses the successive steps in the process. Entering the system at Step I, the raw content is scanned for material in need of interpretation. Four events, E_1, E_2, E_3, and E_4, emerge as candidates for interpretive treatment. Other aspects of the content fed into Step I were considered either useful and understandable in their original form, or not worth the effort necessary to wring some other meaning from them. Step I thus has the function of preparing material for transmission through the rest of the system.

As a result of the interpretive perspectives through which the four events pass at Step II, each event is assigned to one or more classes, K_a, K_b, etc. E_1 is assigned to three classes, while E_4 is assigned to only one class, indicating that Step II does not assume a one-to-one relationship between events and the classes to which they might be assigned. Some events are found eligible at Step II to enter only one class, while others' eligibility is not so restricted.

The function of determining the justification of the class assignments of Step II for the individual case, and therefore of paring them down, belongs to Step III. Here the criteria of consistency with the context of the case in question, the interpreter's purposes at the moment, and so on, operate so as to eliminate some class assignments, reducing those in the illustrations for E_1 by one, those for E_2 by one, those for E_3 by three, and rejecting that for E_4 completely, sending it back via a feedback loop to Step II for another try.

The classes of events emerging from Step III represent the product of the semantic stage of interpretation and may be either used by the interpreter in their present state or permitted to continue on their way to the propositional stage.

Using the conventional logical symbol of implication, $\supset$, in the expression of the generalization, the three inputs into Step IV are shown to result in the output of only a single generalization, $K_a \supset K_b$. Of the four classes entering here the joint operation of the interpreter's schemata and other observations produced the single generalization asserting a relationship between K_a and K_b. For want either of supporting additional data or of representation in the interpreter's schemata, classes K_c and K_l drop out of the system at this point; the interpreter can find no way of using them. They may, however, serve as supporting data for some subsequent generalization.

If the interpreter decides to seek some explanation for the relationship he has just asserted to exist, the generalization moves on to Step V, wherein theories are scanned or orientations are assumed that produce one or more possible explanations or constructions that account for the generalizations. In Figure 1 we find three possible constructions emerging from Step V. As we have seen in Chapter 4, it is quite possible that these are not mutually exclusive.

It is the function of the final step in the model to reduce, where possible, these competing constructions to the single one that best accounts for the generalization. In the illustration, as a result of the application of the criteria of subsumption, prediction, postdiction, and understanding at Step VI, only C_3 survives to reign as the interpretation of some aspect of the content originally fed into the system at Step I.

From the schematic representation of the model we note that Steps I and IV serve to put the message in a form upon which it can be operated by the succeeding steps in their respective stages. Step I does this by isolating those aspects of the content to which the various interpretive perspectives are to be applied, while Step IV accomplishes this same function by producing the generalization for which alternative constructions will be attempted.

Also to be noted from Figure 1 are the analogous nature of

the roles played by Steps II and III at the semantic stage and those played by Steps V and VI at the propositional stage. In each case the first step has an expansive function, increasing the number of alternatives to be carried on through the system, while the second step has a constrictive function, containing criteria that serve to reduce the number of alternatives that pass beyond it.

The functions assigned to each of the steps in this model endow them with their own unique problems by way of the demands they place upon the interpreter, his skills, his knowledge, and his personality, as well as the demands they place upon current knowledge and theory in psychology. The nature of these demands, together with their implications for research, has been discussed at length in connection with each of the steps in the preceding chapters. It remains now only to point out that our model as diagramed in Figure 1 provides an excellent armature around which these diverse research efforts and their findings could be integrated. Possessed of such a model, we are constantly apprised of where the gaps in our knowledge of the interpretive process exist, as well as of where in the process any particular study will make its major contribution.

CHAPTER **6.**

Interpretation
in Psychodiagnosis

PSYCHODIAGNOSIS is a descriptive venture, having as its ultimate goal the provision of a basis for the anticipation of the behavior of the patient under various contingencies. Unless it can be shown that this goal is accomplished by the use of a particular psychodiagnostic approach, continued use of that approach represents sheer ritual. Therefore if the clinician is not to be found guilty of engaging in ritualistic behavior in the pursuit of his professional goals, he must be able to demonstrate that the product of his psychodiagnostic procedures permits predictions to be made about a patient's behavior at a higher level of accuracy than could otherwise be obtained.

Our conceptualization of psychodiagnosis as predictive in intent has the effect of blurring, if not obliterating, the distinction between diagnosis and prognosis. And this is intentional. For diagnoses which do not imply prognoses can serve no purpose other than that of occupying the clinician's time or fulfilling certain compulsive needs for order. Since it does not seem unreasonable to ask that the order established by our psychodiagnostic systems should lead beyond itself, I would propose that psychologists cease to make the distinction between diagnosis and prognosis. To continue in this anachronism is to cut diagnostic procedures off from their only justification and means of improvement—how well they predict behavior.

The present definition of psychodiagnosis is consistent with recent emphases on the diagnostician as decision-maker. In making a decision regarding a patient—whether he should be recommended for outpatient or inpatient treatment, whether he should be subjected to an extensive neurological examination, whether he should be released on trial visit, and so on— the clinician is, in effect, anticipating the behavior of the patient under the various contingent conditions represented by his decision alternatives. His decision is governed implicitly, if not explicitly, by what he predicts will maximize the chances of the patient achieving some desired state as well as by what he predicts will minimize the patient's achieving some undesired state.

Although discussions, such as that by Meehl and Rosen (1955), which focus upon the alternatives of minimizing either false positive or false negative rates imply it, psychologists have yet to exploit fully the potentialities of adopting a minimax criterion in psychodiagnosis. Evidence abounds that certain tests have higher false positive rates than others in the diagnosis of brain damage, juvenile delinquency, psychosis, and so on, and similarly for false negative rates. This would suggest that it may be worthwhile to consider the strategy of developing diagnostic procedures that will guard against one or the other of these alternatives, that will yield information permitting the clinician either to maximize chances of obtaining some desired outcome or minimize the chances of some undesired outcome. The same tests or procedures may not be suitable for both objectives, and reflection suggests that many cases exist where it is more appropriate to aim for one alternative than the other.

The psychological interpretation of content is but one approach to the problem of psychodiagnosis, and as such it plays a role that varies in importance with the predilections and training of the diagnostician. While one clinician will base his diagnosis solely upon a configural analysis of an MMPI profile and assorted other test scores, another clinician will eschew all quantitative data and devote himself entirely to puzzling over the meaning of the content elicited in the course of the anamnesis and projective testing. Our concern in this chapter will not be that of deciding which of these two clinicians should bear the palm, but rather that of determining how interpretation fits into the psychodiagnostic process, what its major contributions are to this process, and how it might be most effectively utilized.

The clinician's diagnostic formulation is constructed out of what we might call a psychodiagnostic matrix, which consists of data obtained from free behavior observations, such as waiting room activity, ward behavior, and interactions with others wherever these may be observed; information from collateral sources, such as parents and relatives, social workers, school records, job supervisors, and police records; artifacts of the patient, such as diaries, letters, and works of art; the anamnesis; psychological tests; examinations made by other disciplines, such as medicine, neurology, dentistry, and biochemistry; and, on occasion, the patient's response to psychotherapy.

Of course, not every case will contain information from all these sources, nor will every psychologist make use of all the information potentially available about a particular patient.

Like any communication system, the diagnostician has a limited channel capacity and therefore must be selective in what he admits into the channel lest it become overloaded and either break down or become markedly reduced in efficiency: he can handle just so much information and no more. Hence, the psychodiagnostic matrix, as I conceive of it, consists of all of the *potential* data available on a patient, the aggregate out of which we select that which we believe to be valuable for our purposes and that which we can use; in no case is all of the data in this matrix ever realized.

In addition to the questions posed by the reason for referral, admission to this communication channel is governed by the clinician's preferred method of treatment of psychodiagnostic data. Although rarely if ever would one find one method followed to the exclusion of the other, it is possible to distinguish two basic approaches: the *formal* and the *interpretive*. The data of psychodiagnosis vary in the extent to which they lend themselves to the application of each of these two approaches, and so clinicians favoring one or the other method will vary accordingly in what information they choose to heed.

Intermediate between the formal and interpretive approaches to psychodiagnosis is another that we might term the prima-facie approach and that shades into these other two at times. It might be considered a sophisticated common-sense approach, typified by the clinician who says, "If you want to know what is wrong with the patient, ask him. He may tell you." Since our interest in this chapter is not in a complete exposition of the nature of psychodiagnosis but only in an understanding of the role played by interpretation in this task, we shall ignore the prima-facie approach and deal only with the two extreme cases; the one that denies any role to the interpretive process, and the other that depends exclusively upon it. As we have defined these approaches, the one serves as a foil for the other; the reader must recognize this and not read what follows as an exhaustive exposition of the nature of psychodiagnosis.

The formal and interpretive approaches to the problem of psychodiagnosis may be thought of as representing two different strategies of attack upon the psychodiagnostic matrix: each aims at maximally exploiting the data contained in it. But, as will become apparent, these approaches to this task differ in many respects, and each may be shown to have certain disadvantages as well as certain advantages when measured against the criterion of how well it serves the ultimate goal of psychodiagnosis, the provision of a basis for the anticipation of the behavior of the patient under various contingencies. Also, when other criteria, such as maximal exploitation of the data, teachability, researchability, and provision for its own future development and improvement, are employed, we shall find that each approach has its own characteristic advantages and disadvantages. It will therefore become apparent that it is not out of an access of bonhomie that I suggest that these two approaches should be viewed as complementary rather than antagonistic, or that we should set our problem as that of determining how they may be optimally combined rather than that of which one should be put into the shade.

CHARACTERISTICS OF THE FORMAL AND INTERPRETIVE APPROACHES TO PSYCHODIAGNOSIS

It is one of the defining characteristics of the formal approach to psychodiagnosis that the data it deals with are phenotypical, taken as they present themselves to the diagnostician, with no attempt at transformation or interpretation other than numerical. The rules by which these data are transformed or combined so as to arrive at a diagnostic formulation are explicitly specified and require little or no judgment by the clinician in their application.

The actuarial or cookbook approach to the treatment of diagnostic material championed by Meehl (1956) typifies the formal approach to psychodiagnosis. Here, for example, by entering a compendium of personality descriptions, each associated with a particular MMPI profile, the clinician finds a description whose MMPI code matches that of his patient's and ideally his job is done. He now has a personality description of his patient. The clinician is not troubled by questions such as just which items in the MMPI did the patient say were true of him and which false, nor does he ask what taking the test meant to the patient. There are no rules of procedure to handle the information that he might obtain from such questions.

The formal approach need not involve experience tables or statistical sophistication of any degree at all. A signs-and-symptoms approach to psychodiagnosis, an essentially binary system, in which the diagnosis hinges upon the presence or absence of certain previously designated attributes, also falls under the rubric of formal, even though the rules for treatment of the clinician's observations do not involve anything stronger than nominal or ordinal measurement. Thus, the clinician who decides to call his patient a reactive depressive rather than a schizophrenic, because he believes that situational factors contributed a greater share than did life-history factors to the depression, may be using a formal approach if his situational and life history data were treated phenotypically, that is, if it was not necessary to interpret any of the situational or life-history events in assessing their significance. Similarly, the use of Munroe's (1945) inspection technique or Klopfer's (1951) prognostic rating scale with the Rorschach as a way of assessing the adjustment of a patient represents a formal approach to psychodiagnosis. Verbal content is not beyond the grasp of the formal approach to psychodiagnosis and is typically treated by the tabulation of type-token ratios (Johnson, 1946), discomfort-relief quotients (Dollard & Mowrer, 1947), adjective-verb quotients (Boder, 1940), or by scoring procedures such as are applied to life history or biographical data blanks.

In the formal approach, the treatment of the psychodiagnostic matrix is invariant from patient to patient and consequently, provided all the elements of the matrix are present, a diagnosis is assured in every case. For this reason the nature of the information collected and the diagnostic procedures used are much more constant from patient to patient than is the case in the interpretive approach. Also to be noted is that, with the possible exception of latency as a measure of emotional disturbance, the rules by which data are to be entered into the diagnostic formulation are specific to the technique or procedure producing them. We have, for example, one set of rules telling us what to make of various MMPI profiles, another set of rules by which we assay demographic data, and still a different set of rules for the use of time-sample data. The interpretive rules are, in effect, part of the procedure.

The extent to which diagnostic formulations follow from either an empirical or a theoretical rationale does not differentiate between the two approaches to psychodiagnosis. The rules guiding the formalist may have been derived empirically, logically, or intuitively. The only criterion for their being considered a part of the formal approach is that they be capable of application without exception to every case containing the necessary data and that they not require any transformation of the data by the diagnostician. At the risk of raising some hoary psychological issues, we might conclude by saying that the formal psychodiagnostic orientation derives from, and contributes to, a nomothetic approach to personality study.

Our discussion of the characteristics of the formal approach to psychodiagnosis has by implication suggested many of the characteristics of the interpretive approach. Nevertheless, it will be helpful to have these stated explicitly. In contrast to the formal approach, the data upon which the diagnostic formulation is based in the interpretive approach are genotypical, in the sense that they are the transformations resulting from the application of the interpretive process to the data contained in the psychodiagnostic matrix. As we have seen, the logic of psychological interpretation permits the clinician to translate data from a wide variety of sources into the same genotypical language. Consequently, the interpretive diagnostician is not so rigidly bound as is his formalist colleague in terms of what procedures he will use or where he will look in the psychodiagnostic matrix for the answers to the questions posed by a particular case; since his rules of interpretation are not procedure-specific, the interpretive diagnostician enjoys considerably more freedom in the execution of his diagnostic responsibilities than does the formalist.

To the extent that the interpretive approach holds sway, treatment of the psychodiagnostic matrix will be considerably more variable from patient to patient than is the case for the formal approach. For this reason the dimensions upon which assessments are made of patients will vary more from case to case for the interpretive than for the formal approach. If, for example, the interpretive diagnostician can find nothing of interest to him involving a particular patient's dependency needs or nothing permitting him to make some estimate of this variable, he may not mention it at all in his report; the formalist, on the other hand, if dependency represents an important variable in his concept of psychodiagnosis, will have a procedure available which will permit him to make some assessment of it for every patient. Thus, except to the extent that he is bound by some outline or standardized schedule, the items reported on, or the variables assessed, by the interpretive diagnostician are apt to vary markedly from case to case.

While the formal approach restricts the diagnostician to only those aspects of the psychodiagnostic matrix for which he has rules of treatment, the interpretive approach permits the clinician to scan the entire matrix, including those aspects usually treated by the formalist, for items that might be found susceptible to interpretation. This has the effect of placing a larger burden of responsibility for maximal exploitation of the psychodiagnostic matrix upon the interpretive diagnostician; every datum he lets pass by unused in his diagnostic formulation is ignored either inadvertently or deliberately, but in either event the responsibility for not using it devolves upon him personally. Not so in the case of the formal approach. Here the responsibility for what parts of the matrix are used and how they are used are completely determined by whether rules are available for their exploitation. This is not to say that the formalist is simply a hack, for much skill may be required in extracting some items from the matrix (intelligence tests, personality ratings, and behavior check-lists, for example) and still more may be required in their integration if this has not been completely routinized. However, between the two approaches it is the interpretive that holds the greater potential for the excitement and challenge of discovery in the individual case.

Perhaps this last point is best illustrated in connection with intelligence testing. For the formal approach the purpose of the test is strictly that of obtaining an intelligence estimate; for the interpretive approach it is more. The test is a sample of the patient's behavior, including verbal behavior, and the interpretive clinician would be remiss if he did not scan this material for additional information. Charlotte Buhler (1938), for example, suggests that the way in which the child executes the ball-in-field test of the Stanford-Binet may be used not only to determine whether or not two months should be added to his mental age, but also as a window into his personality dynamics. Suggestions in a similar vein may be found in the literature concerning the interpretation of maze tests, vocabulary tests, comprehension tests, and so on. But these are suggestions for the ears of the interpretive clinician only; in each case they involve transformations of the data according to the logic of psychological interpretation.

More generally illustrative of the differences between the formal and interpretive approaches to psychodiagnosis is the way in which the interview is regarded and treated. In addition to being a means of obtaining factual information from the patient, the interview has long been recognized as a potentially powerful diagnostic instrument. But there have been marked divergencies with respect to how this potential might be unlocked and these seem to align themselves pretty well along the formal-interpretive dimension.

As the archetype of the formal approach to this challenge we might cite the recent work of Matarazzo and his associates (Saslow & Matarazzo, 1959). By standardizing the interview, breaking it down into five separate periods, with the behavior of the interviewer clearly specified for each of these periods, they investigate individual differences in interviewee behavior without regard to content. For example, by using the Chapple Interaction Chronograph (Chapple, 1949) they are able to describe the interaction between interviewer and patient in terms of fourteen variables, such as the number of times the patient acted, the average duration of his actions, and his tempo. The chronograph record provides no place for recording interview content as such. All measures deal with the morphology of the interview rather than its substance. Evidence of high reliability for these measures from the standpoint of both temporal stability for the patient and observer agreement, together with the finding of correlations between interviewee interaction scores and other clinical variables, lead these investigators to believe that the use of the standard-ized interview together with the Interaction Chronograph should have a place in the clinical psychologist's arma-mentarium.

If we might extrapolate and exaggerate a bit to make the point here, under Matarazzo's purely formal regime we would find every clinical facility equipped with its own Interaction Chronograph, ticking away during the diagnostic interview and inexorably recording every occurrence of a Chapple-relevant event. These records, fed into appropriately pro-grammed electronic computers, would then yield diagnostic formulations in matters of seconds after the interviews termi-nated. Questions of what the patient said, or why he said it, would be irrelevant. The only judgment required in the entire process would be that by the observer using the chrono-graph, and this would be reduced to a minimum. The inter-viewer himself has only to keep his lines straight, remembering when he is to remain silent, when to interrupt the patient, and so on; he does not have the burden currently carried by so many diagnosticians of the interpretive persuasion of hav-ing to decide where to probe further, where to reflect, whether he has gotten all of the information he will need for his diagnosis, and, lastly what it all means. Under Matarazzo's aegis the interviewer has become a part of the apparatus, and an interchangeable part at that.

In the interpretive approach it is not the behavior of the interviewer that is rigidly prescribed so much as the kinds of content he should seek to elicit and be alert to. To be sure, there are recommended principles of interviewing practice (for example, Deutsch & Murphy, 1955), but these have as their aim the elicitation of as much interpretable material as possible from the patient rather than the standardization of approach sought by the formalist. Illustrative of the kind of content and information the interpretive diagnostician seeks

is the following outline for a psychoanalytic diagnostic interview prepared by Saul (1957):[1]

I. *Information from the interview*

A. Anamnestic data

1. Chief complaints, current life, and emotional involvements
2. Habits, routine, a typical day
3. Onset and course of complaints and symptoms
4. Significant interrelationships at various ages in childhood;
   history of period from conception to birth
5. Medical history including symptoms, psychological and
   physical

B. Conscious attitudes

1. Toward others, past (especially during earliest years), and
   present
2. Patient's attitudes toward and understanding of himself,
   his symptoms, and his problems
3. View of the future; his expectations and ambitions
4. Conventional examination for mental status, if indicated
   modified as advisable
5. Major forces in the personality
   a. Psychosexual
   b. Dependence and independence
   c. Needs for love and object interest
   d. Feelings of inferiority, egotism, narcissism, competitive-
      ness toward members of family and toward representa-
      tives of parents and other relatives
   e. Superego images; shame and guilt
   f. Hostility
   g. Mechanisms of flight, including regressive trends
   h. The nuclear emotions, the childhood motivational pat-
      tern at the core of the personality (a fundamental which
      the interviewer is trying to understand)
   i. Ego functions and interrelations with id and superego,
      grasp of reality, prominent defense mechanisms, aesthetic

1 Reproduced with permission of Dr. L. J. Saul and the publishers
of the *Psychoanalytic Quarterly*.

and intellectual capacities, judgment, will, and strength

6. Favorable characteristics: an understanding of the patient's assets, capacities, talents, and potentialities

C. Unconscious associative material
  1. Memories
     a. Earliest
     b. First continuous memory
  2. Dreams
     a. From earliest childhood
     b. Repetitive, in childhood and later
     c. Common types of dreams throughout life and currently
     d. Some current dreams
     e. Dreams of night preceding the interview and of the night just after the appointment was made
  3. Conscious fantasies and daydreams—past, present, and long-continued ones
  4. Nonverbal, such as facial expressions, mode of dress, and mannerisms
  5. Transference
  6. Tendency and themes of interview (treated as if it were free association)
  7. Countertransference

II. Information from other sources (as required and if not contra-indicated)
  A. Interviews with relatives and others
  B. Information from social caseworkers
  C. Psychological tests

This is an exceedingly comprehensive schedule, one that taps many aspects of the psychodiagnostic matrix. Yet it is readily apparent, as I am sure its author would agree, that its entire value rests upon the quality of interpretive skill brought to bear upon the material elicited. Although Saul presents this as an outline for a psychoanalytic diagnostic interview, with but few exceptions it could be used by nonpsychoanalytically oriented clinicians, so long as they accept the legitimacy of interpretation in psychodiagnosis. From this interview outline it should be apparent that while the formalist prospects for the diagnostic lode in the structure and morphology of the interview, his interpretive colleague's shafts are sunk almost exclusively into its content.

Armed with distinctions between manifest and latent content, assumptions and hypotheses about the significance of memories, various kinds of reported feelings, relationships, and activities, the interpretive diagnostician seeks to elicit content from his patient that will permit him to give full reign to all of these through the process of interpretation. As the interview content proceeds through the different parts and stages of the interpretive process, transformations occur that ultimately find their expression in the diagnostic formulation. What begins as a yawn by the patient at the outset of the interview, for example, is interpreted at the semantic stage as an expression of apathy, finds itself part of a generalization asserting that the patient is unwilling to accept responsibility for his present difficulties, and finally contributes to the constructive interpretation that the patient is an asocial psychopath.

The role of the interviewer in the interpretive approach is best exemplified by Saul's statement that, "The interviewer is attempting throughout the interview to 'read' the material and penetrate the essential underlying motivations as rapidly and surely as possible" (p. 77). What a different world this is from Matarazzo's!

But there is a common ground here that should not be lost sight of. Although the language frequently differs, and the methodology certainly differs, both approaches to the interview—as indeed to the entire psychodiagnostic matrix—have the same objective: providing a basis for the anticipation of the patient's behavior under various contingencies. Let us now consider the advantages and disadvantages of each approach in the achievement of this objective.

Advantages and Disadvantages of the Formal and Interpretive Approaches

With regard to achievement of the ultimate goal of psychodiagnosis we are not concerned so much with toting up advantages and disadvantages of each approach to the task as we are with recognizing where each is more appropriate. In order to do this we shall have first to consider in some detail what the various contingencies are for which we wish to make our behavioral predictions, or more simply, for what kinds of situations diagnostic evaluations are considered necessary. As we do this it will become apparent that the requirements of the psychodiagnostic evaluation vary with the use to which the information is to be put, and, in turn, so does the appropriateness of each approach.

If we ask the question, "When is a psychodiagnostic evaluation called for?" we shall quickly discover that the situations arrange themselves into two easily distinguished classes. The first, which we shall call the *bounded class,* contains those situations where the predictions to be made are discrete, circumscribed, and easily specified. Such questions as, "Should this patient be placed on an open ward?" "Will this client stay in group psychotherapy for at least fourteen weeks?" "Does this patient require a neurological examination?" "Is this youngster a potential juvenile delinquent?" and, "To what psychiatric category does this patient belong?" are typical of those in which the predictions made or implied are discrete and permit answers in essentially "Yes" or "No" terms.

In each instance the contingent conditions to which we are asked to predict are themselves known or at least specifiable within certain broad limits. We know what being on an open ward entails, what demands it makes upon the patient and how success or failure on it are defined. Similarly, fourteen weeks of group psychotherapy in a certain setting is a clearly specified criterion that is either achieved or not by a patient.

In all the instances in the bounded class of psychodiagnostic problem, the contingencies are known and the behavior that might be anticipated is clearly specifiable according to some discrete, and (frequently, but not necessarily) dichotomous criterion.

Furthermore, in the bounded problem we know when the psychodiagnostic information is to be used, when we can say that the job has been done, when we can determine how well the job has been done. That is, the bounded problem involves a temporally specifiable point where the psychodiagnostic formulation will be brought to bear, whether it is in making a decision about the disposition of a patient or determining whether there is agreement upon psychiatric classification. Once this point has been passed, the evaluation serves no other purpose, its usefulness is spent.

The second class of psychodiagnostic problem is the *un-bounded class*. While the bounded class is involved with problems of *disposition* of one sort or another, the unbounded class of psychodiagnostic problem arises in connection with problems of *management,* such as occur in psychotherapy, evaluations for foster home placement, and requests for help by parents in child guidance clinics. Here the contingencies cannot be clearly specified in advance nor are discrete predictions often requested. Rather than being used at some circumscribed point in time for the making of a discrete decision, the psychodiagnostic formulation here is used on a continuing basis as a guide in the making of moment-to-moment decisions the nature of which can rarely be foretold.

As soon as the psychotherapist and his patient meet, decision demands begin streaming in upon him and continue throughout the interview: should he take the initiative here; are the tears displayed by the patient cause for alarm; should he comply with the patient's request for advice on some topic. Although there are many therapists who believe that psychodiagnostic information would interfere with their therapeutic effort, for those therapists not so inclined the psycho-diagnosis serves as a schema or framework within which to set the events of the interview and by means of which they can quickly evaluate the alternatives presented to them at the moment. Not only this, it also serves as a guide to areas that should be explored and may provide a forecast of what will be discovered when the area is touched upon. In this way also, the psychodiagnosis prepares the therapist for what is in store for him and is performing an anticipatory function.

In effect, in the unbounded case what is called for from the psychodiagnostic evaluation is a miniature theory, custom tailored to account for a particular patient's personality and behavior, which may be used to deduce the consequences of various decisions according to the circumstances occurring at the time they must be made. Often referred to as personality dynamics, these formulations enter into the predictive and decision-making process according to the same deductive logic by which the discrete predictions in the bounded case are made.

Although the logic in the application of the psychodiag-nostic formulation does not differ between the bounded and unbounded problem, the kind of formulation that will prove most useful does. The formal approach to psychodiagnosis, yielding as it does information of an essentially quantitative nature, would seem best suited to the bounded problem. Here, by the use of regression equations, discriminant function analyses, and the like, the optimal weighting of the informa-tion derived from the psychodiagnostic matrix can be deter-mined. And this is, of course, only possible in the bounded case because the predictions required represent discrete events that can be entered into such statistical analyses. It is, for example, only a matter of patience and ingenuity to find the best combination and weighting of variables to predict academic success, recidivism, or likelihood of benefiting from shock therapy. Such variables must only be quantifiable and maximally reliable, two of the distinguishing attributes of the variables dealt with in the formal approach. A discrete answer is called for in the bounded case and it is a discrete answer that is yielded by the formal approach.

On the other hand, in accounting for the day-to-day behavior of a patient or as a guide in determining the course of a psychotherapeutic interview, the information forthcoming from a purely formal psychodiagnostic evaluation would be of minimal value. Here, instead of discrete predictions or assertions, we need evaluations of strengths and weaknesses, areas of conflict, patterns of behavior, and sources of anxiety, evaluations only rarely produced by formal psychodiagnostic procedures.

While many statements concerning personality dynamics can be made on the basis of observations and anamnestic material not subjected to interpretation but simply taken at face value as representing various personality characteristics and patterns of response, it is nevertheless here that psychological interpretation, by passing new dimensions through the data, may help to generate insights not otherwise possible. While it may, for example, take no interpretive effort to assert that an individual is threatened by authority figures after he tells us that he becomes anxious whenever he is in the presence of a person with any sort of power over him, it may not be possible to account for this generalization without submitting a great deal of material to interpretation. Thus it is in the unbounded case that the interpretive approach to the psychodiagnostic matrix has the most to offer.

It is in the generalizations and constructions of the interpretive process that the patterns emerge which provide the psychotherapist with the schema necessary for him to understand the on-going behavior of his patient, and with the classes of behavior and events into which he can place the current and projected situations of his patient and anticipate the likelihood of various outcomes given certain circumstances. Knowing, for example, that the patient in the past has acted in such a way as to provoke hostility by others against himself, which he then uses to justify his own hostility, the therapist is alerted and is able to understand when he him-self begins to experience hostile feelings toward the patient. He "knows" what his hostility means, and he may know better what to do about it than if he had not been apprised of this by the psychodiagnosis. He is now able to predict what the patient will do if he should express his hostility, and knowing this he can, according to his therapeutic strategy, either express the hostility and so bring forth the patient's char-acteristic hostility, which can then be dealt with in therapy, or not express his hostile feelings toward the patient but instead deal with something else that he believes to be more important at the moment. But the therapist has had to make a decision—perhaps a decision he would not have even recognized as such if he had not known of this patient's pat-tern of behavior—and to make it he has relied in part upon the anticipated outcomes of the courses of action open to him.

Because, as we have noted, the same logic is applied in predicting in the bounded and in the unbounded case, whether from the formal or from the interpretive approach, there is a strong temptation to predict from an interpretively derived psychodiagnostic formulation to a bounded problem. This is where the clinician gets into trouble. In not dis-tinguishing between the two types of psychodiagnostic prob-lems many clinicians will attempt to make discrete predictions on the basis of their assessment of the individual's personality dynamics, and invariably they are embarrassed by the out-come. And this is inevitable, for they are bound to either overinclude or overexclude, either overweight or underweight certain material in arriving at their predictions. In addition to the increased likelihood of error, if a discrete prediction is called for it is grossly inefficient to collect data that will have no bearing upon the prediction and that does not yield a discrete answer, except by extended ratiocination. We therefore find that the interpretive approach to psychodiagnosis is less appropriate than the formal approach in dealing with bounded problems.

Failure to make the bounded–unbounded distinction in psychodiagnostic problems is responsible for much of the current controversy over the utility of actuarial as opposed to clinical prediction (Meehl, 1954). If this distinction were made it would readily become apparent that, parallel to the formal and interpretive psychodiagnostic approaches, actuarial prediction is the method of choice in connection with bounded problems and will be found highly unsatisfactory in dealing with unbounded problems, while the reverse holds true for clinical prediction. Furthermore, the clinician would recognize that, unlike the bounded case where his decisions are guided exclusively by event-probabilities (inductions), in the unbounded case his decisions are based upon his beliefs, which *may* have no relationship to event frequencies. In the unbounded case we have, therefore, no choice but to rely upon the clinician's deductive capacities; in the bounded case we do have this choice and can never justify not making it in favor of the statistician.

The means by which psychodiagnostic instruments achieve their objectives differ for the bounded and unbounded problem and this should be taken into consideration in their evaluation. In the bounded case, the instrument can be said to have accomplished its purpose if it permits a significant increment in the number of correct predictions or decisions *across persons* than could be otherwise obtained; in the unbounded case the significant increment must be *across events* for the same person. In the former case we take a cross-sectional approach to validation; in the latter a longitudinal. Base rates, as most frequently applied (Meehl & Rosen, 1955), therefore have relevance in evaluating diagnostic instruments or procedures only in the bounded case. We must, in other words, ask whether this test permits a significantly larger number of correct diagnoses in the group studied than could be obtained simply by knowledge of the incidence of the diagnosis in the population from which the group was drawn. Such a question can rarely be asked in connection with an unbounded problem.

This is not to say that the validity of instruments used in unbounded psychodiagnostic problems cannot or should not be investigated. But the task is much more formidable. For the question to be asked here is whether the instrument permits a larger number of correct predictions or decisions over time, in each case in which it is applied, than could otherwise be achieved. To answer this question adequately would require some means of equating decision-demands from case to case, the setting up of time intervals during which counts would be taken of the number of correct decisions for each case, and then comparisons made between these counts for cases in which the instrument under study was and was not used. This is no mean undertaking, but until it is done it would seem that clinicians are perfectly justified in discounting much current test validity research as irrelevant for their purposes. And this would hold for psychological interpretation as an approach to the psychodiagnostic matrix as well.

In addition to their achievement of the major objective of psychodiagnosis, we may also compare the formal and interpretive approaches with respect to several other criteria, such as the extent to which each utilizes the data contained in the psychodiagnostic matrix, teachability, the utility of each as both a stimulant and tool of research, and the potential of each for its own development and improvement. While certainly subsidiary in importance to the psychodiagnostic function of providing the necessary anticipatory basis for decision-making, these other criteria each in their own way expose different facets of the two approaches and therefore merit some consideration.

It would seem on the surface that from the standpoint of maximal utilization of the psychodiagnostic matrix, the interpretive approach has the advantage over the formal. In not being restricted by procedure-specific rules of operation, the interpretive diagnostician begins gathering his data at the moment of contact with the patient in the waiting room, continues as they proceed down the hall together to the consulting room, and doesn't stop until he loses sight of the patient passing through the door to his ward or to the street. Every moment bracketed within this interval is potentially critical from the interpretive standpoint; from the formal standpoint much of this is only incidental to the main event.

This is a very real *potential* advantage to the interpretive approach. But it is not without its hazards. For some of the behavior observed will be irrelevant to the understanding of the patient's problem, some of it will be unreliable in the sense of not being characteristic of the patient's general mode of behavior, and some of it will be redundant in the sense of not contributing any information about the patient that the diagnostician does not already have. Nevertheless, the clinician may submit all these behaviors to interpretation. Having succeeded in coming up with a plausible interpretation, he may be loath to cast it aside as noncontributory, especially if some effort was required in its derivation, or at the very least it may be given more weight than it deserves in determining the final diagnosis.

These are hazards, or disadvantages, of the interpretive approach which will vary in significance from one clinician to the next, and it might be argued that they are only likely to arise in the case of the inexperienced or the inept. And to a certain extent this is true. If the diagnostician weighs each interpretation against the criteria of contextual consistency, his purposes in seeing the patient, theoretical consistency, subsumption, and postdiction, he will indeed minimize these hazards. Thus, to enjoy the benefits of maximal utilization of the psychodiagnostic matrix the interpretive diagnostician must be able to suspend his commitment to any particular interpretation until he has been able to apply these various criteria of acceptability to it. He must be willing to accept the proposition that all that is interpretable is not gold.

In contrast to the interpretive approach, the formal approach may be likened to a coarse sieve through which the psychodiagnostic matrix is passed. The quality of what is retained for doing the job at hand is entirely dependent upon the validity and reliability of the procedures employed, as well as upon the way in which they are applied. For psycho-metric techniques in particular, it is usually possible to assess this quality with a fair degree of accuracy. The formalist therefore usually has a more objective basis for knowing how much credence he can put in his diagnostic formulation than does the interpretively oriented clinician.

As recompense for what he has had to ignore of the psychodiagnostic matrix, however, this objectivity is often of dubious merit. For as is only too abundantly obvious, all our diagnostic procedures, no matter how objective, are fallible. Add to this the fact that we are still groping for many of the important parameters of behavior and personality, and we begin to cast covetous eyes at the material passing through the formalist's sieve.

What this would suggest is that where the variables necessary for an adequate diagnostic appraisal are known—in other words where we know what aspects of the psychodiagnostic matrix we wish to mine, a formal approach would seem to hold the most promise. This, as we have seen, is most likely to occur in the case of bounded psychodiagnostic problems. Where this is not the case, an interpretive approach is indicated. If, for example, our job were that of predicting whether an individual would succeed in an executive training program, and previous research had indicated that this prediction could be made with an acceptably high degree of accuracy by the appropriate weighting of certain demographic and sociological variables together with selected job performance measures, it would be foolhardy to take an interpretive approach to the problem. And this would hold true for more conventional clinical diagnostic questions as well.

On the other hand, to delimit the area of the psychodiagnostic matrix scanned intentionally when all the variables involved are not known, or in connection with unbounded psychodiagnostic problems, treating only those that can be treated formally, smacks of scientism. For this is where the interpretive approach can make a major contribution: not necessarily in any individual case, but in the attack upon the diagnostic problem represented by the case, and therefore in providing fruitful leads to be checked out in subsequent cases. In venturing into the unchartered areas of the psychodiagnostic matrix, and in doing this consistently in case after case, the interpretive approach holds the key to discovery of those variables still untapped but necessary to the complete understanding of the diagnostic problem posed originally. In the unbounded case, it is precisely because we cannot anticipate all the demands which will be placed upon the psychodiagnostic formulation, all the decisions which will be referred to it, that we must include as much of the psychodiagnostic matrix as possible. Providing that the interpretive diagnostician is willing to submit his rich store of clinical lore to systematic and critical examination, he may be expected to make a greater contribution to the growth of knowledge in clinical psychology than the formalist. For the interpretive clinician willing to accept the challenge, every diagnostic problem becomes a miniature experiment, and every case should therefore add an increment to his knowledge. To the formalist in his role as diagnostician this opportunity is denied: to take part in the adventure he must shift his role to that of researcher.

In a sense, what we have been saying is that maximal utilization of the psychodiagnostic matrix is not an intrinsic good. Rather, its value increases in direct proportion with our ignorance of the important diagnostic variables involved, of how they might be best assessed, and as we move from the bounded to the unbounded class of problem. It is in this regard that the interpretive approach to psychodiagnosis, in giving the diagnostician license to explore and to speculate, puts him in an excellent position to deal with unusual diagnostic problems and to discover the new and important psychodiagnostic variables of the future. While this opportunity is not denied the diagnostician committed to a formal approach, it is in the nature of the approach that the opportunity is less easily grasped.

There can be little doubt that if it were possible or desirable to train two completely different breeds of diagnosticians, one formal and the other interpretive, it would be considerably more difficult to train the latter. In place of the explicitly stated rules of procedure and analysis entailed by the formal approach, the interpretive approach presents the student with the task of mastering principles that have never been stated systematically—if they have been stated at all; while the one must learn where to locate the proper experience table, the other's training involves developing his own personal norms and hypothesis-forming capacities; in place of the regression equation, the quintessence of the formal approach, the interpretive approach depends upon theoretical and experiential schemata in integrating data.

Although this is a choice we do not have at present, it serves to point up the fact that the formal approach does have the pedagogical advantages of ease of communication and grasp which the interpretive approach can never be expected to match. This differential may unwittingly affect the attitudes of both teachers and students toward each approach. For both, but for different reasons, the interpretive approach to psychodiagnosis will prove the more frustrating: for the instructor because of the greater difficulty in exposition; for the student because of the greater uncertainty of achievement. Therefore, unless instructors and students are constantly on guard against it, they may cast their lot with the formal approach to a greater extent than intellectual considerations would warrant.

This is not to say that because of the looseness and ambiguity inherent in it, the interpretive approach may not hold its own attractiveness for certain individuals. These are often confused with depth and creativity and are considered inherent in the study of the truly significant problems of our time (Maslow, 1955). There is no doubt that these conditions do inhere in certain stages of creative effort and that there probably is some relationship between them and the profundity of the problem being dealt with, but these considerations do not give looseness and ambiguity any virtues in their own right, nor do they suggest that these conditions can ever justifiably be used to support one's claim to either creativity or profundity.

Commitment to either a formal or an interpretive approach to psychodiagnosis can never be total; what I have suggested is that one's major commitment to either approach should not be determined by one's frustration tolerance on the one hand or the potentialities for ego enhancement on the other. Just as the formal approach can degenerate into scientism, so the interpretive approach can lead to obscurantism.

Psychodiagnosis, regardless of approach, enters into a relationship with research as both producer and consumer. As producer, it fulfills its role by providing not only conventional reliability and validity studies, but also estimates of theoretical parameters of behavior and personality for use in both basic and applied research. From this point of view any research that requires the use of populations differing from each other in certain personality variables poses a psychodiagnostic problem. Whether it be a study of thinking in schizophrenics as compared with normals, or the difference between introverts and extraverts in relative amounts of reminiscence in motor learning, or the effect of anxiety on learning, or the personality characteristics of successful and unsuccessful graduates of an executive training program, the research is dependent upon one or more psychodiagnostic procedures. The value of the research effort may well stand or fall with the value of the psychodiagnostic procedures used. In this connection, psychodiagnosis may be conceived of as a tool and as such we may inquire into its utility when approached from either a formal or an interpretive orientation.

Psychodiagnosis becomes a consumer of research because of the never-ending search for more meaningful, more efficient, and more accurate means of personality description. In achieving this end the psychodiagnostician draws heavily upon the work of researchers quite remote from the clinic. This has been true from the time of Jung, who appropriated the word association technique from researchers who used it to study the laws of association in thought, to the present, with the introduction into the clinic of strobotachometers and Archimedes spirals. There is not a diagnostic procedure in which one cannot find—sometimes buried quite deeply, to be sure—a debt owed by way of either rationale or technique to theory and research that was concerned with issues far removed from the clinic.

And so the findings the experimenter casts aside as error variance or individual differences, the psychodiagnostician frequently picks up and fashions into a meaningful personality variable. He is not always successful by any means, but the point is that this is how psychodiagnostic procedures are born. Blind empiricism in the development of psychodiagnostic procedures is more apparent than real; invariably the technique employed has been used previously in some fashion which, either by hunch or by theory, led to the belief that it might have diagnostic potentialities.

In the appropriation of techniques and procedures born of the laboratory the psychodiagnostician invariably begins to speculate as to the variables being tapped; why the technique differentiates between diagnostic groups, and so on. And here psychodiagnosis acts as a stimulus for further research in the definition of new variables and the development of new theories as well as in the testing of deductions from existing theories. How do the formal and interpretive psychodiagnostic approaches compare here?

Especially in its yielding information for all subjects on any specified set of variables, in the predictability of the kind of information that will be obtained by its procedures, the formal psychodiagnostic approach has much to recommend it over the interpretive approach as a tool of research. Also, in its greater control over both stimulus and response variables, the formal approach permits clearer determination than does the interpretive approach of sources of variance in personality and behavioral measures. This becomes obvious if we compare, for example, the use of a pencil and paper inventory such as the Manifest Anxiety Scale (Taylor, 1951) with a clinical interview in the assessment of anxiety. For assessment purposes, the MAS items represent the stimulus, and the subject's answers to them, which are characterized by a single score, represent the response; in the clinical interview—the method likely to be applied for assessment purposes in the interpretive approach—the interviewer's questions, reflections of answers, and total personality represent the stimulus condition, while the subject's response to all of this is represented by the clinician's judgment (rating or free response) of his total behavior, verbal and nonverbal, during the interview.

If our interest were in the effect of two different stress conditions on the development of anxiety, for example, it is easy to see that variations in anxiety between subjects submitted to the two conditions and assessed by the MAS are more unequivocally attributable to the different treatment conditions than is the case for those assessed by the clinical interview. The simplest way of recognizing this is to realize that the credibility of scientific conclusions depends upon replicated observations under replicated conditions. It would be considerably harder to justify calling each clinical interview a replication of its immediately preceding interview, or each clinical judgment of anxiety a replicated observation, than it would to do this for the MAS and its scoring, which obviously remain invariant from subject to subject. This is not to argue for the greater validity of the MAS or related formal procedures in the assessment of anxiety, but simply to point up the fact that as tools of science they cannot possibly be matched by interpretive procedures. How useful these tools will be, of course, depends upon their validity. But even here, for the reason just cited, it is easier to make firm statements about the validity of formal procedures than it is about interpretive ones.

We have only to look at the impact upon psychology and other social sciences of Freud's original observations as well as those of his followers to realize that the interpretive approach may be an exceedingly potent stimulant to research. Documentation of this assertion could run to volumes. In the freedom to speculate imposed upon the interpretive clinician by the very nature of his approach to data, the stage is set for the invention of new theories and hypotheses. Whether this promise bears fruit or not depends upon a complex of variables that need not concern us here. But every hypothesis so formulated becomes a point of departure for further research that will be concerned with tests of its validity and generality.

Of course, as anyone who has ever wondered what a product-moment correlation he has obtained between two variables means will readily testify, the formal approach does not necessarily inhibit speculation on the part of the researcher. But even beyond this, because of the ease and elegance with which formal assessment procedures can be used, they may be expected to act as a stimulant to research and even serve to channel research efforts into those areas susceptible to investigation by them. Levy (1961) found an increment in publication rate for articles dealing with "anxiety" following the introduction of the Taylor Manifest Anxiety Scale (Taylor, 1951), a formal assessment procedure, which was not matched by increments for articles dealing with either "emotion" or "drive," for which no such procedures exist, but which was matched by an increment in articles dealing with anxiety in children following the publication of a children's form of the MAS five years later!

To be sure, not all the articles tabulated were directly dependent upon the MAS or the CMAS, but this is a coincidence to be pondered over. In a sense it provides a graphic illustration of the relative effectiveness of formal and interpretive psychodiagnostic approaches as stimulants of research and clearly suggests that the advantage lies with the formal approach. For throughout the period studied interpretive procedures were available for the assessment of drive, emotion, and anxiety, but it was only after a formal procedure was introduced for the measurement of the latter condition that it, and it alone, increased in attractiveness as an area of study.

It would therefore appear that both approaches may be productive of research, although for different reasons: the interpretive approach because of the provocative nature of assertions generated by it; the formal approach because it expedites the actual business of research. Again, these two functions are not entirely independent of each other, just as in practice the formal and interpretive approaches rarely appear in the pure culture form in which they have been discussed here. Ultimately, it must be recognized, whether the research stimulated by either approach is original and provocative or banal and pedestrian depends less upon the approach than it does upon the practitioner.

Although most studies of psychodiagnostic procedures deal only with their effectiveness in handling bounded problems, such as therapeutic outcome (for example, Rogers & Hammond, 1953; Hammer, 1953; Feldman, 1958), reviews of these studies (Windle, 1952; Fulkerson & Barry, 1961) do not give any reason to be optimistic that the findings in studies of psychodiagnostic treatment of unbounded problems, if such studies were done, would be any more comforting. Therefore the need for further development and improvement is obvious and it is reasonable to compare the formal and interpretive psychodiagnostic approaches on their potential in this regard irrespective of the type of problem dealt with.

The estimation and allocation of error variance—the first step in determining the credibility of any assertions generated by any psychodiagnostic procedure—depends upon replication. Only as a procedure is repeated, and repeated invariantly, can we assign any error estimate to statements generated by it. Without replication, the errors observed cannot be properly estimated or unequivocally attributed to any particular source or combination of sources. This is as true of psychodiagnosis as it is of any other enterprise depending upon statistical evaluation for its certification of soundness. Thus we should not be surprised to learn that, to the extent that these are dependent upon the estimation and attribution of error variance, the highest rate of development and improvement may be expected of formal psychodiagnostic procedures, for, as we have seen, it is only among these procedures that we are assured of replication of treatment of data from case to case.

But estimation and attribution of error variance at best tell us only where we should place our bets, they tell us what needs change and what does not in our system; they do not provide information suggestive of how changes should be made, of what the nature of new elements or variables might be that should be introduced into the system, or of what strategy might prove better than the one in which we have just lost confidence. This is not the proper function of statistics, and so, once we move beyond this point, we find that the advantages gained by formal procedures over interpretive ones through replicability begin to diminish, and the two approaches are once again on almost equal footing with respect to the question of potential for development and improvement. From this point on progress is dependent upon changes in conceptualization and methodology.

For the interpretive clinician this means further development and refinement of the theory or language system he is using in his interpretive activities and, hence, further research concerned with both the interpretive process and the theory to which he subscribes. For the formalist too this involves theoretical research, although it may also be approached via an atheoretic, empirical trial-and-error strategy.

Although the formal and interpretive approaches may be equally endowed with potential at the creative or search stage, when the results of their endeavors at this stage come up for test, it is again the formal approach that may be expected to take the lead. Thus, if we conceive of the entire process of improvement and development in psychodiagnosis as involving repetitive cycles of *test-search-test,* it is evident that it is the formal approach which should progress the more rapidly through each such cycle because of its advantages at the test phase and hence, which should ultimately show the greatest rate of improvement and development.

It should be clear from the foregoing discussion that the interpretation of content is not something one can either be for or against as a psychodiagnostic procedure; it must constitute a part of the preparation of any well-trained clinician. Indeed, if we accept the distinction between bounded and unbounded psychodiagnostic problems suggested in this chapter, the clinician who is unprepared to engage in psychological interpretation is also unprepared to deal with an entire class of problems with which he is likely to be faced in clinical practice. And although we recognize that bounded psychodiagnostic problems are more ably handled by formal procedures, it must also be recognized that because these procedures are still quite primitive and limited in their applicability, even here there is a place for the application of interpretive procedures.

Sifting the Psychodiagnostic Matrix

Having agreed that interpretation is a necessary part of the psychodiagnostic procedure, let us now concern ourselves with the very practical issue of how one goes about applying it. For this one needs a framework that will help indicate where interpretation can be brought to bear or where interpretable material is likely to be found. While the problem here is a practical one, its answering will also serve to further support our argument as to the need for interpretation in psychodiagnosis by pointing up more concretely those elements of the psychodiagnostic matrix that would otherwise pass through the clinician's sieve.

Remembering that interpretation begins with our attempt to answer a question posed by some event, usually not understandable on its own terms, we shall attempt to indicate where interpretive material might be found in psychodiagnosis by listing those questions the clinician should ask or be sensitive to in his contact with a patient appearing for psychodiagnostic evaluation. In any given case many of these questions will not turn up any interpretive material and yet will yield diagnostically significant prima-facie content, such as would be the case, for example, if the clinician observed that the patient had a *mask-like* expression on his face when he met him in the waiting room and that his hands were engaged in a constant *pill-rolling* movement (symptoms of Parkinsonism); in yet other cases nothing of diagnostic or interpretive significance will result; but in all cases, unless these or questions like them are asked, the clinician has not done his job. In each instance, the test of whether or not one has struck a vein of interpretive material by the question is what happens when the answer to that question is followed by the further question, "Why?"

As a perhaps unnecessary caution, I would like to say that it would be a mistake at this point for the student to prepare to copy these questions out of the text. To do so, and perhaps to have them listed somewhere available in the consulting room or on the clip board on which he takes his notes, would be a mistake for two reasons. First, the clinician could not possibly pay thorough attention to his patient and at the same time check off each question to be sure that it has been considered; to do so would result in the clinical evaluation deteriorating into a scene one might encounter between a traveler and a minor European customs official—correct but dull. Second, these questions are intended to indicate and promote a certain attitude or orientation toward psychodiagnosis rather than to prescribe the exact nature and form it is to take; they certainly do not exhaust all the questions that might be asked, nor will they all be appropriate in every situation.

The following is an attempt to divide the encounter between clinician and patient into a set of ten events. Each event is stated in italics and then followed by the questions pertinent to it. For purposes of this illustration I have assumed that the examination consists of an anamnesis followed by two or more psychological tests—a rather heavy order for the clinician and patient in real life, but not in fiction.

1. *Meets patient in waiting room and introduces himself.* What was patient doing when first observed? How had he

been occupying himself? How does he respond to his name being called? How does he respond to clinician's introducing himself? How has he affected others in waiting room? Is there anything unusual about his dress or grooming? Did he come alone or with someone? If with someone, what is relationship to person and what is the quality of the relationship.

2. *Invites patient to come with him to consulting room.* Does patient show any reluctance to come, any hestitation, or does he show eagerness? Does patient make any remarks at this point either to others in waiting room or to clinician? If so, what are they? If patient has come with someone, how does he part company with person? Is there any evidence of startle or confusion at being invited to come with clinician?

3. *Walks down corridor with patient to consulting room.* How does patient respond to "small talk" by clinician? Does patient ask for reassurance during walk, begin talking about his problems, engage in "small talk," or remain silent? How does patient orient himself in relation to clinician as they walk: alongside clinician, behind him, or in front of him? Is there anything unusual about patient's posture or gait?

4. *Opens door to consulting room and enters.* Does patient show any reluctance to enter? Does he wait to be invited in or does he precede clinician into room? Upon entering does patient wait to be told where to sit or does he attempt to determine this for himself and seat himself? Does patient explore room visually or through actual locomotion, or does he simply sit focused on the clinician? How does patient seat himself: deep into chair, on edge, or otherwise? What posture does patient take in chair: alert, relaxed, limp? Does patient make any remarks about any aspects of the room, either physical or functional? Has there been any change in patient's manner during period of observation from public waiting room to private consulting room?

5. *Begins rapport building and explanation of nature of*

contact with patient. Does rapport seem easy or difficult to establish? Does patient inquire about how information will be handled, about confidentiality, about what decisions will be based upon it, and so on? Does patient respond differentially to mention of anamnesis and testing? Does patient take initiative in describing complaints and symptoms or wait to be asked? If patient smokes, does he ask permission first or just begin? Does patient inquire about how long interview and testing will take?

6. *Conducts anamnesis.* Where do the variations in tension, mood, cooperativeness, coherence, and frankness occur during the anamnesis? What areas does patient dwell on? Which ones does he avoid or require prodding on? Does patient bring in apparently irrelevant information? What is nature of this information? How well does patient respond to usual clinical techniques for guiding the course of the interview? If patient is given freedom in shifting topics or in guiding course of interview, what is sequence of topics? Does patient ask for reassurance, suggestions, or advice during interview? Does patient weep at any time during interview or show signs of emotional decompensation? What is the general tempo and control of speech during interview? Where do variations occur? Are there any unusual skeletal or physiological responses during the interview? If so, where do they occur? What kind of relationship does patient seem to be trying to establish with clinician? What is the nature of clinician's response to patient during the interview?

7. *Indicates end of anamnesis and that administration of tests comes next. Suggests short rest break before beginning testing.* Is patient reluctant to terminate interview? Does he try to relate additional material? Does he make any remarks descriptive of his feelings about the interview? If so, what are these? What does patient do with free time offered him during the break? Is there any show or report of apprehension at mention of testing?

8. *Administers tests.* Many of the questions asked during the conduct of the anamnesis are also appropriate here. In addition: Are there any differences in patient's behavior between the anamnesis and testing, and between the different tests administered? How well does patient conform to instructions for tests administered? Does patient confine his activity to that demanded by the tests, or does he engage in test-irrelevant activity as well? If he does the latter, what is its nature?

9. *Indicates to patient that testing and examination are completed. Thanks patient for cooperation and informs him of whatever the next step in plan for him might be.* Does patient give any intimation of his reaction to the total examination? Does he do this spontaneously or guardedly? Is there any reluctance to terminate contact? Does patient request additional clarification of how information gained will be handled or what happens to him next? Does patient thank clinician for anything? If so, how does he put it? Does patient ask for clinician's opinion of his case? Did patient at any time during contact express interest or curiosity about clinician, his age, training, and so on?

10. *Conducts patient to waiting room or appropriate exit and bids him farewell.* If patient had come with someone, how do they respond to each other on meeting after examination? How does patient take leave of the clinician? Is there a change between his comportment during the examination and that when he again emerges into the public?

In making the observations suggested by these questions, as in culling all the material obtained through the anamnesis and psychological testing, the clinician's question must not only be "What does this event mean?" or "How may it be interpreted?" but also, "What does this event mean for *this patient?*" Thus, we ask not only how a dream might be interpreted, but also why the dream was dreamt; not only what a Rorschach response means, but also why it was given.

It is frequently this second question, the *personalizing* question, that permits a choice between interpretations and that spells the difference between simply a clever interpretation and a useful interpretation. Of course, we have implied the asking of the personalizing question in all interpretive activity when we earlier discussed the role of the context as a criterion in judging the adequacy of an interpretation. Here, we simply reiterate it because of its importance in making psychodiagnostic interpretations meaningful.

SUMMARY

In order to understand the role of interpretation in psychodiagnosis, this approach was contrasted with a formal one. While the interpretive approach proceeds on the basis of a set of assumptions and principles not specific to any particular psychodiagnostic procedure, the formal approach is most often found to depend upon procedure-specific rules. Beyond this, the interpretive approach is found to culminate in a set of assertions based upon the clinician's experience, observations, theories, and beliefs, while the formal approach gives rise to assertions ultimately based upon observed event-frequencies. Finally, the assertions of the two approaches tend to differ, with those of the interpretive approach much more often being in the form of hypotheses or propositions and those of the formal approach most likely being in a discrete or quantifiable form. These differences between the two approaches are found to have implications for the most appropriate use of each in psychodiagnosis.

Although we see psychodiagnosis as a predictive venture, it is nevertheless helpful to make a distinction between the two types of problems encountered in it: *bounded* and *unbounded* psychodiagnostic problems. The bounded problem is one involving a discrete prediction or decision, usually circumscribed in time and most often concerned with the classification or disposition of a case, whereas the unbounded case involves problems of case management such as in psychotherapy, where the therapist requires of psychodiagnosis a formulation that will serve as a continuing guide in his moment-to-moment and day-to-day decision making. While in the bounded case we know in advance the conditions under which the psychodiagnostic product will be used, in the unbounded case such information is generally lacking or of the most diffuse sort. Considering the distinctive characteristics of each, the formal approach to psychodiagnosis, of which the actuarial method of prediction is one example, is found most appropriate and efficient when dealing with bounded problems, while the interpretive approach offers distinct advantages in the case of unbounded problems.

From the standpoint of maximal use of available psychodiagnostic data, there is no doubt that the interpretive approach holds the advantage over the formal approach, since the latter can only deal with those portions of the data for which specific rules of operation have been developed, while the rules of operation of the interpretive approach are not procedure-specific. However, since maximal use of psychodiagnostic data is not an end in itself, this is only an advantage where we are still seeking for additional variables or parameters; once these have been defined the efficient course of action is the development of formal procedures for their assessment and use. The interpretive approach is therefore most valuable in early stages of theory development or in approaching new and undefined problems. Beyond a certain point in maturity of theory construction, and as the problems being dealt with psychodiagnostically are of a recurrent and bounded nature, the value of a formal approach increases.

Pedagogically, the formal approach to psychodiagnosis holds certain advantages over the interpretive approach. It is much easier for the teacher to communicate the set of rules or inductions to the student that is required in the formal approach than it is for him to provide the student with the theoretical and experiential background upon which the clinician must draw in the interpretive approach. This is a real advantage, of course, only if the formal approach is, in fact, equal to or better than the interpretive approach in accomplishing the psychodiagnostic task in question. To the extent that this is not the case, the danger exists that both teacher and student will be seduced by the greater simplicity and occasional elegance of the formal approach into focusing upon only those problems where it may be applied.

In summary, the interpretive approach may be expected to make its major contribution in providing the bases for dealing with unbounded psychodiagnostic problems, in charting new areas of research, and in the formulation of new hypotheses and the definition of new variables; the formal approach may be expected to be found clearly superior in dealing with bounded psychodiagnostic problems and in the actual conduct of research. Each approach will be found unsatisfactory to the extent that it is applied in the sphere of activity more appropriate to the other. For this reason, the training and practice of clinicians cannot be restricted to one approach or the other but must rather be directed to an understanding of the proper role of each.

CHAPTER 7.

Interpretation and Tests

THE psychological test, whether of intelligence, interest, or personality, provides a major portion of the psychodiagnostic matrix out of which the diagnostic formulation is constructed. While there is no test totally immune to the efforts of the clinician bent upon taking an interpretive approach to all material in the matrix, it is primarily to "projective" test protocols that his attention is drawn. Why? In trying to answer this question we shall have to come to some understanding about the nature of tests in general and of projective tests in particular. My purpose here, however, is not to provide an exposition of tests and measurements as such, but rather to provide a perspective from which the similarities among *all* tests that are subjected to interpretation will become apparent. If this is achieved, it will help to substantiate the claim made at the beginning of this book that the principles of psychological interpretation are the same regardless of where applied, and we may expect the clinician to move with greater confidence from one test to another as he sifts them for interpretive material. At the same time, it is hoped that the clinician will arrive at some understanding of the limitations and proper role of interpretation in psychological testing.

The Distinction between Projective and Objective Testing

The frequency with which one hears of a patient being assigned for "projectives," and the fact that we have a professional journal, the *Journal of Projective Techniques*, containing articles devoted to projective testing, would surely lead one to believe that there exists a class of tests or techniques distinguishable on firm grounds from other tests or techniques. And this has been a belief held by many ever since Frank coined the term "projective methods" in 1939 (Frank, 1939) and likened them to the x-ray methods of medicine. But as with many other verbal distinctions found in the intellectual history of man, the fact that it exists is no assurance that it is either meaningful or useful. Let us consider the grounds upon which projective tests have been distinguished from other tests. In discussing the points presumed to differentiate between projective and nonprojective tests, for ease of exposition we shall only refer to the Minnesota Multiphasic Personality Inventory (MMPI) in talking about nonprojective tests. The arguments are, however, not in any way limited to the MMPI.

Freedom of response. Sometimes put in terms of the ambiguity or unstructuredness of the stimulus, freedom of response is most often cited as the major distinguishing feature of projective tests. Frequently, to drive this point home, the contrast is cited between a personality inventory such as the MMPI and a projective test such as the Rorschach; while in the former instance the examinee can only respond with "true" or "false" to each test item, in the latter there are no such constraints—the validity of the distinction appears self-evident.

It is this greater freedom of response, the argument goes, that allows the examinee, through the assortment of responses he elects to make, to project his own personality into the test protocol. Therefore, the greater the freedom of response (by which is meant the number of different responses possible), the greater the possibility of projection.

This distinction is a spurious one. It has survived only because no one has ever attempted to determine quantitatively the number of possible different responses that might be made to a Rorschach card or to the entire test, and because of the particular perspective chosen from which to describe the response possibilities to the MMPI. On the first point, it is certainly true that there are a large number of responses possible to the Rorschach—just as there are a large number of different stories which might be told to any TAT card—but the number is not likely to be infinite in any psychologically meaningful sense in either case. On the second point, while it is true that any *single* MMPI item permits of only two responses, if we shift our perspective to the response given to the test as a whole we find that with 550 items, each offering two response possibilities and each being a *constituent of the total response,* there are 2^{550} responses possible to the test as a whole—a not inconsiderable amount of freedom. From the standpoint of freedom of response, it would seem that the eligibility of the MMPI as a projective test is unimpeachable.

On the other hand, we find that such arch projective tests as the Blacky Test (Blum, 1949) contain a multiple choice inquiry; that the concept evaluation technique of McReynolds (1954), in which examinees are given lists of responses and asked to select from among them those which best fit the blot, is used with the Rorschach; and that in the Bender Gestalt Test (Bender, 1946), the examinee is clearly instructed to *copy* the geometrical figures placed before him—even less freedom than in the MMPI, where at least the patient can make one of two responses to each item!

A corollary of the freedom of response dimension, also cited as critical in differentiating between projective and nonprojective tests, is the ambiguity of the stimulus presented to the examinee. Stimulus ambiguity may be created in a variety of ways, but the only way in which it can be measured is by way of the number of different responses given to the stimulus —the larger the number, the greater the ambiguity. But ambiguity does not reside entirely in the stimulus itself; it is also dependent upon what the subject is instructed to do with the stimulus. The inkblot is ambiguous if the subject is asked to report what it might be, but it is much less ambiguous if he is instructed to report whether it is a veridical representation of some object or not, or if he is asked to report on the colors contained in each blot, or on whether he considers the blot a complex or simple structure, and so on.

By the same token, the MMPI can be made, and frequently is made, a more ambiguous task by asking the patient to answer each item as he thinks a healthy person would, or as he thinks a sick person would, and so on. Indeed, the MMPI items themselves are not entirely without ambiguity even if the examinee is asked to answer them as they apply to himself. Certainly, for example, we might expect a variety of interpretations of the terms in the statement: "Once in a while I laugh at a dirty joke." Clearly, individuals will differ in the time span they use as a referent for "once in a while"; what they consider to be laughing, whether a smile or snicker qualifies, or whether it must be raucous; in what they consider "dirty," whether this would be anything sexual, whether it would be restricted to certain sexual activities, or whether nonsexual topics might also be considered dirty; and finally, in what their criterion is for an anecdote to be considered a "joke."

For these reasons, we are forced to conclude that the identity of projective techniques as a unique class of techniques is on very shaky grounds if these are either the amount of freedom of response offered the examinee or the ambiguity of the stimulus presented to him. At best, tests might be ordered along such continua. But that such an ordering would result in a bimodal distribution, with conventionally designated projective tests making up one hump and nonprojective tests the other, seems quite unlikely.

Indirectness of method. This is supposed to be another more or less exclusive property and virtue of projective techniques. It is believed that since the method is indirect, in the sense of the examinee not being aware of just how his response is going to be evaluated, it is less susceptible to faking and less likely to arouse resistance. In comparison to most pencil-and-paper personality inventories, it is true that in general projective techniques are less transparent regarding their purposes and the way a particular response is likely to be evaluated.

But here again there are exceptions. We find, for example, that when graduate and advanced undergraduate students in a course in clinical psychology, who had also had at least two quarters of abnormal psychology, were asked by Seeman (1952, 1953) to indicate which of a selected group of test items would score in which direction for certain scales of the MMPI, only on those items which had previously been designated "obvious" was there any degree of unanimity of agreement on the correct scale associated with the item; for items previously designated "subtle" there was a striking lack of agreement upon the correct scale to which the item belonged. Furthermore, when Seeman repeated this study with these same students after another two quarters of clinical psychology, one of which was devoted to a study of the MMPI under the guidance of no lesser light than Dr. Paul Meehl, they were still not able to fathom the correct MMPI meaning of Seeman's subtle test items. And these were Minnesota students!

Clearly, therefore, indirectness, subtlety, or opacity is not the exclusive property of projective techniques. If any more evidence were needed to demonstrate this, we might point to the fact that new test scales are continually being derived from the MMPI—a fact which suggests that even to psychologists the meaning of much of the behavior manifested by examinees on the test still remains a mystery.

On the other side of the ledger, it is obvious that there is considerable variability among projective methods in their indirectness, ranging all the way from the admittedly rather transparent sentence completion methods to the supposedly enigmatic Rorschach inkblot technique. But even in the case of the Rorschach, and even though individuals may not be able to spell out the scoring system or the interpretation made of certain responses, we find ample evidence that their performance on the test is affected in a predictable fashion by factors which would make for greater defensiveness. Thus, to cite only one illustration, Henry and Rotter (1956) found very marked differences between the summary scores of those subjects who were given the standard instructions and those who were told that it was used in detecting psychopathology. Although the subjects may not have known just how their responses would be evaluated, they apparently knew enough so that when they became defensive F% and F+ increased while the number of aggressive responses tended to decrease. However indirect the Rorschach might be, its ability to circumvent an individual's defenses in the manner claimed for it and for other projective techniques is open to question.

Intraindividual versus interindividual comparisons. Ever since Frank (1939) sallied forth to establish the claim of projective techniques for a place in the clinical firmament, it has been argued that whereas diagnoses based upon nonprojective methods depend upon comparisons between the individual and some norm group and the application of cutting scores and other psychometric paraphernalia, in the use of projective methods diagnoses are based upon intraindividual comparisons, upon an evaluation of the configuration of scores obtained by the individual on the test. As Rosenzweig put it (1949, p. 109), ". . . [since] the aim is largely to understand the individual in his own terms—his productions being considered from within as much as from without—interpretation does not rest heavily upon the statistical determination of 'cut-off scores' that arbitrarily differentiate the normal from the pathologic."

To recognize the lack of substance to this claim for the distinctiveness of projective methods we have only to note the amount of effort expended by Buhler, Buhler, and Lefever (1948), for example, in their development of the Basic Rorschach Score, which purportedly would differentiate the normal from the pathological on the Rorschach, or the publication of the Rorschach Prognostic Rating Scale by Klopfer and his associates (Klopfer, Ainsworth, Klopfer, & Holt, 1954), or the cry by Rosenzweig and Fleming (1949) for norms for the TAT. Furthermore, it should be obvious that no comparison of factors within the individual can have any meaning unless projected against some set of norms. More often than not, in the case of projective techniques, these norms are carried in the head of the clinician rather than on paper, but nevertheless, without them any comparison made within the individual would yield a unique event of which we could say nothing.

Turning again to the MMPI, we find almost from the beginning of its development a continuing flow of strictures against basing diagnoses on single scale scores as against the profile of scores. Gough (1953), for example, would have us attend to the curve formed by the MMPI profile and utilize such attributes of this curve as its phasicality, direction of slope, and over-all elevation, and Meehl and Dahlstrom (1960) report on their extended efforts to develop configural rules for discriminating psychotic from neurotic MMPI profiles.

It soon becomes obvious from a perusal of the recent literature that nonprojective test users are no less concerned with the information contained in score configurations than are projective test proponents. If any difference exists here it is likely to be at the level of objectivity or formalism introduced, but even here we are not dealing with a discrete variable differentiating the two types of methods. And so, once again, we find the justification for setting projective tests apart from other assessment methods quite feeble.

From the foregoing, we are forced to conclude that, as valuable as this distinction between projective and nonprojective tests may have been in providing an entré for a set of procedures that did not conform to the conventional conceptions of the nature of psychological tests at the time Frank issued his manifesto, to persist in making this distinction now will only hinder further growth and understanding. Making the distinction when Frank did may have been good tactics; to persist now would be poor strategy.

In the discussion that follows I shall occasionally speak of projective techniques without such qualifiers as "so-called," or "usually designated," simply as a short-cut way of referring to tests such as the Rorschach and TAT. I wish to emphasize that this is a usage dictated only by convenience and convention; if we were willing to forego the former and able to overcome the latter, the distinction would soon pass into oblivion.

The Instrumental and Expressive Dimensions of Behavior

Any behavioral event may be looked at from two different points of view. First, we may ask whether it accomplished the task set for the organism; how well it achieved the objective toward which it was directed; or most simply, whether it was successful or unsuccessful according to some criterion. When we ask these questions we are focusing upon the instrumental dimension of behavior. For example, we are interested in the instrumental dimension of behavior when we ask how many trials it took a rat to learn a T-maze under certain conditions, whether or not Mr. Jones successfully completed an executive development program, what score Johnny received on a Stanford-Binet intelligence test, and how many responses a patient gave to the Rorschach test. Our interests here are not in the form or content of behavior, except insofar as this might be critical in judging success or failure.

On the other hand, we might ask how the organism went about accomplishing the task set for it, what form his behavior took, regardless of whether it was successful or not. Here we are interested in the stylistic or expressive dimension of behavior. We may, for example, want to know not only whether Mr. Jones successfully completed an executive development program, but how he related to others in the program, whether he required a great deal of reassurance, whether he was very aggressive—all attributes that may be irrelevant to determining success or failure in the program but that do describe his behavior in the program. Similarly, on the Rorschach we ask not only how many responses the individual gave—which is actually the task set for him in the test—but whether they were wholes or details, whether they relied only on form or used other determinants as well, and so on. Here our interest is in the form or content of behavior only insofar as they are expressive of the individuality of the person being observed, not for what they tell us about his success in satisfying the requirements of the task set for him.

The distinction made here between the instrumental and expressive dimensions of behavior is not unlike that made by Vernon (1953) between expressive and adaptive behavior. However, I believe that it is preferable to speak of two different dimensions of behavior rather than two different behaviors in order to emphasize the fact that we are dealing with the same behavioral event merely analyzed from two different perspectives. The term *instrumental* is preferred over *adaptive* simply because the behavioral dimension to which it refers is the same as that involved in behavior theory dealing with instrumental conditioning: that aspect of behavior which either secures the reinforcement or goal for the organism or not. For example, in instrumental conditioning the interest is in the rate of bar pressing by the rat in a Skinner Box (instrumental dimension), not in how it presses the bar (expressive dimension).

The importance of the expressive dimension in understanding human behavior and personality has been explicitly recognized at least since Adler (1927) emphasized the importance of the study of an individual's life-plan in understanding his personality, and it has gained new prominence during the current interest in response sets and biases in personality inventories (Edwards, 1957; Jackson & Messick, 1958) as possible sources of important personality variables. Except where he seeks to account for variance in the instrumental dimension, the major focus of the clinician's interpretive efforts falls upon the expressive dimension of behavior. And so it is to situations, methods, or tests which maximize this dimension that the clinician turns when he wishes to adopt an interpretive approach to psychodiagnosis.

Whether there is any behavior that can be labeled purely instrumental or purely expressive is doubtful. For these are not, strictly speaking, two different kinds of behavior, although any given behavioral event may be said to be more instrumental than expressive, or vice versa. In effect, the instrumental and expressive dimensions of behavior may be thought of as the outcome of an analysis in which behavior is projected against two orthogonal dimensions. Thus it should be possible to design situations which will accentuate one or the other of these dimensions in the behavior elicited. And in fact it is.

If we design a task that is either very easy or very difficult to accomplish but permits of a variety of approaches to its execution, we have a situation that will elicit behavior with maximum variance on the expressive dimension and relatively little variance on the instrumental dimension. If, on the other hand, we design a task that is of intermediate difficulty but permits of only one successful avenue of attack, so that we obtain a distribution of scores vis-à-vis successful accomplishment or the extent to which the individual hit upon or manifested the correct response, we have maximal variance on the instrumental dimension and minimal variance on the expressive dimension. In similar fashion, by appropriate manipulations of the difficulty of the task and the variety of means by which it may be executed, we can produce situations that elicit behavior high in variance on both expressive and instrumental dimensions or low in variance on both dimensions. In addition, it should be obvious situations can be made to vary with respect to these two dimensions by variation in what is recorded of the behavior elicited, whether only its achievement, or only its form, or both.

The personality test, projective or otherwise, presents the individual with a task that will maximize variance on the expressive and minimize the instrumental dimension of behavior. In the pencil-and-paper inventory the task set for the individual is simply to answer each item as true or false—a task easily accomplished, but one that leads to great variability in its manner of accomplishment. The clinical scales of the MMPI are nothing more than objective means by which the particular pattern of response of the examinee (his expressive aspect) may be compared with those of individuals falling in various diagnostic groups or differentiated on the basis of certain personality variables. The empirical derivation and quantitative expression of these scales should not obscure the fact that here we are dealing with the expressive dimension of behavior. To be sure, the opportunities for the clinician to exercise his interpretive talents are markedly diminished. But this is only because the interpretations have already been made for him by the test maker in his empirically derived scale definitions, not because the behavior elicited by the test is not susceptible of interpretation. Indeed, the clinician could, if he had the temerity, throw caution to the winds and embark upon his own interpretation of an examinee's answers to the MMPI. Indeed, though they do not manifest this boldness, we do find many clinicians interpreting markedly elevated MMPI profiles as representing a plea for help and the excessive use of the "Cannot say" response as reflecting either defensiveness or oppositional tendencies. But generally, the clinician using the MMPI and kindred instruments in their orthodox fashion simply agrees to follow the test maker's directions as to how the expressive dimension of behavior elicited by the instrument shall be analyzed.

In effect, any test of ability or achievement may be pressed into service as a tool of personality study if we develop and apply to it some analytic system that focuses upon the expressive dimension of the behavior elicited by the test. This is what Buhler (1938) did when she bade clinicians pay attention to how the child draws his lines describing his search for the lost ball in the Ball and Field Test of the 1916 revision of the Binet in addition to whether or not his plan of search qualifies as the performance of a 13-year-old. Similarly, in teaching the clinician to be alert to and describe whether the examinee on an intelligence test requests much reassurance during the test, how he responds to failure, how he handles difficult test items, the content of his responses to vocabulary items—especially those which were incorrect—and so on, we are focusing upon the expressive dimension of behavior elicited in a situation originally designed to provide information about only the instrumental dimension. How effectively the clinician will be able to use this additional information will depend upon his skill in subjecting it to interpretation and the availability of normative information dealing with the various expressive attributes he has unearthed.

Projective personality tests, like nonprojective ones, present the individual with a task that is relatively easy to accomplish but that permits great variation in its mode of execution. The task on the Rorschach is simply to report on what the inkblots look like, on the TAT to tell a story in some way appropriate to each picture, on the Draw-a-Person Test to draw a person. If the individual fails on the instrumental dimension elicited by these tasks it is usually as a result of noncooperation or profound psychological deficit. And although some variations will be found in the instrumental dimension, the bulk of the analytic systems developed around each of these instruments deals with, and therefore magnifies, variations in the expressive dimension.

Projective tests differ from nonprojective tests here primarily in that the expressive dimension of behavior they elicit is usually described in verbal terms rather than quantitatively, thus rendering it more amenable to interpretation. To recognize this we need only compare the interpretive purchase possible from a behavioral description such as, "T score 78 on Scale 2," from the MMPI, with the vistas opened up by the statement, "Every story involving a man and a woman depicted the man as exploiting the woman," from the TAT, or the statement, "Four of his twelve percepts involved decaying matter," from the Rorschach. It is for this reason that the clinician of an interpretive bent is more likely to be found with a set of Rorschach inkblots tucked under his arm than with an MMPI.

Where quantification is attempted with projective tests, it does not supplant verbal description. It simply serves to indicate to the interpreter how much weight should be given to the various components of the behavior he is interpreting.

But the meaning attributed to the behavior elicited by any projective technique still depends ultimately upon the interpreter's efforts and skill in piloting it through the various steps and stages of the interpretive process. The diagnostic formulation that finally emerges represents the product of the interpreter's generalizations and constructions at the propositional stage of interpretation.

In place of the scoring key provided with the nonprojective test, the projective test usually has one or more analytic systems available for use with it. These systems, it should be noted, perform the same function as the scoring key: they provide a means of describing the behavior elicited by the test. But whereas the description emerging by means of the objective scoring key obtains meaning when it is converted into a standard score and combined with other data according to empirically derived rules, the description resulting from the analytic system developed for the projective test only takes on meaning after it has been subjected to interpretation. There is one exception here, of course, and that is the case where the clinician applies a previously derived set of signs, such as the Piotrowsky (1937) list of signs of brain damage or the Prognostic Rating Scale (Klopfer, 1951). But with this exception, the purpose of the analytic system is simply that of converting the expressive dimension of behavior into a form amenable to interpretation. And while the analytic systems will vary from test to test, once they have done their job the next step, interpretation, follows the same rules and logic regardless of the test used.

To be sure, much of the interpretation may be done for the individual clinician by the author of the test or by other workers in the field, but this does not change the fact that the principles followed in interpreting the behavior described by the analytic system are the same as those applied wherever content is interpreted. Therefore, in approaching the use of a new test from an *interpretive* standpoint, what the student must master is the *analytic* system advocated for use with it; from then on he will begin to recognize familiar ground. Although the student may be expected to profit from the interpretive suggestions made by authorities on the test in question, it is nevertheless the case that these suggestions will be found to follow the same principles and logic which may be found underlying the interpretation of other material. If the student recognizes this he will be that much ahead in mastery of the test.

Whether this mastery will result in a valued contribution on the part of the clinician depends, of course, upon whether the test in question was worth mastering in the first place—in other words, upon the validity of the test. The problem of test validity is an extremely complex one, particularly when the test requires interpretation for its use, and one that we cannot discuss at length here. From the distinction we have made between analysis and interpretation, it should be clear, however, that failure of a test where interpretation is involved may be a function of failure of the analytic system, failure in interpretation, failure in the theory which was to bridge the gap between test and criterion, or some combination of these. As we discuss a variety of analytic systems in the next section, it will become apparent that many represent potentially major sources of error variance as a result of inconsistencies in their application within a particular test, or of making distinctions which may be semantically or logically possible but psychologically meaningless, or of the use of terms such as "originals" which carry surplus meaning. Unfortunately, the interpretive process, by its very nature, can treat the irrelevant as easily as the relevant and so provides no check upon what the clinician accepts for interpretation. Thus, simply because he has been able to arrive successfully at an interpretation of a test protocol, the clinician has no assurance as to its validity or utility. These must be judged on other grounds.

There is one other implication resulting from the distinction we have made between analysis and interpretation that is of particular importance for the future status of psychological interpretation in psychology and psychiatry. It is an open secret that projective tests are not held in the highest esteem by all members of these professions and any cursory survey of the literature dealing with their validity will explain why. However, because the interpretive process is an integral part of most projective techniques, if the distinction between analysis and interpretation is not clearly maintained it is quite easy for a failure of any of these techniques to be counted automatically as a failure of psychological interpretation as well. This would be a case of guilt by association and a grave injustice, unless further evidence indicating that the fault lay with interpretation per se were adduced. It is to be hoped that, if the distinction between analysis and interpretation is maintained, greater discrimination will be exercised in the future in deciding where to place the onus of guilt when a projective test fails on one of the validity ordeals devised for it. Just as interpretation is not the exclusive property of any single theory, so it also stands apart from any single diagnostic procedure.

From the foregoing discussion it would appear that despite our earlier conclusion to the contrary, we have uncovered a real difference between projective and nonprojective tests: the extent to which the test depends upon the interpretive process as opposed to empirical derivation in giving meaning to the behavior elicited by it. This, however, soon poses a dilemma.

Although this may, in fact, be the means by which these two classes of tests are distinguished from each other, such a distinction has implications that make it doubtful whether it would ever be given official sanction by projective psychologists. For this distinction simply represents two different ways of handling data and, to anticipate a point to be made in the final section of this chapter, with regard to tests distinguishes only between test and no test. Consequently, if we agree that this does represent the only real difference between projective and nonprojective tests, we must still conclude that there are not two classes of tests for the reason that projective tests are not tests. That is to say, if projective tests owe their identity to the fact that they require the clinician using them to engage in interpretation in order to derive any value from them, they lose their status as tests, and hence we have only one class of tests. If, on the other hand, we do not accept this interpretive–empirical distinction between projective and nonprojective tests, then we find that we still have no basis for distinguishing between these two classes of tests.

Although it appears that I have tipped my hand here, we shall continue to speak of "projective tests" and refer to them as "tests" in the next section simply for ease of exposition, since it is in connection with instruments conventionally so designated that most interpretation occurs. No harm will come of this if it is kept in mind that our interest in this chapter is with the role of psychological interpretation in testing—as it is currently carried on. I shall return to the problem of the status of projective tests in the final section of this chapter.

SOME ANALYTIC SYSTEMS AND TEST INTERPRETATIONS: AN OVERVIEW

To illustrate the points made in the preceding section we shall now examine some of the analytic systems applied to projective tests as well as some of the interpretations made of the behavior analyzed by these systems. It will be seen that these analytic systems vary in many ways, not the least of which is the degree to which the system is distinguishable from the interpretation to be made of the behavior analyzed by it. At one extreme we find Murray's (1943) need-press system for the TAT, in which there is little attempt to distinguish between the analysis of the TAT stories and their interpretation, and at the other the complex and comprehensive system of analysis of the Rorschach test, where the separation between analysis and interpretation is quite clear-cut. Failure to recognize the distinction between analysis and interpretation is undoubtedly due in part to the fact that this variability exists among tests. And it is this failure, in turn, which is responsible for the impression held by many that systems of interpretation are specific to tests and therefore must be learned anew with each new test encountered. It is hoped that what follows will help dispel this impression.

The Rorschach test

There are several analytic systems available for the Rorschach, those by Beck (1944) and Klopfer and Kelley (1946) being the most popular. The analytic system for the Rorschach consists of a truly impressive scoring system by means of which each response is coded in such fashion as to catch what is believed to be its psychological essence. In the Klopfer system this results in approximately sixty different scores from which the examiner must choose in characterizing a single response. The decision as to how a particular response shall be coded depends upon it location in the five-dimensional space defined by this system. These dimensions are: location, determinants, popular–original, form quality, and content. From an examination of the interpretations made or suggested by Rorschach workers, it becomes apparent that each of these dimensions is treated as though it provides more or less unique information about a different aspect of psychological functioning. The scores allocated to each dimension serve to describe that aspect of the personality of the individual for which the dimension is believed to be illuminating. This will become more apparent as we consider each of the dimensions and the interpretations usually made of scores associated with that dimension.

1. *Location.* Every percept of the examinee's is awarded a

location score, which purportedly describes how much of the blot was used in the percept as well as certain characteristics of the area used. In this way the location scores indicate not only whether the examinee reported using the whole blot or some part of it, but also certain qualitative aspects of the location, such as whether it was a rare or a frequently used detail, or whether the response was justified or not (DW).

Scores on the location dimension are treated interpretively as reflecting certain cognitive aspects of the individual's personality. In particular these scores are presumed to be diagnostic of the individual's organizational ability (number and quality of W's), his preference for the abstract and theoretical as opposed to the concrete and practical, and his intellectual efficiency in coping with problem-solving situations (succession). Of course, this does not do full justice to the myriad ways and nuances of interpretation possible here, but it does serve to indicate the general tenor of location interpretations. Let us now see what the critical assumptions and principles of interpretation involved are.

Two of those assumptions are the equivalence of events within a given class and the nonindependence of members within a class. The first assumption permits the Rorschach interpreter to treat responding to a detail in an inkblot as equivalent to responding to a detail in a social situation or any other situation. That is, having set up the class of "response to details" (or wholes), the interpreter is free to ignore where these responses occur in arriving at his estimate of how concerned the individual is with "detail." And via the nonindependence assumption, each additional detail response given by the examinee increases the examiner's confidence that still more detail-oriented behavior will be observed. Therefore, whatever interpretations inhere in concern with details, may be attached to the personality of the individual whose Rorschach protocol is judged to contain too many details.

These interpretations are also made possible, it should be

noted, as a result of the principle of interchangeability of genus, which in the case of the Rorschach is perhaps stretched to the limit, in that the inkblot confronting the individual is treated as interchangeable with any other aspect of the real world that might confront him.

The perspectives particularly relevant in mediating interpretations of location scores are *metaphor* and *frequency*. Metaphor is most commonly encountered in the interpretation of dreams and other thematic material, but here it is the interpreter rather than the subject who supplies the material viewed from this perspective; the tester, not his subject, has chosen to use the terms "whole" and "detail." Having used the terms he can then proceed to note their frequency of occurrence within the protocol and arrive at some assertion about the individual's tendencies to be concerned with the abstract or theoretical, for which "whole" is a common metaphor, or with the concrete and practical, for which "detail" is the metaphor, or with minutiae, for which "rare detail" serves as the metaphor.

Similarly, treating each inkblot as a separate problem-solving situation, the interpreter notes whether the sequence of location scores for responses to each card is similar, either beginning with wholes and then followed by details (working from the general to the specific) or the reverse, or variable from card to card. If he finds the former condition prevailing he infers that the individual's intellectual methods of attack on problems are orderly and systematic; if he finds the latter condition he concludes that the individual is inefficient, if not confused, in his approach to the cognitive challenges of life.

We thus find that once the response has been located on the analytic dimension of location, it is ready for interpretation. We shall find a similar situation with regard to the other Rorschach dimensions. Our concern here, it should be noted, is not with the validity of these interpretations, but simply with the demonstration that they require no special assumptions or principles other than those required wherever psychological interpretation is undertaken.

2. *Determinants.* This is by far the most important dimension in the analytic framework of the Rorschach, containing more possible scores than any other, and the one to which most space is usually devoted in any exposition of the method. Every response is awarded a determinant score, which in effect is a way of coding the percept for the qualities attributed to it by the examinee: whether it is reported as moving or not, colorful, having tactile qualities, and so on. Many Rorschach workers prefer to believe that here they are actually recording those attributes which truly determined the examinee's perception. Whether we find this notion quaint or not does not alter the ways in which determinants are interpreted.

Inferences based upon determinant frequencies are primarily concerned with emotionality, its quality and control, and more generally with the individual's social orientation and adjustment. We find, for example, that an absence of any determinants other than form in a protocol would lead to its author being diagnosed as emotionally constricted; the reporting of many percepts in which bright colors are used may lead to his being described as emotionally expressive and warm, either with control over his emotionality (FC) or emotionally labile and, perhaps, impulsive (CF). If there are many human movement responses in the protocol the examinee may be reported as intelligent and creative (cognitive virtues), but if these outnumber some weighted combination of color responses, he will also be thought of as generally introverted. The use of achromatic color is presumed to betoken depression, and shading used in certain ways is considered diagnostic of anxiety. When determinant scores are placed in ratios with each other additional interpretations are made possible. But since it is not my purpose here to present a full exposition of Rorschach interpretation, this should suffice to indicate the flavor of interpretations emanating from a consideration of the determinant dimension.

Most of the interpretations here may be seen as the outcome of adopting the perspectives of *metaphor* and *affect*. Either of these two perspectives will, for example, permit bright colors to be interpreted as having emotional import and achromatic color as representing depression. And if we grant these interpretations of the color determinants, and grant other emotional interpretations of the shading determinants on similar grounds, it "follows" that not using these determinants—that is to say, reporting only the use of form—must reflect a repression or constriction of emotionality. In this way also, by only the slightest extension, a general concern with form is interpreted as a concern with control, so that when other determinants are used in conjunction with form we can speak of the person being either able to exercise control over his emotions or not, depending upon whether we score the response so as to indicate that form was more important than the other determinant (for example, FC, Fc, Fk) or less important (CF, cF, kF) for the individual in "determining" that percept.

Movement, either human (M) or animal (FM), occupies a special position among the Rorschach determinants. For while each of the other determinants—form, color, and shading— are attributes of the blots as well as of the percepts, movement can properly be an attribute of the percept only, since inkblots are stationary. Because of this difference between movement and the other determinants, it is believed that the reporting of movement (Rorschachers would say *perception* of movement) requires a special contribution by the examinee not required by the other determinants: he must "create" the movement himself or it must come from within him somehow. This reasoning has, from the perspective of metaphor, endowed the movement response with special value as a sign of creativity and inner directedness. The latter is included, since it is assumed that the person in perceiving movement must have been attuned to certain inner kinesthetic experiences which he has projected onto the percept of the blot.

3. *The popular–original dimension.* Any human act may be located upon a continuum ranging from the banal to the original, and the Rorschach response is no exception. Most analytic systems therefore contain provisions for deciding whether a response is to be scored as popular—one that occurs frequently—or original—one that occurs infrequently: not more than once in one hundred protocols according to Klopfer and Kelley (1946).

This results in a large number of responses in each protocol not being scored as either popular or original, so that in effect we have a three-point scale here. Unfortunately for the examiner (and perhaps for his patient as well) only one end of this scale is adequately anchored: the examiner is supplied with lists of popular responses for each inkblot but is cast adrift when it comes to scoring original responses. According to Klopfer, or Rorschach himself (1942, p. 47), he cannot score original responses until he has administered at least one hundred tests. But to what kind of cases? These problems have never seriously concerned Rorschach workers and are mentioned here only in passing because they illustrate neatly a point made in the preceding section. That is that a failure of the test may not represent a failure of interpretation. It could, in many instances, represent only a failure of the analytic system.

The interpretation to be placed on the number of popular responses in a protocol follows fairly obviously from the label attached to these responses and from the assumption that they are of the same order of importance as any other behavioral events we might observe—that is to say, from the assumption of interchangeability of genus. If there were "too many" it would be acceded that the individual has adequate ties with reality, unfortunately to the extent that he would be considered a conformist. If he produced what might have been considered an average number of popular responses we would credit him only with good reality contact. On the other hand, very few populars and a number of originals may be interpreted as indicating either creativity (an obvious precondition for doing anything original) or psychopathy, depending upon the judged quality of the responses.

It is perhaps most obvious in connection with this dimension that the interpretations made here are no different from those that would be made elsewhere, given the same labels; and this labeling is the responsibility of the analytic system. But should the labels be given inconsistently from one domain of events to another, the validity of their attendant interpretations cannot help but vary also.

4. *Form quality.* Most analytic systems provide some basis for characterizing the extent to which the percept is assigned to an area of the inkblot structurally resembling its actual appearance. Systems vary in how they attempt to accomplish this ranging, from Beck's quasi-empirical tables of F+ and F− responses for each blot, to Klopfer's, in which accuracy is essentially dependent upon the examiner's judgment of fit between blot and percept. And while for Beck responses are scored F+, F, or F−, for Klopfer responses are either F or F−, although his recent presentation of a form-level rating system (Klopfer *et al.,* 1954) seems to be an attempt to introduce quantification here, as well as to cover a quality that Beck handles under a different concept, Z, or organizational activity. However, regardless of variations in scoring, the interpretations remain essentially similar.

The F or F+ score being assigned to responses in which there is judged to be a close fit between percept and blot, the F− response naturally is interpreted as the outcome of inaccurate perception. Since the inkblot is viewed as merely another segment of reality to which the individual is responding, it seems perfectly reasonable to append the same interpretation to his reporting seeing an airplane in Card I as we would to his reporting that messages were being sent to him via the radiator. Thus from this dimension we find interpretations emerging dealing with the quality of the individual's reality contact (amount of perceptual distortion) and cognitive functioning.

The interpretive perspectives involved here are easily discerned if we conceive of perception as functioning so as to inform the individual about the world around him, and of the effect of incorrect information as being deviant behavior. In this way the perspectives of *function* and *effect* jointly serve to produce the interpretations uniquely associated with the form quality dimension applied to the Rorschach test, just as they would in any other situation where judgments of perceptual accuracy of presumably significant aspects of reality are made. Consequently, we see that these perspectives can serve in mediating the interpretation not only of dream content or social interaction, but also of responses to inkblots.

5. *Content.* Not to be confused with content analysis and interpretation, the content dimension gives rise to only a very gross coding of percepts into a relatively small number of categories, and is admittedly (Klopfer *et al.*, 1954, p. 199) one of the underdeveloped areas of Rorschach technology. It therefore figures only minimally in the total interpretative activity stimulated by the test.

Interpretations inspired by content scores center primarily around the attitudes and interests of the examinee. If a large number of different types of content are reported, it is conjectured that the individual has a broader range of interests than if only a limited number were reported. Focusing on human and animal responses only, Klopfer suggests that reporting seeing segments of these creatures more than half as many times as reporting seeing them whole is indicative of an overly critical attitude—the examinee seems to "take people apart." A few specific content categories have their own special interpretations associated with them. Thus "seeing" emblems in any number in the blots will result in the person being suspected of being concerned with social status; more than one or two anatomy responses are likely to be taken as indicative of hypochondriacal tendencies, and the reporting of sex organs among one's percepts will usually result in the most dire of diagnostic formulations.

The analytic system here is the most primitive of the whole test, hardly transforming the actual response at all in many instances. For the most part, the interpretations made of content scores are fairly elementary and similar to those that would be made if under other circumstances the individual seemed to be overly concerned with one type of object or event to the relative exclusion of others—and again, the interpretative principles are the same.

The interpretations emerging from the use of the formal scoring system of the Rorschach depend, as we have seen, upon applying the same perspectives to the inkblots and the responses to them that are applied to other forms of behavior. Treating the response as an event and as a consequence of the occurrence of another event (an inkblot), we have the necessary patterning of events out of which propositions are formed. And it is these propositions, in the form of both generalizations and constructions, that constitute the Rorschach clinician's diagnostic formulation of the case. For example, the assertion that a patient tends to distort reality would be one of the generalizations likely if a large number of F— responses were given by him. Given this generalization, one construction which might follow is that the patient is schizophrenic. If, however, the F— responses occurred in smaller number and only on the brightly colored cards, we may find the generalization being made that the patient becomes disorganized only in the presence of emotionally stressful situations, and the construction offered that he is unable (perhaps for reasons yet to be determined) to tolerate stress or that he is a neurotic.

To many clinicians the Rorschach represents a prime source of interpretive material, not through its formal scoring but rather through the content *qua* content that is elicited by it. For example, we find Zubin, Eron, and Sultan (1956) concluding that (p. 782): ". . . viewing the Rorschach technique as a systematic, controlled interview and basing its evaluation on content analysis of the protocols is the method to be recommended, because it is the only one that can now yield reliable and valid results." Whether or not this sanguine view of content analysis is justified, it is a very popular one.

In contrast to the formal analysis of the Rorschach, in content analysis there is no analytic system to which the material is submitted prior to interpretation—the process of interpretation begins operation as soon as the clinician turns to the content and decides to treat it interpretively. The systems of content analysis that have been proposed from time to time for the Rorschach are simply attempts at systematization of the interpretations that would normally be made of content obtained from any source at the semantic stage.

To illustrate this let us consider the "Palo Alto Aggressive Content Scale," proposed by Finney (1955) for use with the Rorschach test as a means of assessing hostility. The scale consists of five categories according to which each response is evaluated. In Table 4 are listed the category labels together with examples of responses falling under each, and the interpretive perspectives that would lead to a response being so classified. It is interesting to note in this regard that Finney describes the principles involved in constructing the scale as "essentially rational and *a priori* rather than empirical," representing ". . . speculations as to the most probable standards used by the general public to determine their reactions to the destructive nature of any given object or animal" (p. 10).

TABLE 4

CATEGORIES AND EXAMPLES FROM THE PALO ALTO AGGRESSIVE
CONTENT SCALE AND THE INTERPRETIVE PERSPECTIVES INVOLVED

Categories	Examples	Perspectives
1. Non-destructive responses		1. Effect, affect
2. Derogatory remarks	"A fat slob of a man"	2. Effect, affect
3. Victim of destruction responses	Dead animal; scarred; torn up	3. Effect
4. Possible destructive responses	Wolf; savage, gun; lightning	4. Effect, function, intensity
5. Active destruction responses	Killing; spitting on someone; arguing	5. Effect, intensity

Many content interpretations are quite involved and ingenious, clearly reflecting the theoretical biases of the interpreter, yet aside from the differences in language used these do not rely on any principles of interpretation unique to the Rorschach. For example, when Brown (1953, p. 262) betrays his psychoanalytic commitment in suggesting that a "jet propelled plane" reflects anal-aggressive impulses we can see how he arrives at this by using the perspective of *function* or *affect* to justify the aggressive interpretation being placed on the jet plane (which is typically used in combat), and the perspective of *structure* for the anal component of the interpretation, since the jet comes out of the rear of the plane.

As a final bit of evidence supporting our position on interpretation and the Rorschach test, we might note that Lindner (1950), an early proponent of content analysis, maintained that "most responses except those which are exceptionally common and to which the blots so readily lend themselves—are produced only after a process of distortion, displacement, condensation, and, indeed, the operation of perhaps every mechanism that lies behind the dream. It is my belief that there is little if any difference between the dream and the Rorschach response" (p. 89). By implication, whatever principles are found useful in interpreting dreams will also be found useful in interpreting Rorschach content.

Other tests

Because the Rorschach test is by far the most frequently used diagnostic test today (Sundberg, 1961), and because it possesses the most completely elaborated analytic system of any test on the market, we have gone into the nature of its analytic system and the interpretations stemming therefrom in some detail. To consider other tests in as much detail would not be warranted, both because they have not reached the same stage of maturity as the Rorschach and because many of the points we would make would be repetitious with those already made. The point would seem to have been well enough established with the Rorschach that the interpretation of the test can be completely derived from the principles and logic of the interpretive process presented in the first part of this book. This was found to hold for both the scores derived by way of its analytic system, and for the content itself when treated as content. Now let us simply take samples of statements made about other types of projective tests and the behavior elicited by them to see whether in any instance interpretive principles are necessary that are unique to a particular test. In taking this sampling approach I am fully aware that I am leaving myself open to the charge of bias in the selection of illustrations, but there is no help for it and I shall have to risk the criticism so as to get on with the job. To do otherwise would be impossible in view of the ever-growing catalogue of tests available to the clinician.

In approaching this section, I would like to suggest that the reader might find it interesting if in each instance where a statement is presented about the meaning of some aspect of a test or the meaning of some test response, he pause after reading it and ask himself whether the statement was necessary, or whether anyone armed with knowledge of the general principles of psychological interpretation could not have made the same statement unaided if he had been presented with the material in question. These are statements taken either from test manuals or from authorities on the tests and presumably are intended to inform the uninitiated in the use of the test. The question is how much special information one needs beyond a knowledge of general interpretive principles to arrive at the same level of sophistication as the authority about a particular test. This is not intended to disparage the authorities in question or to discourage the publication of test manuals or their reading. Especially is it not intended to suggest that interpretive plausibility be substituted for empirical validity. However, in very few of the instances we shall encounter were the assertions founded upon, or subsequently subjected to, empirical verification.

In his brief manual accompanying the TAT pictures Murray (1943) maintains that the test's "special value resides in its power to expose the underlying inhibited tendencies which the subject, or patient, is not willing to admit, or can not admit because he is unconscious of them," and that "as a rule the subject leaves the test happily unaware that he has presented the psychologist with what amounts to an x-ray picture of his inner self." With complete candor he goes on to state that what is needed in interpreting the test is "a rigorously trained *critical intuition*," and that "to get much below the surface, knowledge of psychoanalysis and some practice in translating the imagery of dreams and ordinary speech into elementary psychological components" will be found necessary. In view of its author's beliefs, it is surprising to find so many expositions (Henry [1956] lists fifty-six articles and books) devoted simply to the administration, scoring, and interpretation of the TAT, as though it did, in fact, require some very special principles and training. It would seem either that Murray was hopelessly naive about the interpre-

226 · *Interpretation and Tests*

tive problems involved in his own test, or that these workers failed to see the forest for the trees and hence believed that the TAT situation was unique and called for their special efforts in illuminating it.

Examination of this literature, however, reveals that neither of these two conclusions is quite justified. For while Dr. Murray may have been guilty of some naiveté with regard to the nature of his test and its interpretation, in no instance do we find conceptualizations of the test or interpretive suggestions that require or imply the need for special or unique interpretive rules. On the other hand, while many of these writers do offer illustrations of their interpretive approaches to the TAT without mentioning that these follow from a general knowledge of psychodynamics and principles of interpretation, for the most part they each also offer different ways of approaching or organizing the interpretive attack upon the TAT—different analytic systems. Some of these analytic systems may be genuine contributions. Once the attack is under way however, they appear united under one flag and most seem in agreement with Stein (1955, p. 41), either implicitly or explicitly, when he states that "in analyzing and interpreting a TAT protocol the psychologist should adopt the same set of principles that he employs in analyzing and interpreting situational behavior. . . ."

Consequently, we find Bellak (in Shneidman, 1951, p. 50) interpreting falling asleep in a story to Picture #1 as resolving a conflict situation by withdrawal, which would be consistent with viewing this event, regardless of where it occurred, from the perspectives of *effect* and *sequence*. In like manner, Stein (1955, p. 72) takes a *functional* perspective when he informs us that the hero seen "going up and down" the rope in Picture #17 may indicate preoccupation with masturbation, and Henry (1956, p. 90) a *structural* perspective when he reminds us that the violin in Picture #1 is sometimes a phallic symbol. Henry (p. 104) provides evidence of the use of *metaphor* and of the essential similarity in the interpretive approaches to different projective tests when he suggests that "organization and logic of intellectual approach" may be evaluated by considering the story teller's "mental approach in terms of inclusive whole concepts (W's), large-detail (D) responses, and small-detail (d) responses."

The problem of one event being susceptible to more than one interpretation is recognized by Rotter (1946) in his contribution to the literature on the TAT and is solved by him by the application of "only one major principle . . . consistency in personality"—in other words, by the application of the principle of contextual consistency in selecting between alternative interpretations. We also find the principle of analysis and synthesis in the relationship between symbols and referents in operation when Murray (1943, p. 7) speaks of an "endopsychic thema" in which the story teller is represented by two different heroes in the same story—each representing a different aspect of his personality.

There are a variety of sets of pictures available to the clinician, most of which differ in the kinds of scenes depicted or in certain characteristics of the characters involved. Some have been constructed to facilitate investigation of certain personality variables such as the McClelland pictures (McClelland, Atkinson, Clark, & Lowell, 1953) used in studies of achievement motivation, while others have been constructed for use with special groups such as crippled children (Greenbaum, Qualtere, Carruth, & Cruickshank, 1953) and Negroes (Thompson, 1949), and even with groups as groups (Henry & Guetzkow, 1951). But regardless of the pictures used, we find that once we move beyond the analytic system there is little difference between them in the way they are interpreted.

An interesting variant on the TAT method is the Make a Picture Story (MAPS) Test, developed by Shneidman (1951), in which the examinee not only must tell a story to a picture, but must also, first, construct the picture out of backdrops and cut-out figures. It can be easily seen that such a procedure adds a new realm of potentially interpretable data in the form of the kinds of figures selected, how many, how arranged, and so on. Nevertheless, when fifteen recognized authorities on the TAT were presented with TAT and MAPS protocols on the same patient and asked whether they found any difficulty in applying to the MAPS their interpretive methods developed for the TAT, thirteen reported no difficulty at all (Shneidman, 1951).

The drawing of the human figure, once thought to be of value primarily as a means of estimating intelligence, has reached under the aegis of Karen Machover (1948) and the body-image hypothesis, a level of popularity with clinicians second only to the Rorschach (Sundberg, 1961) as a means of studying personality. Interpretations of figure drawings depend upon an analytic system that focuses upon and assigns differential significance to each part of the body and to various structural and formal qualities of the drawing. Thus, we find Machover suggesting that disproportionately large heads, as well as disproportionately small ones, indicate the presence of some type of psychic malfunctioning, frequently of an intellectual or control nature. Hands drawn in such a fashion that the fingers taper to points (spears) are interpreted as reflecting aggressive impulses, and problems in drawing the waistline are believed to reflect conflict between those aspects of personality characterized by the body above the waistline— strength, nurturance, and so on—and sexuality, which is associated with the lower part of the body. Shading for Machover, as for Klopfer with the Rorschach response, reflects anxiety, and the area of the body shaded is the cue to the source of the anxiety. Locating the figure high on the page represents an optimistic outlook, locating it low on the page a pessimistic one.

In these few examples it is evident that viewing the figure drawing from the perspectives of *function* (head as a control center), *structure* (fingers drawn like spears), *association* (lower part of body connotes sexuality), *metaphor* (the optimist is "high" while the pessimist feels "low"), and *sequence* (anxiety is associated with body area shaded), will yield practically all the interpretations suggested by Machover. In effect, Machover's manual saves the clinician the trouble and responsibility of scanning each feature of the drawing from a variety of perspectives to decide which ones he should apply, or which of several interpretations yielded by a particular perspective should be adopted. She has done this for him. But the processes by which these interpretations were developed appear to be in no way unique to the figure drawing test.

Despite the fact that Frank (1939, p. 403) claimed as one of the definitive characteristics of the projective method the fact that it "involves the presentation of a stimulus situation designed or chosen because it will mean to the subject not what the experimenter has arbitrarily decided it should mean (as in most psychological experiments using standardized stimuli in order to be 'objective') but rather whatever it must mean to the personality who gives it, or imposes upon it, his private, idiosyncratic meaning and organization," we find that Symonds (Kinget, 1952, p. vi) describes as a "signal contribution to the difficult field of the projective significance of drawing," a monograph in which the author freely attributes particular meanings to each of the stimuli presented to the examinee for completion, and derives diagnostic interpretations from the extent to which the drawing completion is judged consistent with the meaning of the stimulus. Thus we learn from Kinget (p. 36) that *"Stimulus 2, the wavy line,* suggests something lively, mobile, loose, fluttering, growing or flowing"; that *"Stimulus 3, the three vertical regularly increasing lines,* expresses the qualities of rigidity, austerity, regularity, order and progression"; and that *"Stimulus 5, the two opposed slanting lines,* expresses predominantly the idea of conflict and dynamism." Although she assures us that these descriptions are "not derived from armchair procedures" (p. 35) the temptation to believe otherwise is difficult to resist. But if these descriptions were empirically derived, it is surely encouraging to find that they are also consistent with those which might have been born of the perspectives of *metaphor* or the *reactions of the interpreter*.

It would seem pointless to continue this exercise any further. We have seen the same interpretive principles and perspectives represented in the TAT, in the Rorschach and the Draw-a-Person Test, and in the Drawing-Completion Test and the MAPS Test; to go further in this effort would not rest our contention upon any firmer grounds, for we are in the position of trying to establish confirmation of an assertion by marshaling positive instances in its favor. The diagnostic use of any of these tests rests upon an amalgam made up of varying proportions of assertions based upon interpretive principles and of assertions that have been empirically derived, with those based upon interpretation invariably possessing the greater leverage. Unfortunately, the language used by many test authorities is confusing in this regard and gives no clue as to which type of assertion is being dealt with, thus leaving the reader with the task of determining whether he is being asked to accept a statement upon interpretive or upon empirical grounds. It is this indiscriminate commingling of interpretive and empirical assertions that undoubtedly has also served to obscure the extent to which commonality does prevail in the interpretation of these different tests.

INTERPRETATION AND VALIDITY

In the preceding section, we avoided any discussion of the validity of the various interpretations or of the tests from which they came because our interest was only in examining the role played by common principles in these tests and interpretations. To engage in such an evaluation would be far beyond the intent of this chapter, which is to further illustrate the nature of psychological interpretation. However, there are some points with regard to interpretation and validity, and with the role of interpretation in testing, which need making here. For here as elsewhere, the clinician using psychological interpretation should "know what he is about." And to do this, to avoid succumbing to the illusion that he is exercising some gift from the gods when he interprets a Rorschach or TAT, he must have some perspective in which to set this activity. To a certain extent he should already have obtained this perspective from his reading of the first chapter in this book, but here it may be well to examine briefly its implications for the role of interpretation in testing.

Any process having as wide an applicability as does psychological interpretation is indeed a powerful intellectual tool. To find similar principles useful in the interpretation of such a variety of tests as we have just considered, as well as in the interpretation of such other material as dreams, overt behavior, and literature is truly impressive. Unfortunately, it is also intoxicating. For how else can we explain the fact that thirteen out of fifteen psychologists in Shneidman's study (1951), many of whom admitted that they had never used the MAPS test before, claimed that they found no difficulty in adapting their usual methods of analysis and interpretation of the TAT to it, with hardly a demurrer entered over the question of validity. Bellak, for example, assures us on the same study that "the method I use for the TAT can be used with advantage for the MAPS" (p. 276), and Korchin testifies, "I have never worked with the MAPS test before but I am most impressed from this experience with its possibilities" (p. 281). Intoxication here seems to have taken the form of an alteration in otherwise normally working thought processes whereby plausibility and facility have displaced empirical validity as the criteria by which tests are to be judged.

And not only is it judgment that is affected; once having enjoyed the heady experience afforded by the interpretive act, many psychologists also, we find, develop some fairly impermeable barriers to any messages that might upset their cognitive structures or habit patterns. We find, for example, that after more than four decades of experience and research, not a single one of Hermann Rorschach's original interpretations of scoring factors on his test has been changed. While this may attest to his genius, it should also give one pause to reflect upon the possibilities of an intellectual encapsulation of rather dangerous completeness.

That this encapsulation is, however, not restricted to Rorschach workers is suggested by several other instances where interpretations remain unperturbed by the accumulation of data. Stein (1955), for example, in the second edition of his manual on the TAT, appearing seven years after the first edition, still refers to the figure in Picture #3BM being seen as a girl as representing a perceptual distortion and suggests that it will be found most frequently in the protocols of patients with strong feminine tendencies, despite the fact that during this intervening period at least one paper (Rosenzweig & Fleming, 1949) appeared reporting that twenty-five of the fifty ostensibly normal males in that study saw the figure as a female. In like manner we find Machover in 1960 (Rabin & Haworth, 1960) confidently describing sex differences and developmental patterns in children as a result of her interpretations of their figure drawings, despite the fact that a comprehensive review of the literature in 1957 (Swensen, 1957), dealing with empirical evaluations of many of her interpretations, concluded with the statement: "Machover's hypotheses concerning the DAP have seldom been supported by the research reported in the literature in the past eight years" (p. 463).

If this is the price we have to pay for the use of psychological interpretation, many may decide that it is too high.

But I believe that psychological interpretation is too valuable a tool to be cast aside that easily. Furthermore, I believe that if set in the proper perspective it may be used by the clinician with no untoward effects upon his cognitive faculties.

The fact that a statement is interpretively rather than empirically derived does not automatically serve to deprive it of the possibility of possessing either validity or utility, any more than finding the reverse to hold true would serve to confer these virtues upon the statement. These questions must be answered empirically, not by fiat. Ultimately our evaluation of any assertion must be in terms of its utility as a basis either for decision-making and management, or for simple classification and prediction.

Psychological interpretation, as we have seen, is nothing more than a process of encoding material according to certain rules of procedure. We engage in this activity when we find material that we believe will be more valuable for our purposes, more easily worked with, if it is interpreted. But whether this is the case or not, whether interpretation does the job we set for it must always be determined empirically. For the interpretive process depends upon a system of logic not unlike mathematics, which, although a part of the real world, contains no guarantee that its application will be of value in the real world. We can always judge whether an interpretation is consistent or not with a particular theory and with the logic of the interpretive process itself, but this does not imply that it will be either valid or useful in any particular instance of its application. These are empirical questions for which we must seek independent criteria outside of our interpretive system. Plausibility cannot be substituted for verifiability.

It would seem, if we accept this line of reasoning, that the clinician is generally on safer grounds dealing with empirically derived means of interpreting test material. And to some extent he is. But sampling error, measurement error, inappropriateness of norms, and so forth exact their toll here so that his safety is only a relative affair. In addition, if he were to choose this course he would find the use of certain tests completely ruled out for him. And though some may not find this a lamentable loss—as we observed in our discussion of psychodiagnosis—we are far from that stage in the development of psychology where we can cavalierly dismiss any potentially usable source of data in the study of personality. The problem is that of finding the proper role for interpretation in testing, not that of ruling it out.

In our earlier discussion of the interpretive process a strong emphasis was placed upon the personal element in it, upon the intellectual acumen of the interpreter, his willingness and ability to entertain alternative perspectives and interpretations in dealing with the material before him, and his ability to accept the tentativeness, indeed the riskiness, of interpretation. Interpretation was portrayed, not unintentionally, as an adventure—an adventure undertaken when the interpreter encounters a situation that in some fashion does not make sense on its own terms. If we accept this view of psychological interpretation, we cannot accept the institutionalization of its use in the form in which we find it in projective tests. To label a technique or procedure as a test is to imply that its use is so regularized and its results so reliable and valid that we can turn to it with confidence that it will serve whatever purpose it was purportedly designed to serve, and do this independently of the person using the test. Testing should not involve adventure—at least not for the clinician.

This may seem to be a naive view of the nature of tests, but I believe that it represents the *implicit* view held by practically all who use them. Thus, for the TAT to depend as heavily as it does for its usefulness upon the interpretive skills of the clinician, would be, according to this view, to deny it status as a test. And to the extent that we have been correct in our analysis of the nature of projective techniques in general, this would hold for other projective tests as well. So long as they depend upon the individual clinician and the interpretive process for their utility, they do not qualify as tests. This is not to deny them any value; it is simply to deny them status as tests.

The interpretive process requires content for its operation. This it gets from a variety of sources, as we indicated in the last chapter. The function of projective techniques is best understood as simply that of providing another source of content additional to that obtained in the interview, free behavior observation, artifacts, and life history data. They would be best thought of as *response elicitation techniques*. Thought of in this way, whether the responses they elicit will be interpretable or the interpretations rendered of value would be recognized as being problematical to the same extent as is true of the clinical interview itself or of any of the other sources of content available to us. It would serve to put the clinician on guard against placing any more confidence in their results than he would in any other yet-to-be-tested hypothesis.

Introducing the concept of response elicitation techniques for the broad range of instruments now called projective tests does not prevent our investigating such questions as which techniques most often elicit "useful" responses, which ones are most easily interpretable, and whose interpretations most often serve our purposes. Indeed, it would seem to focus research on some questions that heretofore have been overlooked in connection with projective tests. For from this point of view it becomes reasonable to ask not only if a particular interpretive approach can be used with the content elicited by an instrument—we have seen that any content is susceptible to interpretation from one or more perspectives—but also if the content elicited will yield useful interpretations. True, this is the point of many validity studies at present.

But the present view would serve to emphasize the fact that interpretation alone is not at stake in these studies, that also involved is the possibility that the analytic system and the content elicited, no matter how easily interpreted, are totally irrelevant. It is in the nature of the interpretive process that it can be applied to the most irrelevant material and still yield convincing assertions, and so we must concern ourselves with the question of whether certain types of content should ever be admitted to the interpretive process.

It is reasonable to think of the individual as possessing several response systems, some of which are only minimally correlated with each other, and it is quite possible that certain tests yield faulty interpretations simply because they tap fairly isolated response systems of the individual. Where this is the case, where a test has tapped a response system only tangentially related to the system of primary interest, the interpretive approach to the content elicited is very likely to lead us astray. Here only a straight-forward empirical approach will point up the irrelevancy of the responses elicited.

With regard to tests, the interpretive process can only lead to hypotheses. To the extent that a test is solely dependent upon interpretation for its usefulness, whether carried on by the individual clinician or by a single authority, it is not a test but a response elicitation technique and a source of hypotheses. Should a set of hypotheses be formulated that exhaustively accounts for all of the types of responses elicited by the instrument, and should these hypotheses be verified, then the instrument may be considered a test. Tests then need not be born of blind empiricism, they may indeed be conceived through an avowedly interpretive approach, but ultimately they must stand the ordeal of empirical scrutiny to be considered tests. From this standpoint, projective tests are abortions. They represent cases of instruments that have never progressed beyond the first stage of test development—

the tentative attribution of meaning to the responses elicited by them. It seems that only Hermann Rorschach himself, among all the luminaries in this field, recognized the unfinished nature of his technique when he insisted upon referring to it as an experiment.

Those instruments currently called "projective tests" may be with us for some time yet—perhaps they should be. Their place in the total psychodiagnostic process is that of providing content which is susceptible to interpretation, and as such they provide a service not strictly performed by tests and only partially performed by the anamnesis and free behavior observation. We do not see projective tests as operating at a "deeper level" of personality than do any other psychodiagnostic procedures—we have found the concept of "depth" psychologically meaningless—but we do see them as potentially valuable contributors to the psychodiagnostic matrix. Consequently, it may be necessary for clinicians to develop a new category into which to place projective tests—perhaps simply "response elicitation techniques"—which will provide them with a status in the psychodiagnostic process coordinate with that held by the interview and by tests, but which will also serve to emphasize the hypothetical nature of their contribution to psychodiagnosis.

What does this imply with regard to the role of interpretation in testing? Simply this: interpretation plays the same role here as it does elsewhere—it is a means of transforming data and as such it is a potent tool. It may play a significant role in the development of new tests, in the attribution of meaning to the responses elicited by them, that is, in tying the behavior elicited by the test into some theory. But beyond this role in test construction, in the work-a-day clinical situation interpretation permits the clinician to approach every test—every true test, that is—in a more comprehensive fashion. After gleaning from the test the information it was designed to provide, he may then focus upon those aspects of the individual's performance that are unique, for which the test contains no standardized and verified means of analysis and interpretation, and sift these for material that may be fashioned through the interpretative process into valuable generalizations and constructions not otherwise obtainable. But this is purely in the nature of a bonus that interpretation provides in connection with testing, and the propositions so formed must be treated with much more caution than those generated by the test itself. For while interpretively derived propositions may in many cases be the more valuable ones, at the same time they are also the ones most subject to error. The clinician's use of interpretation in testing will prove to be an asset only so long as he fully understands its functions and limitations in the psychodiagnostic process; in the hands of a clinician failing to grasp these, interpretation becomes a snare.

SUMMARY

In order to discuss the role played by interpretation in psychological testing, the distinction between projective and nonprojective tests was first considered. It was concluded that insofar as this distinction rests upon such attributes as *freedom of response, indirectness of method,* and the making of *intra- rather than interindividual comparisons,* the distinction is a tenuous one. Tests are found to differ in the extent to which they permit variance in either the instrumental or expressive component of behavior, but even here a hard and fast distinction between the two types of tests cannot be maintained. However, it does seem to be the case that it is with the expressive component of behavior that most psychological interpretation is concerned and, in turn, that conventionally designated projective tests depend upon psychological interpretation for the analysis of this component of behavior. Nonprojective tests, while also dependent upon the expressive component of behavior, do not depend upon the interpretive activity of the clinician for their utilization; their usage is based upon empirical and psychometric treatments of the test protocols. On the basis of these considerations, it was suggested that currently designated projective tests might be better thought of as "response elicitation techniques" rather than tests, and that their sole function is to provide the clinician with an additional source of content for use in the interpretive process. Reserving the test designation only for standardized and empirically verified procedures, we further suggested that it may be helpful for the clinician to think of his psychodiagnostic data as coming from three coordinate sources: the anamnesis and collateral sources, such as school records, case history records, and free behavior observations; response elicitation techniques; and tests.

With regard to tests, psychological interpretation, because of the nonspecificity of its principles, may in many cases add another dimension to their usage: they may be used conventionally as tests and, in addition, they may be treated as behavior samples to be scanned for interpretive material.

The use of interpretation with response elicitation techniques or projective tests was illustrated and analyzed in detail with regard to the Rorschach and supplemented with the analysis of statements frequently made in connection with other projective tests. It was suggested that a distinction be made between the analytic system proposed for use with a particular test and the interpretive principles applied to the material resulting from the application of the analytic system. When this distinction is made it becomes increasingly apparent that the same interpretive principles are applied regardless of the test in question; only the analytic system changes. In many instances it is quite likely that the analytic system, which tends to be specific to the test, may be a major source of error in subsequent test interpretations. Thus, in evaluating the findings of investigations of projective test validity one must seek in each instance to determine the extent to which these should redound to the analytic system as opposed to the interpretive principles involved.

CHAPTER 8.

Interpretation in Psychotherapy

Directions for a Theory

VIEWING interpretation as a particular activity engaged in by the psychotherapist in the course of his work with the patient, let us now try to develop a theory to account for its effects in psychotherapy. Can we account, for example, for the change reported in a patient after informing him that his dream indicated that his fear of competing with others is due to his equating competition with hostility and aggression? If such an interpretation helps in making the patient less fearful in competitive situations, how does this come about? Why will such an interpretation in one instance be immediately acknowledged by the patient as correct (with, perhaps, a report of an accompanying *aha-erlebnis*), while in another instance it is greeted with skepticism if not outright rejection, and in yet another it leads the patient to question his therapist's professional qualifications? A theory of interpretation should answer these questions. Although it would be both premature and presumptuous to offer a full-blown theory of interpretation at this point, because such a theory must draw upon certain areas of knowledge which themselves are not fully developed, I do believe that the view of the interpretive process that has been developed in the preceding chapters indicates the directions which such a theory must take in its development.

The traditional view of interpretation, the psychoanalytic view primarily, takes as its model the archeologist who makes discoveries about mankind by *uncovering* artifacts of previous cultures. Although shifting disciplines slightly, Menninger's (1958) assessment of the value of dream interpretation is typical of this view when he says, "Dreams serve the psycho-analyst as core-drilling samples serve the geologist—except that our samples are spontaneous! They are coded com-munications from the unconscious which in that form can elude the repression barrier. When they are translatable, they —with the aid of association—illuminate and clarify whole areas of obscurity in the life history, the clinical picture and the transference situation" (pp. 149–150). The present view of interpretation, having rejected such concepts as depth and the unconscious, takes as its model, instead, the scientist or theorist himself who makes his "discoveries" by means of a special language system that permits him to deal differently with events than does the layman or, in many instances, his own predecessors.

In rejecting the traditional view of the nature of interpre-tation, we must perforce also reject its conception of how interpretation influences behavior. For if we have rejected the substantive and topographic concept of personality held by psychoanalysis, it makes little sense to maintain that " . . . interpretation splits the ego into an observing and an ex-periencing part so that the former can judge the irrational character of the latter" (Fenichel, 1945, p. 26), or that "the therapeutic task . . . is to reunite with the conscions ego the contents (both unconscious anxieties of the ego and instinctual impulses of the id) which have been withheld from consciousness. . . ." (p. 570). The present concept of the nature of interpretation requires that we advance a theory regarding its behavioral and therapeutic effects which does not rely upon such views.

Interpretation is clearly a cognitive activity that might be variously described as being concerned with the coding and recoding of information, concept formation, abstraction, induction, and deduction. But a new dimension becomes involved once we think of interpretation as an activity in psychotherapy, and one that is intended to bring about some modification in patients' behavior. For we are no longer concerned with describing and accounting for merely the cognitive activities of the interpreter. We must also concern ourselves now with questions of how interpretations made in therapy are communicated from the therapist to his patient, and how behavior changes as a function of interpretation, when it does. The interpreter is no longer a lonely man, he is not engaging in interpretation simply for his own edification, as a therapist he is trying to both understand and influence another individual by this means. The construction of a theory of interpretation in psychotherapy therefore represents a problem in communication and influence, in the relationships between perception and behavior, and in interpersonal relations, as well as one in cognition.

After listing the requirements of a theory of interpretation in psychotherapy, interpretation will then be considered from the standpoint of each of the problem areas just mentioned. Although these problem areas are surely not independent of each other, for purposes of discussion we shall treat them as such. For although we may agree that interpersonal relations also involve problems of communication, and that communication and influence may be construed as but a special case of perception and behavior, to try to bring together what others have torn or kept asunder would lead us too far afield.

As it happens, there are certain aspects of interpretation that are more easily discussed in terms of one type of problem than another, and so, considering this chapter more in the nature of a working paper than a formal exposition of theory, we shall proceed, neglecting for the most part the lines of relationship between areas which certainly exist. Finally, drawing upon this discussion, I shall present a set of propositions that I believe may provide the groundwork for a theory of interpretation in psychotherapy and a point of departure for research therein. But before proceeding further, it is necessary to consider the status of interpretation in psychotherapy.

The Status of Interpretation in Psychotherapy

Of all of the techniques in the therapist's armamentarium, interpretation probably enjoys the most ambiguous status. At one extreme we find Rogers, who has been constant (1942, 1951, 1961) in his proscriptions against the use of interpretation in psychotherapy and in his warnings that "interpretations are usually threatening and tend to slow rather than speed the process of therapy" (1961, p. 13), while at the other we find, among others, Fenichel (1945), Fromm-Reichmann (1950), and Rosen (1953), for whom interpretation represents one of the nodal points of the entire psychotherapeutic process. Precisely what role interpretation does or should play in psychotherapy is a difficult question to answer because of the sparcity of research evaluating the effectiveness of specific therapeutic procedures. But such has been the influence of Rogers and his followers that his observation of a decline in the use of interpretation by nondirective counselors over an approximately six-year interval (1951, pp. 30–31) probably reflects equally well practices with regard to interpretation by other therapists as well. It is because of this influence that the position of the client-centered group must be critically examined.

Why the subject of interpretation evokes the kind of

partisan spirit it does among client-centered therapists is hard to understand and not to the point here. However, it does appear that just as "damnYankee" has become a single word for the Southerner, so has "intellectualizedinterpretation" (Rogers, 1942, p. 25) been added to the demonology of the client-centered camp and with about as much dispassionate thought. In this regard it is curious to note that while Rogers (1961, p. 13) in a recent symposium cites Bergman's (1951) research, which was conducted at Chicago, in support of his contentions regarding the deleterious effects of interpretation, he neglects to acknowledge the existence of the contradictory studies by Dittman (1952) at the University of Michigan, which reported that therapeutic movement was associated with interpretations somewhat deeper than pure "reflection," and by Auld and White (1959) at Yale, in which no evidence was found that patient resistance increased following interpretation!

Perhaps the clue to understanding here actually rests with "intellectualizedinterpretation." For we find that Rogers has never had any qualms about the use of "reflection," "clarification," "reformulation," or "summarization" (1942), and that he cites with approval (1951) the "increasing variety of attempts to communicate the fact that the therapist is endeavoring to achieve the internal frame of reference of the client" (p. 31). The therapist is adjured by Rogers to attempt to achieve "a deep understanding of the private world of the client" (p. 31), and "to reconstruct the perceptual world of the individual at the moment of expression, and to communicate this understanding with skill and sensitivity" by Hobbs (1951, p. 289). One begins to wonder just what the nondirectivists mean by interpretation, and we are brought back to "intellectualizedinterpretation" as the possible answer. One begins to suspect that much of the fuss and fury has been directed at the technique itself when it was actually elicited by misuses of the technique, and that there has, in fact, been a continuing failure on the part of Rogers and his coworkers to discriminate between interpretation and its misuses, damning the technique because some have wrongly applied it much as one might damn x-rays as a diagnostic device because some practitioners have misused them.

The point is that problems of focus in interpretation, of format, and of timing are the real issues here, not whether interpretation per se is good or bad. The therapist following Rogers' strictures regarding interpretation would probably not perform in a discernibly different fashion from one following Fenichel's (1945) warning against bombarding the patient with "deep interpretations" instead of dealing with material that is unconscious "by naming it at the moment it is striving to break through to consciousness" (p. 25). With due allowances for differences in vocabulary it is reasonable to believe that Rogers would agree with Fenichel when he says that "To name unconscious contents that are not yet represented by preconscious derivatives, and therefore cannot be recognized as such by the patient merely by turning his attention to them, is no interpretation" (p. 570). Interpretation as described in the first five chapters of this book is an activity difficult to conceive of as absent from any therapeutic endeavor, regardless of its theoretical orientation. Our problem therefore is not to vindicate its use, but rather to attempt to understand its function in the therapeutic process.[1]

Interpretation is no less present in the choice of what the Rogerian therapist shall summarize of the client's preceding statements—from which some material must be ignored or edited—or in his reflection of feeling, than it is in the massive

[1] As should be clear from our earlier discussion of the nature of interpretation, we do not identify interpretation with any particular theory of personality or behavior nor with any single mode of communication or usage. Not every interpretation is communicated to the patient—some are for the guidance of the therapist only. But these are interpretations nonetheless. One of the most powerfully impressive illustrations of the operation of interpretation in psychotherapy is Margaret Sechehaye's (1952) report of her treatment of a severely regressed schizophrenic girl by means of what she called "symbolic realization" in which interpretations were rarely if ever verbalized, but rather acted out by the therapist in her handling of the patient.

interpretive assaults mounted by Rosen (1953) upon his schizophrenic patients. In each case events are being recast in different terms, and in each case the hope is that this transformation will promote some desired change in the patient's behavior.

Interpretation actually plays a dual role in psychotherapy: the one intentional and the other less so. In its first role its function is to help the therapist make sense out of the material presented to him by the patient, to serve as a guide in his work with the patient, and where interpretation is communicated to the patient, to provide the patient with a new and (hopefully) more productive approach to his problems. That interpretation has a second role as well in the therapeutic process is becoming increasingly recognized. In making an interpretation to a patient we cannot help but communicate to him something of what we think of him, of ourselves, and of the nature of therapy itself. Therefore, interpretation also serves to define the relationship between patient and therapist, and, as we shall see, it may be a potent source of threat or reassurance, depending upon how it is used. Once we cease to identify interpretation only with verbal intervention, and once we cease to identify it with ineffectual verbal intervention in particular, the answer to the question of the status of interpretation in psychotherapy is obvious: it cannot be avoided in psychotherapy—at least as psychotherapy is currently practiced.[2]

REQUIREMENTS OF A THEORY OF INTERPRETATION

The requirements of a theory of interpretation can be thought of as being of two kinds: specifications or ground rules that must be followed in its construction, and a listing

[2] An exception to this might be the case of what I would call the content-free psychotherapies advocated by Wolpe (1958) and by Haugen, Dixon, and Dickel (1960), which rely almost exclusively upon counter-conditioning and progressive relaxation techniques.

of those phenomena for which the theory must give a satisfactory account. Scientists, and perhaps psychologists more than any others, have grown increasingly concerned—not to say entranced—with the philosophy of science and its canons concerning the nature of scientific theory and explanation, so that very little needs to be said about the ground rules we intend to follow in constructing our theory of interpretation in psychotherapy, except to indicate a few special rules to which we subscribe.

Like any human enterprise, the development of a scientific theory must follow certain accepted rules of procedure if its undertaking is to have more than personal and private significance. These rules are implied in our understanding of the nature of scientific theory, stated perhaps most succinctly by Braithwaite (1955) when he said: "A scientific theory is a deductive system in which observable consequences logically follow from the conjunction of observed facts with the set of fundamental hypotheses of the system" (p. 22). The theory, in other words, must have empirical content and it must contain statements in a language sufficiently unequivocal so that their truth value may be determined by comparing their logical implications with empirical observations.

Beyond these general specifications, however, an additional one will be imposed: the theory must be able to account with uniform success for the effects of interpretation in psychotherapy, without regard to whether the interpretation is of a psychoanalytic nature or derived from some other theoretical position. While we shall hope to develop a theory of interpretation which is continuous with general psychological theory, we are imposing the condition that it be theory-free with regard to the kinds of interpretations for whose effects it will try to account. This will require that we develop concepts as applicable to the interpretations of the Freudian as they are to those of the Adlerian, or the Jungian, or the Sullivanian, or the Rogerian. The theory is to be catholic, for we are dealing with a catholic phenomenon. To attempt to do otherwise would be to imply that one could rationally utilize interpretation in psychotherapy only if he subscribed, in part at least, to that particular personality or therapeutic theory for which interpretation was a meaningful process.

For this reason, interpretation cannot be described as being concerned with "uncovering" meanings, with "making the unconscious conscious," or with a splitting of the ego into a "reasonable judging portion and an experiencing portion" (Fenichel, 1945, p. 570), because these are all dependent upon one particular view of personality and psychotherapy. If these were the only terms upon which we could rest a theory of interpretation, a therapist would indeed be taking a psychoanalytic approach in his treatment of a patient if he engaged in interpretation. But my contention is that interpretation is not the exclusive property of any single theory of personality and psychotherapy. A theory that will support this contention must be one that will make interpretation a plausible endeavor for the therapist regardless of his theoretical persuasion. The particular personality theory to which the therapist subscribes dictates *what* will be interpreted and, in most instances, *how* it will be interpreted, but beyond that, when we concern ourselves with the *why* of interpretation, we are dealing with a different level of theory. And it is on this level that the present theory of interpretation is designed to operate.

Let us turn now to the phenomena for which the theory must account. Here we indicate the range of phenomena that have been identified with interpretation in psychotherapy and thus rough out the area of ignorance for which an adequate theory of interpretation should provide the map. In describing these phenomena we are, in effect, establishing a set of job specifications and criteria, which will serve both as guidelines in the construction of the theory and as means of evaluating the final product.

This is a crucial part of the process of theory construction: if one chooses to account for too little he is likely to come up with a theory that does the job but is trivial; if one sets one's sights too high and chooses to account for too much, he endangers his theory by trading rigor for profundity. Obviously, "too little" and "too much" are points on a largely subjective continuum and so little agreement can be expected here as to the direction in which I have erred. Nevertheless, the problem exists and must be recognized. If anything, my guess would be that I have leaned in the direction of "too little," but hopefully not too "too little."

Another problem, considerably more important and no less vexing than the first, also exists at this point and must be recognized. Simply put, this is the question of whether the phenomena we propose to explain are real or imaginary. We are dealing with phenomena that are reported to occur by a variety of observers, but we are also working in an area practically unsullied by controlled research, so that these reports must always be somewhat suspect. Although the psychoanalyst would have us believe that he is in the ideal position to make observations on the nature of psychotherapy and the human psyche, so far as he is human his own theory betrays him with its constant reminders of the roles of the unconscious and irrational in producing distortions in the conscious and the rational. Thus we must acknowledge the possibility that we might be trying to build a theory to explain the hoped for rather than the real; that we might be trying to explain the imagined rather than the observed.

This is a peculiar position to be in. It is not quite like developing a theory to account for why the moon is made of green cheese, why the cheese is green, and why it doesn't spoil, but it is rather like trying to develop a theory to account for the living habits of the "abominable snowmen" of Tibet. Recognizing this problem, perhaps the wisest course would be to abandon the enterprise right here rather than to leave oneself vulnerable to the dangers of waking up one day to find that he has been pursuing a will-o'-the-wisp. But to do this would leave our knowledge of interpretation in psychotherapy no further advanced. Besides, it seems possible that the very construction of a theory to account for certain phenomena associated with interpretation in psychotherapy may go a long way toward helping us determine their existential status.

Theories, in addition to their major purposes, also perform a winnowing function. For in erecting a theory any fragility in the supposed phenomena for which it is to account is soon exposed: first, through problems that become evident in developing a logically coherent formulation to account for these phenomena, and second, through the speculation, controversy, and research that inevitably gather over the head of any newborn theory. Thus, by making an act of faith at this point in the reality of the phenomena for which we are trying to account, we may produce the vehicle that will allow us to determine whether or not this faith was justified. Hence, we shall now proceed to list the phenomena with which a theory of interpretation in psychotherapy must deal with no further qualifications about their reality status: these are our givens.

1. *Interpretation changes behavior.* In one way or another this is the ultimate goal of any interpretation. In most instances, where the interpretation is one made by the therapist and expressed to the patient, it is the patient's behavior that is asserted to change. This change may be at the level of complaints reported to the therapist; at a physiological level, as in a diminution of physical symptomatology; or at a social-interactional level. Although the goal of interpretation is often stated to be that of giving the patient insight, it must be recognized that behavioral change is still the issue, since it is only through such change that the attainment of this insight can be evaluated. Illustrative of the power to modify behavior that has been attributed to inter-

pretation expressed to the patient, is a case reported by Josselyn (1957), in which an adolescent, literally at the point of death as a result of severe ulcerative colitis, manifested a dramatic change in his behavior and remission of his symptoms following a single dream interpretation.

Not every interpretation made in psychotherapy is communicated to the patient, but nevertheless an uncommunicated interpretation may figure strongly in the course the therapy takes through its modification of the therapist's behavior. Thus, for example, Sechehaye's (1952) interpretation of the meaning of apples to her patient governed the kind of apples she fed her and the way in which the apples were dispensed, and this was equally true in connection with the various dolls given the patient, her bathing routine, and so on. Here the patient's behavior is modified also, but only indirectly, and the point is that whether of the patient's behavior alone, or of the therapist's as well, interpretation alters its nature and subsequent course. If this were not the case, interpretation could not be justified as a therapeutic technique. A theory of interpretation must explain how this alteration comes about.

2. *Interpretations have affective consequences.* While strictly speaking these too are changes in behavior, the phenomenon referred to here is the reaction of the patient to having had an interpretation given to him by the therapist or to his having arrived at an interpretation himself. This seems to be a phenomenon that merits separate consideration by a theory of interpretation. Specifically, it has to do with reports that interpretations are frequently threatening to patients, sometimes reassuring, and sometimes gratifying. Horney (Slater, 1956) informs us that affective reactions to interpretations may include anxiety, attack, and relief, and Fromm-Reichmann (1950, p. 151) maintains that "if a patient gets upset or angry about an interpretation, this is usually indicative of its being correct or at least in the immediate

neighborhood of correctness." The implication of reports in this connection is that many of these reactions are as much due to interpretation per se as they are to the particular content conveyed by the interpretation. How can we account for this?

3. *There is an optimal frequency and timing of interpretations.* After making the observation that interpretations have affective consequences, most authorities agree that these consequences may be controlled or mitigated by manipulation of the frequency and timing of interpretation. Too high a "dosage" of interpretation, disregarding content, may in some instances encourage dependency upon the therapist in the patient, in others raise the patient's anxiety level and subsequent defensiveness to a point where therapeutic progress is seriously impaired, and in still others, according to Menninger (1958, p. 132), so gratify the patient as to reduce the frustration necessary for him to move forward in therapy. On the other hand, too niggardly a dispensation of interpretation may increase the patient's frustration level beyond desirable bounds, with equally untoward consequences.

That timing of interpretations is also important is agreed by most authorities. Ill-timed interpretations are held responsible for increases in patient anxiety, hostility, and resistance, as well as for occasional recrudescences of symptomatology. That such consequences may follow upon an inappropriately timed interpretation is further testimony to the affective potency possessed by this procedure. Here, however, the phenomena of interest are the relationships between frequency and timing and other variables as they might determine the potency of the emotional impact of interpretation upon the patient.

4. *There is an optimal relationship between the patient's conceptualization of an event and the conceptualization represented by the interpretation.* Having foresworn use of the concept of "depth," we might point out that the phenomenon

involved here is usually expressed by the statement: *there is an optimal depth for interpretation.* Although there is wide divergence of opinion on just what the optimal relationship may be, there is very good agreement that such a relationship exists, and it is the existence of this relationship that constitutes the fourth phenomenon for which a theory of interpretation must account. At perhaps one extreme we find the point of view represented by Berg (1948), who advocates "deep" interpretation because of its comparability to "instinct gratification" in the relief of "bottled-up libidinal tension" and the "discharge [of] the energy which is causing the intra-psychic stress and symptoms" (p. 383); at the other extreme, of course, is Rogers (1951), for whom interpretation is anathema; and located at various indeterminate points between these extremes are found writers such as Fenichel (1945), cautioning against interpretations that go much beyond the preconscious, and Dollard and Miller (1950), observing that "interpretations should not be too deep. The time to make an interpretation is when the behavior in question is occur-ring, when the patient is unlikely to see the point for himself, but when he is near enough to it so that undue fear will not be aroused" (p. 402).

When the optimal relationship does not obtain between a patient's conceptualization and his therapist's expressed con-ceptualization, the interpretation may simply be rejected, it may be confusing to the patient, it may arouse undue re-sistance, or it may constitute a threat to the patient, toward which he may respond with either anxiety or hostility. Two empirical investigations (Dittman, 1952; Speisman, 1959), which were concerned expressly with this phenomenon, are in agreement that the most effective relationship, from the standpoint of reducing resistance and forwarding therapeutic progress, is one which might be described as "intermediate," somewhat beyond "reflection" but not such that it would be considered "deep" in the sense that the interpretation lacked plausibility from the patient's viewpoint.

The demands we are making upon a theory of interpretation in psychotherapy by requiring it to provide a satisfactory account for these four phenomena are not immodest. And while it may appear that the list could well be extended to include many other phenomena, we shall find it difficult enough to come up with a single, coherent theory which will account for what we have listed. Indeed, it would be presumptuous to believe that at this time we could achieve anything more than a first approximation of such a theory. This should not be surprising since the phenomena listed actually represent manifestations, in a particular context, of problems that psychologists have been grappling with from the very birth of our science. In the next section we turn to a consideration of these general problems and consider the implications for a theory of interpretation of some of the most recent thinking and research devoted to them.

Certain Problem Areas in Psychology and their Implications for a Theory of Interpretation in Psychotherapy

In order to narrow our quest for the nesting place amongst the problem areas of general psychology of the interpretive phenomena for which we intend to develop a theory, it will be helpful to begin by sketching out the psychological context in which these phenomena manifest themselves. It is here that we begin our pilgrimage from the intimate, idiomatic, and troubled world of psychotherapy to the public, universal, and troubled world of science. We can hope that what is lost of the intuitive and idiographic quality of psychotherapy in this journey will be compensated for by the increased benefits accruing to patients from a better understanding by practitioners of one of its major techniques.

The Psychological Context of Therapeutic Interpretation

Despite its more impressive descriptions as a transaction, an encounter, a contractual arrangement, a dialogue, and an I–thou relationship, the therapeutic situation is fundamentally and universally understood as a helping situation: the individual in the role of patient seeks and expects to obtain help from the individual in the role of therapist. Theories of psychotherapy concern themselves with, and differ on, the question of how this help can be most effectively given. But this is not the point here. Rather, the point is that this universal understanding of the therapeutic situation contains certain implications for our understanding of interpretation. For in seeking help and taking the role of patient, the individual so doing is acknowledging either implicitly or explicitly that there is something wrong with his approach to life.

Rightly or wrongly, in our culture the existence of psychological discomfort or disturbance of such magnitude that the individual seeks help, or finds himself in a psychotherapeutic situation, is interpreted as indicative of the existence of some defect on his part. Similarly, and with no greater justification, the individual in the role of therapist, and therefore in a position to render help, is assumed not to possess the same defect—to be, in those aspects salient to the problem bringing the individual into psychotherapy, superior to him. A *status differential* between patient and therapist exists from the very start.

Although we may wish to question certain aspects of the desirability of this status differential, its existence cannot be gainsaid. Protestations to the contrary notwithstanding, neither therapist nor patient truly believes that they meet each other on an equal footing. This need in no way interfere with psychotherapy being a collaborative endeavor, nor need it rule out its taking on the characteristics of any other form of human relationship. This is not to say, however, that either therapist or patient may not, as a result of certain distortions resulting from personal needs or irrelevant learnings, so generalize this status differential that it would preclude the development of any kind of therapeutically valuable relationship. But properly handled, the status differential existing in psychotherapy exists only vis-à-vis those matters properly falling within the province of this enterprise, and as we shall see, represents one of the major variables mediating the effects of therapeutic interpretation.

Closely aligned with the status differential is another one that we might call a *phoric differential*. It soon becomes apparent to the patient as he relates his thoughts, feelings, and behavior that these are less disturbing to the therapist than they are to him. Ostensibly, at least, the therapist is able to bear up better under them than he could. Similarly, the causes for feelings of triumph, gratification, and elation for the patient do not appear to result in like feelings in the therapist, or at least not to the same degree. While this phoric differential probably serves an equilibrating function through such mechanisms as counter-conditioning and extinction, from the standpoint of a theory of interpretation in psychotherapy the important point is that it probably also causes the patient to begin to question the validity of some of his reactions and feelings—to anticipate later discussion, it introduces what might be called *incongruity* (Osgood & Tannenbaum, 1955), *dissonance* (Festinger, 1957), or *imbalance* (Heider, 1958) into the situation for the patient.

Finally, there exists in psychotherapy a *cognitive* and *perceptual differential* that becomes manifest whenever an interpretation is communicated to the patient. Our distinction between perception and cognition here is not crucial and is essentially one of degree of complexity: interpretations at the semantic stage may be viewed as establishing a perceptual differential between patient and therapist; interpretations at the propositional stage establish a cognitive differential. It is also quite likely that those cues, lingual, motor, and paralingual, which go toward establishing the phoric differential also help establish for the patient the existence of the perceptual differential. By simple inference, if the therapist's phoric responses are different from the patient's, he must perceive certain events differently as well.

To a greater extent than is true of the phoric differential, the cognitive and perceptual differential is confined to certain areas: patient and therapist do not disagree on everything. This, of course, is as important in maintaining the therapeutic relationship as it is in maintaining any other type of working relationship. And where perceptual and cognitive differentials do exist, their magnitudes may vary markedly from area to area, or from event to event. To establish a familiar landmark, it is where the cognitive differential between patient and therapist is quite marked that the therapist is likely to be described as making "deep" interpretations.

The status, phoric, and perceptual and cognitive differentials are characteristics of the therapeutic situation *qua* situation. In addition to these, we must include certain characteristics of the patient and therapist as individuals. Most important, in the case of the patient, is his distress and his consequent desire for relief. Psychotherapy itself is a painful business and, as many have pointed out, if the stress incurred in the course of undergoing psychotherapy is greater than that which brought the individual into psychotherapy, he may not continue. This is important because it places an outer bound on the amount of stress the therapist can permit his patient to suffer if he hopes to continue treating him. More important for our present purposes, however, is the fact that the distress and desire for relief which bring the patient into therapy combine with the stress experienced during therapy to make the patient highly motivated for change. True, the situation is often a complex one and frequently involves apparent paradoxes in which patients appear both to want change and no change at the same time. But nevertheless, there is a desire for change, or growth—as one wishes—on the part of the patient, and this represents another important variable in the psychological context in which interpretation takes place.

The characteristic of the therapist that is an important variable in this context is his own desire for change. The therapist in accepting his role has committed himself to helping his patient, and so long as his patient continues to suffer, he suffers also. This is not a matter of counter-transference, identification with the patient, or narcissism—it is simply a matter of the therapist's humanity. He cannot help but suffer with the patient, perhaps not in the same way as the patient, or even for the same reasons, but nevertheless, he suffers. Hence, he too is motivated for change. And it is in the nature of the situation that the change he seeks is in the patient—although, to be sure, along the way he himself may change also.

This motivation in the therapist results in his engaging in many different operations, all with the same end in mind: that of helping the patient, of instituting some change in him. These operations will differ depending upon the school or theory of psychotherapy subscribed to by the therapist and may run the gamut from cajolery and argumentation to sitting quietly and patiently and offering only an occasional "uh huh." But among these operations will be interpretation. Again, the interpretation may or may not be communicated to the patient. But the point is that the therapist cannot help but engage in interpretation so long as he is acting under the impetus of a desire for change, because interpretation by its very nature, through its recasting of events, represents change.

Decisions as to how the interpretation will be used are only a matter of strategy and tactics.

Thus we find that, status, phoric, and cognitive and perceptual differentials to the contrary notwithstanding, both therapist and patient are in complete harmony in agreeing that change is necessary—there may be some disagreement about the locus of change, but that it is necessary and desirable is not subject to disagreement. It is, in fact, likely that a goodly proportion of the time taken by psychotherapy is concerned with the problem of determining this locus—whether in the individual or in others; if in the individual, then where, and so on. The interpretations made in psychotherapy may be considered, in part, as concerned with determining the answers to these very questions. For if an interpretation is offered in a particular area and accepted, this, *ipso facto*, establishes that area as containing one of the loci of change; if an interpretation is offered and rejected, this leaves the question of locus in doubt; if no interpretation is made in a given area, this is presumptive evidence that no change is considered necessary in that area.

Finally, we must recognize that the *modus operandi* of all psychotherapy is through communication—primarily verbal, but not exclusively so. Change in psychotherapy can therefore come about only through, and be explained only in terms of, language and communication; it cannot include physical or chemical manipulations of any sort and still be considered due to psychotherapy, nor can it be referrable to any other process that does not have communication as one of its constituents. And as for change, so for interpretation: without communication the therapist lacks for material to subject to interpretation, and without communication interpretation can have no effect upon the patient. Thus, the existence of communication between patient and therapist becomes the final aspect that must be included in the context in which interpretation takes place.

Interpretation as a Problem in Communication and Influence

From the concerns of small town library committees over the moral and political hygiene of their bookshelves to the millions of dollars spent for advertising concerning feminine hygiene, from the Sunday morning church sermon to the brain-washing techniques attributed to Communist powers, evidence abounds as to the universality of the belief that communication influences behavior. Business management engages consultants to study communication flow as a way of coping with the organizational ills of their corporations, while psychiatrists turn into communications engineers in trying to cope with the mental ills of their respective patients. That the behavior of people is influenced by what they hear and see is an observation hardly needing documentation: communication influences behavior.

But once we go beyond this observation and become concerned with questions of the mechanisms by means of which this influence operates, of the various determinants that might increase or decrease the influence of a given communication, of the characteristics of the communicatee that will be most and least susceptible to such influence, and so on, we enter an area of less certain ground that has only recently come under the scrutiny of science. If we define interpretation as communication, research bearing upon the effects of various characteristics of the source of communication in producing attitude change, and upon the effects of communications upon the receiver as they relate to changes in his attitudes become particularly relevant.

Much research over the years has been concerned with the role of prestige upon suggestion. Expanding their perspective somewhat, Hovland, Janis, and Kelley (1953), in summarizing these and other studies, conclude that "research evidence indicates that the reactions to a communication are significantly affected by cues as to the communicator's intentions, expertness, and trustworthiness." By and large, the greater the credibility of the source, the more influential will be any communication issuing from it. We might therefore expect that both the status and phoric differentials of psychotherapy would combine to increase the probability of interpretations made by the therapist to his patient having some effect upon the latter's behavior. However, more must be considered before we can speculate upon the kind of effect this might be.

Coming back to communications research again, Hovland *et al.* point out that while fear-arousing appeals are generally very effective in influencing behavior and attitudes, the danger always exists that they may make the communicatee too uncomfortable, in which case he will defend himself by failing to pay attention to what is being said. Consequently, in considering the effect of any interpretation, we must concern ourselves not only with the way in which the therapist is perceived but also with the discomfort produced by the interpretation: apparently, as with other forms of communication, a "flop-over" point exists at which the discomfort accompanying an interpretation ceases to enhance its effectiveness, and begins instead to have the opposite effect, simply because the patient has "tuned" it out in self-defense. This latter behavior, of course, we commonly refer to as resistance, and it may take many different forms.

A point which may have considerable relevance to our understanding of interpretation in psychotherapy is that the fear-arousing appeals studied by Hovland and his associates were always accompanied by recommendations of actions which the audience was assured would protect them from the dangers alluded to in the appeal. Thus the audience was in a simple instrumental conditioning situation, in which the appeal raised their drive level, the recommended response was made, and the drive level was reduced, thereby reinforcing the recommended response. While of little interest to the advertiser or propagandist, one becomes curious about the effects of fear-arousing appeals in which the recommendation cannot be accepted by the audience, or in which the recommendation is only vaguely or ambiguously given, or left to the audience to discover. What effect does this have upon the way in which the source of the communication is perceived? Upon the way in which the communication is treated by the audience? Upon the audience more generally? These questions, of course, allude to situations more analogous to those that might occur in psychotherapy, where an interpretation raises anxiety, but where, for one reason or another, the patient is barred from responding in such a way as to reduce this anxiety. We might well guess, however, that it is under conditions like these that patients either quit psychotherapy entirely or begin to develop ways of tuning out interpretations.

Messages will vary in the degree to which they present a position similar to that held by the receiver, and a number of studies have investigated the relationship between the degree of similarity or difference between the positions advocated in a message and that held by the receiver, and the extent of subsequent change in position by the receiver. The findings here are surprisingly consistent and are generally in agreement with French's (1956) second postulate in his theory of social power: "The strength of the force which an inducer A exerts on an inducee B, in the direction of agreeing with A's opinion, is proportional to the size of the discrepancy between their opinions." However, Hovland and Pritzker (1957) note that while the amount of change does increase with increases in the amount of change advocated (as one would predict from French's postulate), the amount of change relative to that advocated declines as the amount advocated increases. Furthermore, they sound a cautionary note to the effect that "boomerang" effects may be induced if extreme amounts of change are advocated.

That interpretations, like other messages, may vary in the degree to which they represent a position similar to that held by the receiver, is implicit in our definition and understanding of the nature of interpretation and contributes to the perceptual and cognitive differential existing in psychotherapy. This was recognized by Fisher (1956), who suggested that depth in interpretation might be considered a form of "distance" as this is defined in studies of influence in two-person games. However, a difference exists between these two situations that must be considered. This is that while discrepancies in attitudes or judgments are generally quantitative in nature and describable in terms of a positive–negative, or evaluative, dimension, the discrepancies attending interpretations in psychotherapy are generally qualitative and would be quite inadequately described if limited to a single dimension: for the most part the perceptual and cognitive differentials in psychotherapy represent differences in kind rather than in degree. Although I do not believe this distinction to be crucial for the validity of the kinds of generalizations we shall make from the one situation to the other, this must, of course, be determined empirically.

For the present, however, we may read the implications of the studies in communication and influence as suggesting that the more positively valued the therapist is by the patient, the more likely that his interpretations will have some influence upon the patient's subsequent behavior. In addition to this, however, two other variables must be considered: the extent to which an interpretation is anxiety arousing and the amount of change required of the patient if he is to act in a manner consistent with the implications of an interpretation. Increases in the first variable up to a point will enhance the effectiveness of an interpretation; beyond that point it will have the opposite effect; increases in the second variable will result in increases in the extensiveness of change wrought in the patient's behavior, although here too a point may be reached where any further increase results in a diminution in the effectiveness of the interpretation and possibly of the therapist as well. The interaction of these three variables—perception of the source, affective reaction to the communication, and extensiveness of change demanded by the communication—represents a major problem for a theory of interpretation and has received considerable attention recently by psychologists concerned with problems in cognition and interpersonal relations. It is to a consideration of these problem areas that we turn next.

Interpretation as a Problem in Interpersonal Relations

We shall consider here only one small segment of the research which has been done in this problem area: that which involves the paradigm of at least two persons and an assertion made by one of them which represents a position discrepant in some fashion from that held by the other. In effect, this paradigm represents the situation in psychotherapy when the therapist communicates an interpretation to his patient just as well as it does the social situation where two or more people express differences of opinion or attitude to each other on some subject. The only difference, it seems, between these two situations is that while the latter has been the object of much speculation and research, the former has only had the benefits of speculation lavished upon it.

It is striking evidence of the working of Boring's *Zeitgeist* (1950) that within the period of a single decade, we find no less than four theories (Osgood & Tannenbaum, 1955; Festinger, 1957; Heider, 1958; Newcomb, 1961) proposed to deal with this paradigm. Although their terms often differ, mercifully, for our purposes, their major hypotheses are in very good agreement. Nevertheless, it will be helpful to consider each in turn briefly, since it seems that each theory, by having a slightly different focus, may also have its own unique contribution to make to our theory of interpretation. Thus, in their discussion of the principle of congruity, Osgood and Tannenbaum, who are primarily interested in predicting the direction and extent of attitude change, assert that "changes in evaluation are always in the direction of increased congruity with the existing frame of reference" (p. 43), and from this predict that, among other things, "the more favorable the attitude toward a source, the greater the effect of a positive assertion on raising attitude toward the concept and the greater the effect of a negative assertion upon lowering attitude toward the concept. Strongly unfavorable sources have just the opposite effects" (p. 54). This seems to imply, more simply stated, that the more favorably the source is regarded, the more favorable will be the consideration given any assertions by it—a point well documented by Hovland *et al.* (1953) in their work on communication and persuasion. The implication for psychotherapy is that for an interpretation to be given favorable consideration by the patient, the therapist must be favorably regarded. To a good extent this is assured by the existence of the status and phoric differentials in psychotherapy, although it is conceivable that these could still exist and the therapist not be favorably regarded in terms of such qualities as sympathy and empathy. It also raises for speculation the questions of the advisability, value, and fate of interpretations made during periods of negative transference.

Festinger, acknowledging the work of Osgood and Tannenbaum and of Heider, nevertheless proceeds to elaborate his own theory of cognitive dissonance which he apparently believes to be somewhat more generally applicable and precise. He defines dissonance as follows: ". . . two elements are in a dissonant relation if, considering these two alone, the obverse of one element would follow from the other . . . *x* and *y* are dissonant if not-*x* follows from *y*" (p. 13). It is clear from his discussion that the elements referred to may cover the whole range from bits of information to attitudes toward individuals to behaviors in the broadest sense of the term. The important point which Festinger makes for our purposes is contained in the statement that "the presence of dissonance gives rise to pressures to reduce or eliminate the dissonance. The strength of the pressures to reduce the dissonance is a function of the magnitude of the dissonance. In other words, dissonance acts in the same way as a state of drive or need or tension" (p. 18). In this, Festinger adds an important element not stressed by Osgood and Tannenbaum: that dissonance or incongruence is an unpleasant state which the individual will strive to avoid by any of the means available to him.

Heider, with something of a Gestalt cast to his thinking, prefers to think in terms of "balanced states," by which he means "a situation in which the relations among the entities fit together harmoniously; there is no stress towards change. If a change is not possible, the state of imbalance will produce tension" (p. 201). However, by speaking in terms of entities and fit, it is clear that Heider has moved somewhat beyond Osgood and Tannenbaum and Festinger, whose concepts seem more closely tied to differences in attitudes or actions that can be best described in a unidimensional framework. Heider's language permits him, also, to treat discrepancies between self-concepts, actions, and sentiments of the sort that might arise as a result of differing interpretations of events and behavior in psychotherapy, although he, himself, does not extend his theory this far.

Taking Festinger and Heider together, we find that both emphasize the stressful nature of dissonance or imbalance— let us agree to use only dissonance in the remainder of our discussion—although Heider emphasizes to a greater extent the interpersonal consequences of dissonance than does Festinger. Both, however, are in agreement that the individual will be moved to do something to reduce dissonance, and it is likely that both would agree that this may result either in a revision in the individual's frame of reference, attitudes, and actions which are dissonant with the new element which has been introduced, *or* in a revision in the individual's relationship with, and evaluation of, the source responsible for introducing the material producing the dissonance.

Here at last we have an explanation for Osgood and Tannenbaum's findings, as well as for all the previous work on prestige suggestion and on the more general effects of evaluations of the source upon the amount of influence exerted by communications coming from it studied by Hovland *et al.* (1953): to think highly of the source but to disregard or disagree with his assertions would be to experience dissonance. Because of the aversive qualities of dissonance the communicatee accepts, and is influenced by, the communication. Furthermore, reinforcement of a drive-reduction type is a built-in feature of this situation just as it is in the use of fear-arousing appeals; as soon as the communicatee agrees with the source and acts accordingly, he experiences relief from dissonance.

In pointing out that the individual may also reduce dissonance by devaluing the source, Festinger and Heider join Newcomb (1961), who provides documentation for his proposition "that change in attraction is influenced by existing attitudes" (p. 20), thereby indicating the interpersonal, and hence therapeutic, implications of dissonance theory. Thus, if a patient is to deal with the dissonance produced by an interpretation which for some reason he cannot accept or act upon, he has only one alternative and that is to devalue, in some fashion, the therapist. In this way, the therapist risks his relationship with the patient every time he makes an interpretation, and for this reason we might suspect that the therapist who interprets too often and too deeply may lose more patients or encourage more negative transference than the one who refrains from interpretation completely or uses it very sparingly.

There are two other ways in which the dissonance produced by interpretation probably colors the nature of the therapeutic relationship. Any relationship between two persons depends upon their possessing some small universe of shared meanings; without this, communication is impossible. In making each interpretation, the therapist adds another increment to the perceptual and cognitive differential that must of necessity exist in the therapy situation. If the interpretation is grasped and accepted by the patient, the magnitude of this increment is probably small. But if it is not easily grasped and becomes a source of dissonance, this increment may be large. And as the perceptual and cognitive differential increases in magnitude, the perceived core of shared meanings upon which the relationship depends, decreases, by definition. The patient begins to wonder whether the therapist understands him or whether he understands the therapist. In either event, the relationship suffers some diminution in effectiveness with each increment added to the perceptual and cognitive differential. Thus, although the existence of this differential is inevitable in any psychotherapeutic endeavor in which interpretation plays any part, the effect of any interpretation upon its magnitude must always be considered before the interpretation is expressed to the patient.

The therapist making an interpretation to the patient, the subsequent increase or decrease in total dissonance for the patient, the consequent increase or decrease in discomfort, and the repetition of this sequence during the course of a single therapy interview or set of interviews, conforms to the paradigm for classical conditioning. Herein lies another way in which interpretation may be expected to affect the relationship between patient and therapist. In this paradigm dissonance plays the role of unconditioned stimulus, its unconditioned response is tension or anxiety, and the conditioned stimulus is the interpretation. The patient "learns" during the therapeutic encounter that interpretation will generally lead either to increases in dissonance and, hence, to anxiety, or to decreases of dissonance and, hence, to comfort. Since the therapist is at the spigot controlling the flow of interpretation, it is only natural that whatever response is conditioned to interpretation—comfort or discomfort—will soon generalize to him as well. In this way, the therapist becomes perceived as a source of relief or of distress, of security or of danger, depending upon the nature and effect of his interpretations. If interpretation thus poses a risk for the therapist, the patient is not much better off. For him, each interpretation throws him into a potential conflict situation, and an avoidance-avoidance one at that. For if he finds the dissonance produced by the interpretation too much for him to handle, he has the alternative, as we have just recognized, of rejecting the therapist. But of course, this would serve only to open up an entirely new area of danger—to devalue the therapist is tantamount to saying that he has placed himself in the hands of an incompetent or to deny himself access to a promised source of relief from his primary source of stress. Thus the issue is joined for the patient: to endure the discomfort of dissonance and maintain the status of the therapist, or to reduce the discomfort of dissonance by devaluing the therapist and to suffer the stress which this would entail. Small wonder that interpretation is threatening to patients.

First, because of the dissonance evoked by any interpretation, and second, because of the conflict precipitated by many interpretations, anxiety as a natural reaction to interpretation becomes readily understandable. There is no need for recourse to fears of hidden impulses or any of the other denizens of the unconscious postulated by psychoanalytic theory to account for this phenomenon. Of course, added to both dissonance and conflict in contributing to the anxiety evoked by many interpretations is the actual content of the interpretation and its personal and social implications for the patient. Whether accurate or not, to interpret an individual's behavior as representing hatred of his mother—this is going to be hard to take. This requires neither dissonance, nor conflict, nor the unconscious to understand.

While interpretation undoubtedly does produce a certain amount of cognitive dissonance and conflict in every case, it also serves to reduce dissonance as well. This, at least, is the intention behind the use of interpretation. For it will be recalled that interpretation is resorted to when events occur or are reported which *do not make sense* on their own terms, and that we look to interpretation as a way of understanding these events so that they will make sense. Interpretation is therefore born out of dissonance, albeit not the same dissonance as that which it in turn evokes, and the very meaningful question arises of the extent to which the relative strengths of these two dissonances determine the acceptance of an interpretation. It is reasonable to expect that should the dissonance introduced by an interpretation be less than that which it is intended to reduce, the interpretation will be accepted; should the reverse be the case, the interpretation will be rejected. And by virtue of the conditioning paradigm, as well as by the possible dissonance-controlling tactic used by the patient, the fate of each interpretation may be expected to be paralleled, in part, by the fate of the patient's perception of the therapist and the status of the psychotherapeutic relationship.

Interpretation as a Problem in Cognition and the Control of Behavior

Here we come to the crux of the problem of interpretation: if it does influence, modify, or control behavior, how? If there is any comfort in it, we might begin by recognizing that, under various guises, this is also the central problem of psychology itself—at least it has been from the time of Watson's behaviorist manifesto to the present—the prediction and control of behavior. Because prediction and control can be manifested only in instances of behavior change, it seems that to ask such questions is very quickly to find oneself in the company of learning theorists. The temptation to say that the question of how interpretation controls or modifies behavior is a problem in learning is very strong indeed. But to say this is small comfort, for if we take this assertion seriously and consult the works of our new-found confreres, we soon find ourselves immersed in a confusion of tongues rivaled only by that which halted construction on a certain tower in biblical history— perhaps the earliest recorded commentary on the problem of communication in the human enterprise. There are theories of learning, but no learning theory.

So that we may escape a similar fate, of the various approaches to learning that might be taken we shall consider only one, a cognitive approach. While I have no doubt that other learning theories might be just as capable of accounting for the phenomena under consideration, it seems to me that a cognitive theory, one which attempts to account for changes in behavior in terms of information, perception, and beliefs, is most congenial with our analysis of the nature of psychological interpretation and with the intellectual and behavioral capacities of man.

It would seem again that we are in danger of succumbing to that occupational hazard of psychology, documenting the obvious. Historians find no difficulty in chronicling the rise and fall of nations in terms of the dominant ideas and beliefs of certain eras, and the power of belief as a determinant of behavior could be no more compellingly illustrated in our present time than by the threat of war that hangs over the Communist-Anticommunist division of world powers. Finally, no one questions the role of cognition in the form of delusional systems in the behavior of paranoiacs. The problem, of course, as with communication and influence, is in describing the mechanisms by means of which behavior is controlled by cognition: how thoughts and beliefs are translated into action.

Fortunately for our purposes, we find in the latest flowering of cognitive theory as nurtured by Miller, Galanter, and Pribram (1960) several notions which not only seem to obviate

one of the major criticisms of cognitive theories in the past—
that they fail to bridge the gap between thought and action—
but which also make for relatively easy generalization to the
problem of interpretation. In this speculative and far-ranging
work, Miller, Galanter, and Pribram propose to account for
the organization of behavior in terms of *images* and *plans,* and
an "incongruity-sensitive" mechanism, the TOTE unit. The
Image (they prefer to capitalize their constructs) is the individual's internal representation of the world about him, the
cognitive map of Tolman (1948), or the schema of Bartlett
(1932). The Image also includes the individual's system of
values and attitudes and is the storehouse of his Plans as well.
The Plan, on the other hand, is equivalent to the program in
computer technology in that it is the means by which behavior
is organized in the proper sequence to secure a given objective.
Plans may operate on the simplest level as well as on the most
complex, as is indicated by their definition: "A Plan is any
hierarchical process in the organism that can control the order
in which a sequence of operations is to be performed" (p. 16).
Both Plans and Images are subject to modification through
experience or the input of new information.

The organism is considered to be in a continual state of
activity—he was born alive and kicking—and so the problem
for the theorist is not one of discovering motives or drives
that will maintain activity or get it started, but rather one of
accounting for which activity is engaged in at a particular
time, or for the way in which the activity is organized. And
here, according to Miller *et al.,* is where the TOTE unit,
which stands for Test-Operate-Test-Exit unit, comes in. In
the simplest instance—as illustrated in Figure 2, one not involving a hierarchy of TOTEs—an act enters the TOTE unit
and is subject to Test against certain criteria provided by the
Plan under which the individual is operating at the moment
and by his Image of what the desired state of affairs at this
point would be. If the act is found "congruent" it is allowed

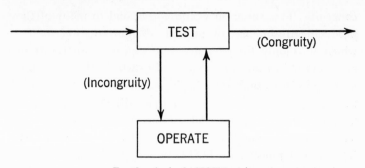

FIG. 2. A single TOTE unit
(from Miller, Galanter, & Pribram [1960])

Exit—the individual performs it, it becomes overt; if the act is found "incongruent" in the Test phase, it is sent into an Operate phase in which the act is modified so as to remove this incongruity. Activity that goes through the Operate phase is then subject to the Test phase again and if found congruent, permitted Exit, if not, returned for further modification. In this way the individual's behavior is always being guided by his Plan of what he is trying to accomplish and his Image of the situation in which he is operating and of what he considers to be a desirable state of affairs. Complex forms of behavior, Miller *et al.* assert, differ only in degree from the simplest reflex in that instead of being dependent upon a single TOTE unit they are controlled by TOTEs within TOTEs, organized in a hierarchical structure.

The TOTE unit can just as well be used to explain the cessation of an activity as it can its initiation—it depends entirely upon the nature of the activity upon which one is focusing, whether it is one associated with the Operational phase or one that is being subjected to Testing before being permitted to become overt. Thus, for example, if it is an event or state of affairs that is being subject to Testing and found incongruous by some criterion, then the organism engages in some Operation (initiation of activity) so as to remove the incongruity. This situation would correspond to many of those producing dissonance, or to that of interpretation itself, in which it is only those events that appear incongruous that are subjected to interpretation, and in which, therefore, interpretation (Operation) only begins when the therapist and his patient are faced with material that will not pass the Test phase in unaltered form, and ceases when the incongruity has been removed. The nature of the activity constituting the Operational phase of a TOTE unit depends upon the Plan the individual is working under at the time as well as the kind of Image he has of the desired state of affairs and the means for attaining it.

An interesting feature of the TOTE unit is that it can be used to account just as well for the acceptance or rejection of information as it can for the organization of behavior. Thus, if the information represented as an input is such as to prove upon entering the Test phase threatening to or incongruous with other information at present included in the Image, it is conceivable that it would be rejected or at least cause the initiation of some Operation which would remove or reduce its threat or incongruity. In this way, the TOTE unit handles very nicely the various approaches to dissonance reduction discussed by Festinger (1957), Heider (1958), and Newcomb (1961), and can equally well account for the viscissitudes of interpretations in psychotherapy.

The control or modification of behavior by means of cognition, therefore, comes about in three possible ways from this point of view. First by means of the Image, second by means of the Plan, and lastly, in a correlative fashion by means of the TOTE unit incorporating these two. The TOTE unit is a stable arrangement not subject to modification itself, but rather providing the means by which modifications in Images and Plans result ultimately in modifications in behavior. Thus it is that information and interpretation, in the role of input into the organism, alter behavior. For the adult human being, language is one of the major carriers of these two commodities and so it should be no mystery why psychological interpretation, or, more generally, talking in psychotherapy, would alter behavior. These bring about alterations in both Plans and Images, which in turn remove the support from certain types of behavior and make others more accessible.

To offer an interpretation in psychotherapy can be viewed as an attempt to alter some aspect of the person's Image. But since all Plans require certain amounts of knowledge in their formulation and execution, alterations in Images quickly ramify to Plans, and by means of their representation in the TOTE structure, to overt behavior as well. Alterations in behavior come about through alterations at the Test level as a result of changing evaluations or perceptions of various events and behaviors, which in turn alter the conditions under which incongruity will be sensed. But while the proximal stimulus for behavior change is incongruity, the form which this change takes is governed once again by the content of the Images and Plans available to the individual. Thus it is that interpretation may function first to make certain behaviors less available to the individual and second, to provide the form which new behaviors might take.

Because, as we have seen, interpretations as well as behaviors must pass the ordeal by TOTE, the interesting problem arises of under which conditions an interpretation will be permitted to enter unmodified into the Image and consequently into some TOTE hierarchy (thereby modifying behavior), and under which conditions it will be the interpretation itself that is modified by the patient (his behavior remaining essentially untouched). Much may depend here upon the relative amounts of incongruity each alternative would entail for the individual: if the interpretation is not found too incongruous with his present Image it may not be Operated upon but may instead bring about an accommodation in the Image necessary to produce incongruity when next certain behaviors apply for exit via some TOTE unit; if, on the other hand the interpretation does produce incongruity with the person's existing Image above some threshold level, it itself may be accommodated to fit the Image and consequently very little behavioral change may result. Of course, questions of how much incongruity is too much cannot be answered at this time, but this line of thinking would seem to provide a blueprint around which measurement operations could be coordinated. And if we think of the degree of incongruity of an interpretation with the individual's existing Image as corresponding with amount of depth we come again to a point where the strictures of Fenichel (1945) and the findings by Dittman (1952) and Speisman (1959) that interpretations of "moderate depth" are most effective in promoting the objectives of psychotherapy, make sense—once again we have a means of accounting for this phenomenon of interpretation.

For the more stimulus–response bound, we might relent briefly and conclude this section by pointing out that, if one wishes to, it is a relatively simple matter to conceive of Plans and Images as themselves stimulus configurations to which responses of varying complexity have been conditioned. The expression of an interpretation, by contributing new stimuli to the situation, alters behavior by altering the stimulus context in which the behavior normally occurs—in the altered context the behavior may no longer be called forth or may have to compete with some other behavior the new context has made prepotent. Each behavioral act also possesses stimulus characteristics of its own and contributes these in some measure to the context in which subsequent behaviors are called forth. In this way it is possible to avoid speaking of cognition but nevertheless to accomplish the same end. For some analytic purposes stimulus–response language is more appropriate; for ours, I believe that it makes for a spurious aura of precision. It may be necessary, ultimately, to have recourse to stimulus–response language to account completely for the phenomena described by cognitive theories, but not in our present stage of development.

A Theory of Interpretation in Psychotherapy

We are now in a position to attempt an integration of the material we have gleaned from a variety of sources having some relevance for interpretation in psychotherapy. Besides the intellectual and esthetic gratifications to be derived from the axioms-and-postulates approach that we shall adopt for this task, there are certain practical values to recommend it as well. Intellectually, such an approach forces us to determine those minimum assumptions and constructs that are necessary for a logically coherent accounting of the phenomena of interpretation in psychotherapy. Lacunae in our reasoning become more readily apparent by this approach, just as do excesses in constructs and assumptions. This becomes a handy intellectual tool in determining whether we have pared too much or too little from traditional theories of interpretation in psychotherapy: can we do without the unconscious, the splitting of the ego, and so on, of psychoanalysis and still provide a rational accounting for the same phenomena for which these concepts have been proposed? Scientifically, formalizing our thinking in terms of axioms and postulates helps provide a clearer frame of reference within which research efforts might be coordinated. Parameters in need of measurement become more obvious, hypotheses are more readily deducible, and the import of their testing more readily interpretable. Finally, it would seem that developing a theory of interpretation in this fashion would have practical value for the clinician in providing him with a clearer understanding of the why and wherefore of the phenomena which he observes and in which he participates in psychotherapy. He should as a result of such understanding proceed with greater assurance, and as many have come to recognize (Frank, 1961), this may be a major factor in determining his therapeutic effectiveness.

The terms that will be used in our axioms and postulates—interpretation, dissonance, image, and plans—should by now be familiar to the reader; they will be used as they have been in the foregoing text and so I shall refrain from giving formal definitions of them.

Axioms

1. *All behavior is controlled by the individual's images, plans, and interpretations.*

We conceive the manner in which this control is exercised to be along the lines of the TOTE unit described by Miller, Galanter, and Pribram (1960), with the more complex the behavior the more complex the organization and structure of the TOTE units involved. *Interpretation* in this axiom might just as well have been replaced by *perception*—its function is that of assigning events to classes, of formulating generalizations and constructions, or more generally, of processing the information out of which the individual's images and plans are built and revised. As is also true of the other axioms we shall state, this assertion is not susceptible to empirical verification or confirmation, but must rather be accepted as given in order for one to operate within this systematic framework.

2. *Events and behavior are multidimensional and hence are subject to alternative interpretations.*

The first part of this axiom simply acknowledges a point with which no one is likely to disagree: it is virtually impossible to conceive of any event or behavior that exists in a unidimensional space. Since each dimension possesses its own set of identifying attributes, and since interpretation begins with the assignment of events and behaviors to classes on the basis of their possession of certain attributes, it follows that they would be subject to alternative interpretations as focus is shifted from one dimension to another.

3. *Dissonance is aversive.*

The aversive quality attributed to dissonance by Festinger (1957), Heider (1958), and Newcomb (1961) is thus built into our system as an axiom. As such it will do yeoman's service in helping to account for the various phenomena of interpretation. In this we follow Miller, Galanter, and Pribram (1960), who rely upon incongruity as the proximal stimulus for the instigation of operations and behavior directed toward its own removal.

4. *Dissonance is never totally reduced for the individual.*

Here we adopt a position which has become increasingly common vis-à-vis anxiety. Because of the complexity of modern existence, multiple group memberships—each with their own value systems, the incompleteness of knowledge in any area and yet the need for choice despite uncertainty, as well as the multidimensional nature of all events and behavior, it is inevitable that for the normally functioning individual there must always be some residue of dissonance in some area for him. To maintain otherwise would be utterly unrealistic.

But it is not only out of respect for realism that we adopt this axiom. For implied in it is the notion that individuals must and do learn to live with dissonance, and that the problem posed for them is one of seeking means for its minimization rather than its elimination. This implication finds expression in our third postulate.

5. *Individuals differ in their tolerance for dissonance.*

If an acceptable means of measuring dissonance could be developed this axiom would be subject to direct test. As matters stand this is not possible, but the axiom is included nonetheless so as to account for the individual differences that all phenomena of interpretation make manifest. This axiom implies that we may anticipate individual differences in the frequency and readiness with which any available means of dissonance reduction is utilized in the face of a given quantum of dissonance. How such individual differences come about is an interesting question in its own right, just as it would be with regard to individual differences in frustration tolerance, anxiety tolerance, or conflict tolerance.

6. *All interpretation is productive of dissonance.*

This axiom, of course, recognizes a point that is implicit in the nature of interpretation in psychotherapy: if interpretation did not represent a position in some way discrepant from that now characterizing the patient, there would be no point in making it—it would not be interpretation. More importantly for the purposes of our theory, however, this axiom, together with our third axiom, provides the *raison d'être* for our expecting interpretation to influence, in some way, the subsequent behavior of the patient. While the form which this influence might take will be a function of a variety of factors and may more properly fall within the province of learning theory, the fact that it exists and the reason for its existence should be accounted for by a theory of interpretation in psychotherapy.

Postulates

I. *The effect of interpretation is predictable to the extent that therapist and patient possess a common core of language meaning and usage.*

While this postulate could be read as the escape clause in the contract offering to present a theory accounting for the phenomena of interpretation in psychotherapy, I would rather it be read as our tribute to reality or common sense, call it what one will. The implication, more specifically, of this postulate is that interpretation with children, psychotics, and persons of cultures grossly different from that of the therapist is a risky business. Put more positively, this postulate implies that to the extent that the therapist has assured himself, by whatever means appropriate in the particular case, that he and his patient can attribute the same meanings to words and use them in the same way, he can proceed safely with interpretation following the strictures entailed by the present theory, or by any other well-founded theory of interpretation for that matter.

By this postulate, we also establish interpretation as a linguistic enterprise that depends, as does any other such transaction, upon agreed-upon rules on the part of the participants —if one of the participants cannot follow the rules then the value of the product of the endeavor must be in doubt (as would be the wisdom of undertaking it in the first place). This is not to say that interpretation such as practiced by Melanie Klein (1933) with children, or Rosen (1953) with psychotics may not have some beneficial value, but I am inclined to agree with Rogers' (1961) comments on Rosen's use of interpretation, that when it is beneficial it is probably because "occasionally they [interpretations] communicate a deep empathy. More often they seem to communicate the fact that he [the therapist] cares enough about the patient to argue with him violently *as an equal*" (p. 148).

From this postulate one might expect that, other things being equal, interpretations undertaken late in psychotherapy would be more successful than those undertaken early, for the simple reason that as psychotherapy progresses therapist and patient come increasingly to share the same frame of reference, as witness Stekel's (Nagel, 1960) observation that "patients dream in the dialect of whatever physician happens to be treating them. . . . Sadger's patients will dream about urinary eroticism; mine perhaps of the symbolism of death and religion; Adler's of 'top-dogs' and 'underdogs' and of the masculine protest" (pp. 49–50).

II. *The magnitude of dissonance produced by an interpretation is directly related to the magnitude of the discrepancy between the present state of the individual, including his images, plans, and behavior, and that represented by the interpretation.*

Having stated as our sixth axiom that interpretation produces dissonance, in this postulate we indicate the manner in which the magnitude of this dissonance may be expected to vary with interpretation. By so doing, we are also providing a bridge by means of which the implications of dissonance theory (Festinger, 1957) can be brought to bear upon the problems of interpretation in psychotherapy. This postulate implies that the responsibility for control of the effects of interpretation—and, hence, of dissonance—in psychotherapy rests squarely upon the therapist's ability to make an accurate assessment of how the position represented by his interpretation compares with that currently held by the patient. The importance of this point becomes more evident in our consideration of the next postulate.

III. *Of two alternative states, that which results in the greater reduction of dissonance, or that which results in the lesser increase in dissonance, will be the one chosen by the individual.*

This postulate is a logical consequence of our third and first axioms, if we assume that one of the plans controlling behavior according to this latter axiom involves the instruction to minimize aversive conditions. The "alternative states" between which the individual makes his choice are several and not all of the same order of significance or implication, some being contingent upon previous choices. In the corollaries which follow, we shall spell out what these choices are and in this way demonstrate that by means of this postulate it is possible to account fairly adequately for the vicissitudes of interpretation in psychotherapy. To forestall any misunderstanding, it might be well to point out that by *chosen* in this postulate we do not mean to imply anything relating to consciousness or volition, but simply to indicate that the individual is faced with a choice situation in that two or more mutually exclusive alternatives are present; we leave the matter of consciousness and volition in this process indeterminate: Postulate III only states that the prevalence of one alternative over another is a function of the relative amounts of dissonance associated with each.

Corollary IIIA. *To the extent that the dissonance induced by interpretation (postinterpretation dissonance) is greater than that existing prior to its presentation (preinterpretation dissonance), the interpretation will either be rejected or distorted, or the therapist will be devalued. To the extent that the reverse is the case, the interpretation will be accepted as intended and the therapist will not be subjected to devaluation.*

Although, as we have seen, interpretation is born out of dissonance, and has as one of its express functions the reduction of dissonance, it is always possible that its effect upon presentation to the patient is the creation of even more dissonance than that experienced prior to its presentation. For example, a student is not able to "understand" why he is doing so poorly in college. His performance is dissonant with his knowledge or beliefs about his ability. The therapist, upon consideration of all the information available, makes the interpretation that the student's poor performance is his way of rebelling against his father's insistence that he become a physician like himself—the son, a Strong Vocational Interest Blank indicates, would much rather be a psychologist! While this interpretation makes the student's poor performance understandable and thereby reduces the dissonance associated with it, he had always thought of himself as being a loving and obedient son, and had been brought up in a home where obedience to one's parents as well as others in authority was regarded as a cardinal virtue. Consequently, the therapist's interpretation—suggesting as it does that there is a marked discrepancy between how he has thought of himself vis-à-vis his father and his own values, and how he is actually behaving—may produce considerably greater dissonance than that which it was intended to reduce.

Under such conditions, the patient may attempt to ward off the increased dissonance by denying the truth of the interpretation, thus rejecting it, or he may introduce some distortion so as to minimize the dissonance so introduced, or he may attempt to discredit the source of the interpretation by questioning the therapist's competence, understanding of his case, or feelings toward him. Forms that this distortion might take are many, but most prominent among them would be agreeing with the interpretation but quickly "forgetting" it, agreeing with it but depersonalizing its implications by commenting upon the frequency with which this state of affairs occurs in the general population (intellectualizing), and simply misunderstanding the import of the interpretation. This is not the place to attempt to catalogue all the means by which the effects of an interpretation may be minimized by the patient; they can usually be found in any text on psychotherapy under the heading of "resistance," and more generally follow the patterns used by individuals trying to reduce dissonance in other situations (Festinger, 1957). The point is that as postinterpretation dissonance increases over preinterpretation dissonance, our expectation increases that patient will engage in one or more of these maneuvers. There are a variety of means by which the competent therapist can forestall these, and we shall discuss them in the next chapter.

Of course, where postinterpretation dissonance is greater

than preinterpretation dissonance, it is possible that the patient will reduce this dissonance in a therapeutically desirable fashion by revamping his plans and images rather than by engaging in the maneuvers just described. Where this happens, however, it is probably due to extrainterpretive factors, such as the patient's over-all plans and images that have prepared him to handle the extra burden of dissonance encountered as a consequence of interpretation or the nature of his relationship with the therapist. The competent therapist will therefore prepare the patient for interpretations which lead to large temporary increases in dissonance so that he does not engage in maneuvers which vitiate the intended effects of the interpretation. It is for this reason that interpretation of any sort, and "deep" interpretations in particular, are not advisable in the early stages of psychotherapy.

If postinterpretation dissonance is less than preinterpretation dissonance, then by virtue of Postulate III we may expect the interpretation to be accepted, and without distortion. Reduction in dissonance here functions as reinforcement in the same way as does any other reduction in drive following some response or state of affairs—it perpetuates or makes more probable the response preceding its occurrence.

Corollary IIIB. *The greater the status or phoric differential, the less probable that the patient will either reject an interpretation or devalue the therapist, and the more probable that he will either resort to distortion or will alter his plans, images, and behaviors appropriately, in attempting to reduce the dissonance introduced by the interpretation.*

This follows fairly obviously, since either to reject an interpretation or to devalue the therapist would be behavior dissonant with the condition of a high status or phoric differential between patient and therapist. Either of these two behaviors would be just the opposite of that which would follow from either a high status or phoric differential: we learn that we should accept the views of those who are superior to us in situations where this superiority is relevant just as we should honor the views of one who seems better able than ourselves to cope with a problem. On the other hand, it is possible to introduce distortions into our understanding of a message without implying anything about our evaluation of the message or its source. Hence this alternative and that of making appropriate modifications in one's plans, images, and behavior become the ones with the lesser dissonance associated with them, particularly as status and phoric differentials increase.

Consequently the therapist in a psychotherapy situation in which either the status or phoric differentials are great will have an easier time of it in making interpretations; he will neither have to argue the validity of his interpretations nor fear the patient's questioning his skills, understanding, or attitudes. On the other hand, for this very reason, he must be doubly on guard against being seduced into believing that his interpretations are not being subjected to distortion by the patient. Before celebrating his success in an interpretation, he must ascertain that it has, in fact, led to the appropriate changes in the patient's images, plans, and behaviors. The means by which the therapist can make this assay will be discussed in the next chapter.

For the therapist operating in a situation characterized by low status and phoric differentials, as would be the case with a therapist obviously in training or otherwise not possessing the trappings of prestige and authority, this corollary serves as a warning that should he attempt interpretations likely to induce dissonance of any great magnitude, he may find himself plying rough seas.[3]

3 It is, perhaps, because client-centered therapy grew out of Rogers' experience in training clinical psychologists, social workers, and others of fairly low status (in the eyes of the lay public, of course), that he looks with such jaundiced eye upon the use of interpretation.

Corollary IIIC. *Except as the patient engages in some other means of reducing postinterpretation dissonance, or in contravention by countervailing plans and images, he will alter his images and plans, and consequently manifest changes in his behavior.*

If the therapist has been able to counter the patient's various strategies for introducing distortions, and has so conducted his relationship with the patient that devaluation of himself by the patient is not likely, this corollary implies that his interpretation may be expected to have its intended effect upon the patient. It is important to note, however, that unless changes are noted in the patient's behavior, it cannot be assumed that he has altered either his plans or his images; if behavior does not change following interpretation it must be assumed either that the patient has selected some other avenue to dissonance reduction, or that he has chosen to endure the increased dissonance because of some countervailing plan which would contravene the changes implied by the interpretation. Thus, for example, a 27-year-old engaged woman agrees with her therapist's interpretations asserting that many facets of her relationship with her fiancee are of a hostile sort, portending ill for their future marriage, but she does not break the engagement because of an image of herself as reaching the end of marriageable age, and a countervailing plan that says, in effect, get married first, worry about these things later. Unless this plan and the image upon which it is predicated are themselves modified, little change in her marriage plans could be expected to follow from the interpretation. Behavior thus becomes the final arbiter here as elsewhere in psychology; the therapist cannot rest content with having "instilled insight" via his interpretation if there are no observable changes in behavior.

The frequently made distinction between emotional and intellectual insight, like the faculty psychology from which it derives, becomes obsolete according to this corollary. If interpretation is intended to instill insight—which we have earlier in this book seen to mean agreement in viewpoint with the interpreter, and which can now be read as revising one's images and plans in accordance with some interpretation— and if we accept Axiom 1, that all behavior is controlled by images, plans, and interpretations, there can be no room for the distinction between emotional and intellectual insight. The only distinctions that make sense are between cases where appropriate modifications were made in images and plans and those where either distortions were introduced into the interpretation, or where the existence of countervailing images and plans prevented appropriate modifications of behavior.

Corollary IIID. *Other things being equal, the greater the magnitude of postinterpretation dissonance, the greater the change in the patient's images, plans, and behavior.*

This corollary is consistent with the finding in attitude change research, that the greater the change advocated by a message, the greater the actual change which occurs (Hovland & Pritzker, 1957), and is deducible from Postulate III, since for every increment in postinterpretation dissonance, if the patient did not make a corresponding change in his state, this would leave him in a situation of greater dissonance than if he did make the change. Thus, insofar as the patient's upper limit of dissonance tolerance has been determined, this corollary counsels the therapist interested in promoting maximal movement in a minimum amount of time to pitch his interpretations so that the dissonance they create reaches this upper limit of tolerance. Axiom 5 asserts that this tolerance level will vary from one individual to another and consequently the therapist must make this assessment in the case of each patient if he is to make optimal use of each therapy hour.

IV. *Events or conditions present at the time of increases in dissonance will themselves acquire aversive qualities; events or conditions present at the time of decreases in dissonance will themselves acquire appetitive qualities.*

The similarity between this postulate and the concepts of secondary drive and secondary reinforcement is, perhaps, obvious; its implications for a theory of interpretation in psychotherapy, perhaps less so. If the individual functions as assumed in Postulate III, selecting that alternative from among those available which will either maximize decrease in dissonance, or minimize increase in dissonance, then by virtue of simple contiguity learning theory, he should respond in a corresponding manner, as postulated here, to the incidental aspects of the situation as well. For our purposes there are five such incidental aspects of the situation—events or conditions present at the time an interpretation is made and the patient either experiences an increase or a decrease in dissonance—which are most important. These are the presence of the therapist, the context of psychotherapy, the activity of interpretation, the patient's experience of himself making an interpretation, and the increase in dissonance associated with the interpretation itself, which may precede a further increase or a decrease in postinterpretation dissonance. Patients vary in the extent to which they discriminate between these different aspects of the interpretive situation, rarely responding in a uniform fashion to all, and for this reason we shall make each the subject of a separate corollary.

Corollary IVA. *To the extent that the interpretations made by the therapist tend to result in increases in dissonance, the therapist will acquire aversive qualities for the patient. To the extent that the reverse is true, the therapist will acquire appetitive qualities for the patient.*

The therapist being present at the time the patient experiences either decreases or increases in dissonance, it is reasonable to expect that his attractiveness to the patient would wax and wane accordingly. This is particularly likely since in most instances he is also responsible for the interpretation that resulted in the change in dissonance level. The important consideration here is with the long-term trend of interpretations, whether they generally result in increases or decreases in dissonance, rather than with any single interpretation. While this in itself may not affect the patient's tenure in psychotherapy, it is of importance in governing his reaction to the therapist and, hence, in making him either easy or hard to work with. Undoubtedly, this represents one of the components of what is usually described as transference. Consequently, the therapist who finds that he is evoking a strong negative or positive reaction from his patient should look to the effects of his interpretive efforts as much as he should to the significant others in the patient's life with whom he is being confused.

Corollary IVB. *To the extent that the interpretations made by the therapist tend to result in increases in dissonance, the context of psychotherapy itself will acquire aversive qualities for the patient. To the extent that the reverse is true, the context of psychotherapy will acquire appetitive qualities for the patient.*

This corollary seems so obvious that merely to have stated it would seem sufficient. In any learning situation, it is usually the case that responses conditioned to the intended stimulus also become conditioned in varying degrees to the incidental stimuli of the situation. We should therefore expect that the patient's reactions to all those stimuli present—the clinic, the office and its furnishings, the arrangements, economic as well as social, that are the context of psychotherapy, if not its concrete representation—will vary as he tends to find these associated with comfort or discomfort, with increases or decreases in dissonance. To be sure, interpretation is not the only factor determining comfort and dissonance, and the actual magnitude of its importance will vary with the extent to which it is used at all by the therapist, but this corollary serves to indicate the means by which it contributes to the patient's feelings about psychotherapy, whatever the magnitude of this contribution might be in the individual case.

Corollary IVC. *To the extent that the act of interpretation tends to result in increases in dissonance, interpretation will acquire aversive qualities for the patient. To the extent that the reverse is true, interpretation will acquire appetitive qualities for the patient.*

Emphasized by this corollary is the possibility that interpretation may comprise a separate and discriminable aspect of the total stimulus situation in psychotherapy, and that, as such, it may suffer increases or decreases in attractiveness to the patient depending upon its general consequences for him with respect to dissonance. As a result, one might expect variations between patients as well as temporal variations within patients in their willingness to cooperate in interpretive efforts, independent of their attitudes toward psychotherapy or the therapist. This corollary thus suggests one of the bases for extraceptiveness or resistance in patients that is not rooted either in their personality make-up or in their fear of repressed impulses and thoughts.

Corollary IVD. *To the extent that increases in dissonance following interpretations tend to precede further increases in postinterpretation dissonance, or failures in reduction of pre-interpretation dissonance, dissonance itself will suffer a further increase in its aversiveness. To the extent that the reverse is true, dissonance will undergo some diminution in aversiveness for the patient.*

Axiom 5 states that individuals differ in their tolerance for dissonance; this corollary suggests one explanation. If drives can function as stimuli (Hull, 1933), then it seems reasonable that dissonance, which also has drive properties, should be capable of so functioning. Treating dissonance as a stimulus, we can therefore conceive of it as acting as a conditioned stimulus for the expectancy of increases or decreases in its own level, and in this way as either increasing or decreasing in aversiveness. If, for example, the patient regularly finds that the increases in dissonance following an interpretation lead to subsequent decreases, we might easily imagine him tolerating progressively higher increases because of the expected subsequent decreases, in much the same way that some people enjoy horror films because of the relief they experience afterward. On the other hand, should the increase in dissonance come to be only a precursor of more of the same there is every reason to believe that its aversiveness would tend to increase. Therefore, depending upon his experiences, we might expect the patient to be able to tolerate either more or less dissonance as therapy progresses.

Corollary IVE. *To the extent that interpretations produced by the patient himself tend to result in increases in dissonance, the activity of self-interpretation as well as his self-concept will acquire aversive qualities. To the extent that the reverse is true, the activity of self-interpretation as well as the patient's self-concept will acquire appetitive qualities.*

This corollary is supported by the same reasoning as that underlying Corollaries IVA and C, and together with them may explain the universally held belief that insofar as possible, the patient should be helped to arrive at interpretations himself. In this way the onus of increased as well as decreased well-being rests with the patient; the therapist's valence remains undisturbed. Where patient-produced interpretations generally lead to decreases in dissonance, in addition to the possible beneficial results accruing from the ensuing changes in his images and plans, the over-all effect upon the patient

should be one of increased self-confidence and self-acceptance
—he recognizes that he can cope successfully with his own
problems. Where such interpretations have the reverse effect
upon dissonance, we might expect the patient to be still less
self-accepting than he had been and have even less confidence
in himself. Consequently, although it is desirable for the
patient to attempt interpretation himself, the therapist should
recognize that this is not without its risks also, and should
encourage or discourage this activity accordingly.

Earlier in this chapter we wrote a job specification for a
theory of interpretation in psychotherapy in terms of four
phenomena for which it should give an adequate account.
These were:

1. Interpretation changes behavior.
2. Interpretations have affective consequences.
3. There is an optimal frequency and timing of interpretations.
4. There is an optimal relationship between the patient's conceptualization of an event and the conceptualization represented by the interpretation.

It must be for the reader now to judge how well the proposed theory is likely to fill the bill. This can, of course, only
be put in terms of likelihood at the present time, since the
true test of the theory rests in its fertility as a source of viable,
substantive, research hypotheses. In making this test, all are
invited to join.

Summary

In attempting to indicate the directions in which a theory
of interpretation in psychotherapy may be expected to develop, recent research and thinking in the areas of communication and influence, interpersonal relations, and cogni-

tion and the control of behavior were reviewed. In addition, an analysis of the psychological context in which therapeutic interpretation occurs was undertaken. This analysis suggested that the relationship between psychotherapist and patient might be described in terms of the existence of a *status differential,* reflecting the fact that in some way the therapist enjoys a higher status than does his patient in the patient's eyes, a *phoric differential,* resulting from the fact that the therapist does not respond emotionally in the same way as does his patient to the events reported by the patient, and a *perceptual and cognitive differential,* implying that therapist and patient do not agree in all instances in their perception or understanding of the events considered by them in the course of their collaboration. As a result of these considerations, the following set of axioms and postulates were proposed:

Axioms

1. All behavior is controlled by the individual's images, plans, and interpretations.
2. Events and behavior are multidimensional and hence are subject to alternative interpretations.
3. Dissonance is aversive.
4. Dissonance is never totally reduced for the individual.
5. Individuals differ in their tolerance for dissonance.
6. All interpretation is productive of dissonance.

Postulates

I. The effect of interpretation is predictable to the extent that therapist and patient possess a common core of language meaning and usage.

II. The magnitude of dissonance produced by an interpretation is directly related to the magnitude of the discrepancy between the present state of the individual, including his images, plans, and behavior, and that represented by the interpretation.

III. Of two alternative states, that which results in the greater reduction of dissonance, or that which results in the lesser increase in dissonance, will be the one chosen by the individual.

Corollary IIIA. To the extent that the dissonance induced by interpretation (postinterpretation dissonance) is greater than that existing prior to its presentation (preinterpretation dissonance), the interpretation will either be rejected or distorted, or the therapist will be devalued. To the extent that the reverse is the case, the interpretation will be accepted as intended, and the therapist will not be subjected to devaluation.

Corollary IIIB. The greater the status or phoric differential, the less probable that the patient will either reject an interpretation or devalue the therapist, and the more probable that he will either resort to distortion or will alter his plans, images, and behaviors appropriately, in attempting to reduce the dissonance introduced by the interpretation.

Corollary IIIC. Except as the patient engages in some other means of reducing postinterpretation dissonance, or in contravention by countervailing plans and images, he will alter his images and plans, and consequently manifest changes in his behavior.

Corollary IIID. Other things being equal, the greater the magnitude of postinterpretation dissonance, the greater the changes in the patient's images, plans, and behavior.

IV. Events or conditions present at the time of increase in dissonance will themselves acquire aversive qualities; events or conditions present at the time of decreases in dissonance will themselves acquire appetitive qualities.

Corollary IVA. To the extent that the interpretations made by the therapist tend to result in increases in dissonance, the therapist will acquire aversive qualities for the patient. To the extent that the reverse is true, the therapist will acquire appetitive qualities for the patient.

Corollary IVB. To the extent that the interpretations made by the therapist tend to result in increases in dissonance, the context of psychotherapy itself will acquire aversive qualities for the patient. To the extent that the reverse is true, the context of psychotherapy will acquire appetitive qualities for the patient.

Corollary IVC. To the extent that the act of interpretation tends to result in increases in dissonance, interpretation will acquire aversive qualities for the patient. To the extent that the reverse is true, interpretation will acquire appetitive qualities for the patient.

Corollary IVD. To the extent that increases in dissonance following interpretation tend to precede further increases in postinterpretation dissonance, or failures in reduction of pre-interpretation dissonance, dissonance itself will suffer a further increase in its aversiveness. To the extent that the reverse is true, dissonance will undergo some diminution in aversiveness for the patient.

Corollary IVE. To the extent that interpretations produced by the patient himself tend to result in increases in dissonance, the activity of self-interpretation as well as his self-concept will acquire aversive qualities. To the extent that the reverse is true, the activity of self-interpretation as well as the patient's self-concept will acquire appetitive qualities.

It is believed that these axioms and postulates provide a reasonable accounting for some of the major phenomena attributed to interpretation in psychotherapy and that they also provide a framework within which a program of research on interpretation in psychotherapy may be developed.

CHAPTER 9

The Practice of Interpretation

in Psychotherapy

THEORY and practice in psychotherapy have had a notoriously tenuous relationship with each other. This has been documented by Fiedler (1950a, 1950b, 1951) and seems to be as true of psychoanalytic (Hendrick, 1948) as it is of client-centered psychotherapists; although Strupp (1955) has reported some differences in practice between adherents of these different schools, the extent to which these differences are specifically and uniquely determined by corresponding differences in theory remains obscure. Nevertheless, despite this inauspicious augury, in this chapter I shall discuss the practice of interpretation in the light of the theory just proposed. In this way, while awaiting the much slower returns from the laboratory, the viewpoint and theory of psychological interpretation proposed in this book may be tested against the pragmatic criterion: the extent to which they provide a frame of reference and guide for the practice of interpretation in psychotherapy.

It seems appropriate to enter a caveat at this time. This is that because this book is concerned only with psychological interpretation, the present chapter might easily be misread as suggesting that this is the essence of psychotherapy. In this chapter we shall be concerned primarily with practical problems involving interpretation communicated to the patient, but I wish to emphasize that this is the whole neither of interpretation nor of psychotherapy. Although interpretation plays a major role in psychotherapy, this chapter is not intended as a treatise on the latter.

PHASES OF INTERPRETATION

The practice of interpretation in psychotherapy may be broken down analytically into a sequence involving three distinct phases, each of which serves a different function from the standpoint of the theory of interpretation in psychotherapy proposed in the preceding chapter. To be sure, it may be difficult to isolate and recognize these phases in every instance of interpretation in actual practice, but I would contend that they "exist" nevertheless, and that it may be salutary for the practice of interpretation and psychotherapy if the clinician were aware of them and the functions they serve.

Phase One: Preparing the ground for interpretation

Thanks to adult education, popular novelists, and paperback psychology, the sophistication of the lay public has reached the point where certain material, such as bizarre behavior, dreams, free associations, slips of the tongue, and certain types of relationships, are taken for granted as in need of interpretation; indeed, to suggest that they might be taken at face value would be considered a sign of naiveté, indolence, or lack of *joie de vivre*. In such instances Phase One poses no problem for the therapist so long as he fulfills the patient's expectations of offering an interpretation or of encouraging the patient to develop his own interpretation.

However, it is not uncommon for patients to relate material or to manifest behavior that to them requires little interpretation; its meaning is self-evident. In most such instances the patient has settled upon his own interpretation or rationalization quite unconsciously and feels little need for—and may, in fact, vehemently resist—any new interpretation offered by the therapist. Yet to the therapist's way of thinking interpretation is called for. How shall he proceed? This is the problem of Phase One.

It will be recalled from our previous discussion that interpretation becomes necessary only with the introduction of incongruity or dissonance, as a way of making sense out of events which cannot be understood on their own terms. Furthermore, according to the theory proposed in the preceding chapter, much of the fate of an interpretation hangs upon the balance between the levels of pre- and postinterpretive dissonance. From this point of view, Phase One has as its function developing the incentive or need for interpretation where this may not have existed, or of so raising the dissonance level prior to an interpretation as to insure that the interpretation when made will be given a hospitable reception.

Although the relation between pre- and postinterpretive dissonance depends upon many other factors as well, the importance of the operations engaged in during Phase One cannot be minimized. Unless these are successfully executed, the patient feels no need for interpretation; unless these are successfully executed the dissonance induced by an interpretation will be so much greater than that which it was intended to reduce that there would be no point in the patient taking it seriously. In this way Phase One serves to prepare the ground for interpretation, but it also serves a second purpose, to indicate to the therapist the patient's readiness for interpretation. For as the therapist engages in Phase One operations he can determine the extent to which these are having their desired effect upon the patient, the extent to which the patient experiences dissonance, and therefore the extent to which the patient is ready for Phase Two, interpretation proper. Should the therapist's observations indicate that dissonance has not been raised as a result of Phase One operations, he would in most cases be well advised not to proceed with Phase Two.

All the various Phase One techniques involve, in one way or another, the juxtaposition of two or more items of information, observations, events, or behaviors that point to a discrepancy or pattern of a dissonant nature from some frame of reference. Occasionally it is enough simply to juxtapose the two events to induce dissonance—to show, for example, that a patient's behavior is not consistent with his professed feelings; at other times it is necessary to project these against some frame of reference (also juxtaposition) to create dissonance. A particular pattern of events—for example, always developing a headache before meeting one's mother-in-law—in this way becomes dissonant when juxtaposed with a frame of reference that says such a pattern should not exist. Regardless of grammar, syntax, or format, juxtaposition is the essential feature of the techniques employed here.

The inept or hostile clinician here can easily fall into the role of grand inquisitor or police detective, and a major danger which the therapist encounters in this phase is that the patient may hold him rather than the dissonance in the material responsible for the discomfort he experiences. The techniques we shall discuss vary in the likelihood that the therapist will become identified with the dissonance they engender, and so apart from examining his own motives in engaging in Phase One operations, the clinician can to some extent guard against these dangers in his choice of technique.

On the other hand, the insecure clinician or the therapist who has strong needs to be liked and always seen as benevolent runs the risk of stereotypy in his handling of Phase One, since he is likely to shy away from any of the techniques in which he may appear responsible in the eyes of the patient for his discomfort. This too would be unfortunate, since stereotypy in any degree will seriously diminish the therapist's value to his patient. Perhaps the point for the therapist to recognize, if he is to avoid this pitfall, is that one cannot avoid pain in dealing with people who need psychotherapy. In fact, one of the therapeutically valuable experiences for the patient may well be the discovery that someone cares enough about him to suffer with him and even to take on some of the responsibility for his suffering in the course of his efforts to grow into a happier and more productive individual. Indeed, if the clinician cannot accept this responsibility perhaps he should stay away from interpretation entirely, if not from psychotherapy as well.

The techniques to be discussed are not the exclusive property of Phase One and do not, in every case, give rise to interpretive material. Frequently they are used simply to obtain additional information, for clarification, as stimuli to get the patient talking, or for some other therapeutic purpose. Therefore to the extent that the therapist does not approach Phase One in a stereotyped fashion, it should not be discernibly different in the eyes of the patient from any other portion of the psychotherapeutic interaction. This may be advantageous in those instances where it becomes apparent that the patient is not ready to move into Phase Two, for the therapist can then decide not to proceed further with the interpretive sequence without any awkwardness for either him or his patient.

Every interpretation in psychotherapy is certainly not deliberately prepared for by the clinician. Since the techniques relied upon to accomplish Phase One have other purposes as well and are continuous with techniques used for other purposes in psychotherapy, it will often happen that material will present itself for interpretation quite spontaneously and without any planned effort on the therapist's part. In other words, the therapist will in many instances find that Phase One has been completed through no effort of his own and it would be unfortunate if he were not always prepared to seize upon the opportunity to proceed with Phase Two, interpretation proper, if this were otherwise deemed advisable. The three-phase sequence in interpretation is analytic and is intended to facilitate the therapist's spontaneity, not inhibit it.

Questioning is probably the most pervasive general technique among psychotherapists of other than a strictly client-centered persuasion (Strupp, 1955), and is used in Phase One to point up either discrepancies or patterns. By virtue of simply asking a question, in many cases the therapist suggests that there is something puzzling, something dissonant, something for which the patient's current interpretation is inadequate, in the material under discussion. As in rhetoric, the question serves to focus the patient's attention upon this material or to suggest a certain perspective, the discrepancy or pattern only becoming fully explicit with his answer to the question. The question posed the patient may be either factual or hypothetical, the actual form being dependent upon the context and particular material being dealt with: in some instances it will be a request for an explanation or opinion or description of feeling; in many instances it will be implicitly stated in the intonation of the therapist's reflection of content or feeling; in almost all instances it places the responsibility with the patient for whether or not the dissonance should be acknowledged and dealt with.

From the standpoint of the dangers inherent in Phase One, questioning is probably the safest technique one can use. The therapist himself never explicitly states that there is a problem, a need for interpretation, he merely sets the stage in which the patient can either follow his lead or not. Thus the therapist becomes minimally identified with the dissonance resulting from Phase One—unless, of course, he conducts his questioning in the manner of a cross-examination. Generally, though, if the question is put so that the patient can either profess ignorance of its answer or ignore the implications to the answer, it is the safest and perhaps gentlest way of handling Phase One of the interpretive sequence.

Recollection and observation is a technique especially suited to the exposure of patterning or recurrences of events under certain conditions. It usually takes one of the following forms or variants thereof:

a. "It seems that whenever you . . . you also . . ."

b. "It is interesting that we were just talking about . . . and now somehow we have moved into talking about . . ."

c. "This is also what your mother said to you when you were a child."

d. "These situations seem to be especially frightening to you."

e. "All of these people (situations) seem to have . . . in common."

f. "This happened at about the time that . . ."

The recollections and observations are always put in a qualified form, conveying a certain tentativeness about them, and thus permit the patient to deny their accuracy with little threat to his relationship with the therapist should they, in fact, be inaccurate, or should he not be ready to face their implications. The therapist is likely to be somewhat identified in the eyes of the patient with the dissonance ensuing from the observation—more so than in the case of questioning— but not to any dangerous degree. If the patient accepts the recollections and observations as accurate he can then be invited to speculate as to their implications, thereby leading into Phase Two, or the therapist can offer his own interpretation if this seems the more desirable alternative for proceeding to Phase Two; if they are rejected as inaccurate, the topic of which they were a part might be dropped for the time being and the patient might be invited to give his version of the circumstances alluded to by them, thereby giving the therapist some insight into the patient's perception of them, or if the therapist's strategy calls for it, he may offer some interpretation to account for the patient's refusal to accept the recollection or observation as accurate and thus proceed to Phase Two.

Exposure of discrepancies is the most direct approach to accomplishing the objectives of Phase One, and although grammatically it may use either simple declarative sentences or questions, it may be regarded as a technique apart from either questioning or recollections and observations because, unlike these, it leaves the patient no freedom of movement in deciding whether or not to face the need for interpretation. Typical of the forms that exposure of discrepancies might take are the following:

a. "But if you feel . . . about . . . , why do you . . . ?"

b. "This doesn't seem to fit with what you said about . . . ?"

c. "Although you say you love him, you still seem to do things which will make him unhappy."

d. "Why would you . . . if you really felt . . . ?"

e. "With your ability you should not be making grades like these."

f. "This doesn't seem to make sense."

In each example the therapist is fully and totally responsible for the assertion that a discrepancy exists. Consequently, whatever dissonance the patient encounters here is obviously the result of the therapist's actions; the patient has no control, no out, should he not be ready or able to cope interpretively with the material involved. While the therapist could still decide not to proceed to Phase Two should it be apparent that the patient is not ready, he has played his hand so that such a decision would be a fairly obvious one—and a fairly awkward one, since it would imply either that he had bungled the affair or that the patient had failed to measure up to his expectations.

Despite the dangers involved in this technique, it is not to be avoided. For to be weighed against these dangers is the expediency and clarity with which the interpretive problem is crystallized; the method is direct and clean; it is obvious to the patient that the therapist is alert and on his toes; it teaches the patient that the therapist expects him and the world about him to behave in a rational fashion and hence may aid in reducing loose thinking in some cases. The problem is then that of knowing when to use this approach to Phase One rather than that of being sure to avoid using it.

As a general rule, of the three techniques discussed, exposure of discrepancies should not be used early in the therapeutic relationship. Because of its dangers the therapist should use it only after he knows the patient well enough so that he can predict how well he will be able to cope with the problem posed him and how well he will be able to handle the dissonance so produced. It should not be used if the therapist is trying to encourage the patient to speak freely and unguardedly and perhaps even to think loosely for a while. The better the relationship between patient and therapist, the more sophisticated the patient, the more the therapist is attempting to encourage reality testing and rationality, the more he should turn to this approach in Phase One of interpretation in psychotherapy.

Phase Two: Interpretation proper

With the completion of Phase One to the therapist's satisfaction, the interpretive sequence is ready to move into Phase Two, interpretation proper. Interpretation, as we have seen, may be either semantic or propositional, and in the case of the latter, either a generalization or construction. Having discussed their rationale earlier, in this section we shall consider where each of these types of interpretation is most appropriate, what effects one might expect of each, and the actual forms they might take.

Behavioral change in psychotherapy, as a result of interpretation or some other factor, is a slow and often tedious process. However, the ways in which these changes come about as a result of different types of interpretation are, I believe, essentially those I shall describe. In the discussion of each type of interpretation I have presented a schematic of how it works; to paint the actual picture would require that we use a palette heavily loaded with frustration, evasion, fear, disillusionment, bewilderment, hostility, patience, courage, and faith. But above all, for success in psychotherapy: patience, courage, and faith—on the part of both patient and therapist.

Interpretations at the semantic stage. These, it will be recalled, are cases involving only a recoding or reclassification of events. What the patient describes as "being truthful" would, we suggest, be better labeled "being hostile"; what the patient takes as "a simple nose cold" we believe is an instance of "avoidance"; and, although the child thinks that he enjoys "painting," we "know" that what he is really enjoying is "smearing." Interpretations at this stage may be expected to both alter behavior and reduce dissonance.

Whatever stimulus values or evaluations inhere in the class *qua* class to which an event is assigned are conferred in some degree upon the event as well. Therefore by altering the class membership of an event through interpretation at the semantic stage we alter those images and plans (Miller, Galanter, & Pribram, 1960) of which it is a constituent, and this ultimately results in behavioral change. When, for example, we say that the bugs, which a patient had said he feared and which he saw as being dirty or dangerous, are symbolic representations of his sexual impulses, we alter in some degree the meaning of bugs and consequently the ways in which the individual is likely to react to them in the future. Similarly, to say that the hunger for food which a patient reports is actually a hunger for love and affection is to alter the meaning of eating and its utility for the patient in gratifying his needs for love and affection. In every instance of successful interpretation at this stage there is an alteration in the valence of some object or event or in the availability of some behavior.

Interpretations at this stage have the effect of reducing dissonance through altering the meanings of certain of the dissonant elements under consideration. Thus, for example, although a patient's fear of premature orgasm appeared to be dissonant with the fact that he had had only once in his life experienced it, the fear became less dissonant when interpreted instead as fear of loss of control or perhaps of sexual inadequacy, for which other information in his case yielded supporting evidence. It is, according to our theory, this reduction of dissonance that insures the interpretation's acceptance by the patient, just as earlier in this book in our discussion of the logic of psychological interpretation we saw that consistency with other elements in the context was one of the criteria used by the interpreter himself in deciding upon the correctness of an interpretation. But while this is an intellectual judgment for the interpreter, dissonance being what it is, it is far from this for the patient. For him the issue revolves around distress and relief from distress; should the patient begin to consider the cognitive merits of an interpretation the therapist should beware: all is not well.

The reduction in dissonance by an interpretation may, unfortunately, be purchased in some cases only at the expense of a far greater subsequent increase in dissonance. In the case above, for example, should the patient have the image of himself as a sexually adequate and potent male, the interpretation of his fear of premature orgasm as fear of sexual inadequacy may produce so much dissonance in its wake as to vitiate its effectiveness. On the other hand, this new dissonance might precipitate a change in the patient's sexual image of himself and thus pose a new problem for the therapist and patient to deal with. Which alternative will prevail is frequently difficult to predict, but the problem must nevertheless be considered in the decision to make an interpretation at this stage. This will be considered further in our discussion of problems in interpretation.

The forms interpretation might take at this stage should all normally convey a certain tentativeness, and are illustrated by the following:

a. "This sounds like . . ."
b. "Suppose instead that we thought of this as . . ."
c. "You seem to be treating . . . in the same way that you treated . . ."
d. "Another way of looking at this would be as . . ."
e. "Very often this sort of thing really means . . . "
f. "Now if we considered this . . . then . . ."

Obviously, the possibilities are many here, but generally they fall into a limited number of categories: *tentative assertions,* such as *a* and *c*; *normative references,* such as *e*; *suppositions* or *invitations to speculation,* such as *b* and *f*; and *invoking alternate perspectives,* such as *b* and *d*. Whether any psychological significance should be attached to this categorization, I would not be prepared to say at this time. Conceivably, excessive use of normative references in interpretation might encourage a greater degree of intellectualization than would be desirable, invoking alternative perspectives may encourage a greater flexibility in general in the patient's thinking, and so on. But this is a proper subject for research, not for speculation. Recognizing the existence of such categories, however, may have some heuristic value, and in terms of practice, may be expected to sensitize the therapist to his own biases in interpretation, thereby encouraging him to expand his repertoire accordingly.

There are two good reasons for tentativeness here: first, because the interpretation is, in fact, only a plausible or desirable alternative codification, not a pronouncement of absolute truth, and it would be well if the patient came to think of all interpretations, his own included, as only plausible constructions of reality, not as absolute representations of reality, and as subject to change should better constructions become available. The second reason for the desirability of tentativeness is that should the patient find the interpretation unacceptable for any reason, there is much less at stake in its rejection by him than had a simple declarative form been used. The tentativeness of formulation implies a much smaller personal investment by the therapist in the interpretation, and hence its rejection implies to a much lesser extent rejection of the therapist as well. Of course, should the therapist desire for some reason to make *verbal* rejection of an interpretation very difficult for the patient, should he wish to throw the weight of his prestige and the therapeutic relationship itself into the breech, he may well phrase his interpretation as a flat-footed assertion that admits of no possibility of error. But this should always be done advisedly.

There is perhaps yet another reason for tentativeness in form here, and this lies in the psychology of the therapist. It seems likely that to the extent that the therapist phrases his interpretations in a declarative form he actually does invest more in their acceptance than if they had been presented more tentatively. We might anticipate that his own willingness to consider alternative formulations, to tolerate a patient's rejection of an interpretation, will be affected by the way in which he phrases the interpretation. He may paint himself into a corner with his interpretation or begin to convince himself that he is really performing an oracular function rather than a therapeutic one. For patients seeking oracles this may be fine; for patients seeking psychotherapy, this is unfortunate.

Probably the one legitimate use of dogmatic or ex cathedra interpretations is in the case where the therapist is using them not as interpretations but rather as ways of manipulating his relationship with the patient, as ways of communicating something of his concern about the patient, or in precipitating some kind of reaction from the patient. Thus, as Rogers (1961) surmises, it may be that Rosen's (1953) interpretive bludgeoning of the psychotic is intended less to impart the knowledge presumably contained in the interpretation than to convey his feelings to the patient, or perhaps simply to shock the patient out of his autistic involvement.

Interpretations at the propositional stage. In the form of generalizations, interpretations at this stage function so as to indicate to the patient patterns of events or behaviors that in turn provide him with causal explanations at an empirical level for some of his experiences. For example, when the therapist informs the patient that the rejection he suffers from others seems to be provoked intentionally by himself so as to justify his own hostility, he is giving the patient a way of understanding why he finds himself rejected by others. Generalizations also serve as a means by which the patient can anticipate the consequences of certain of his behaviors. He learns, for example, that he can expect to feel anxious whenever he is in an authority situation, thereby learning the source of his anxiety, and further, that whenever he feels anxious he counters this with some act of hostility. These new cognitions with regard to anxiety, authority, and hostility may then provide a basis for the patient's working out a new approach, a new plan if you will, for dealing with his authority problems and may possibly also result in a change in his image of authority figures, particularly if the interpretation is given him that his perception of such figures represents a confusion of them with his father.

In addition, generalizations, in providing structure where perhaps none existed for the patient before, are reassuring in that they indicate to him that his life and experiences are understandable, that all is not chaos, and that there is, therefore, some reasonable basis for engaging in the development of plans for coping with his problems. As for the scientist, so for the patient: if there were no lawfulness in his existence, if no patterns or generalizations were possible, there would be no point in his trying to improve his lot, in trying to understand himself and his situation.

While generalizations are concerned with questions of what leads to what—that is, with the contingencies between events—constructions are attempts to account for these contingencies. Generalizations reduce dissonance primarily through demonstrating that there is order of a sort, constructions reduce dissonance through explaining why the order is of the sort that it is. For example, the patient we have cited may readily, or perhaps not so readily, accept the interpretation that he responds with hostility toward authority figures—this is a generalization for which there is much supporting evidence once the appropriate semantic interpretations are made—but he is at a loss to understand why he should do this, since such behavior is dissonant with some of his most fundamental values. Here is where the constructive interpretation comes to the rescue in explaining this as due to his hatred of his father and to his generalization of this hatred to all persons having certain attributes in common with his father.

Of these two types of interpretations at this stage, generalizations probably are the more effective in promoting immediate behavioral change and may, generally, be expected to be of more immediate therapeutic value than constructions. Let us see why.

To begin with, constructions make sense only in connection

with some generalization. Consequently the generalization must be accepted prior to the construction. Next, if we conceive of behavior as constantly guided by the individual's expectancies, it is obvious that it is generalizations rather than constructions which have more relevance for the images or schemata out of which these expectancies are derived. As a result of generalization, behavior becomes locked into a system of antecedents and consequents where none existed before, and it is thus subjected to controls of a sort that did not exist prior to the interpretation. The patient "knows" that in such and such a situation or relationship (antecedent) he will behave in such and such a fashion (consequent), and that this behavior (antecedent) in turn will have such and such an effect (consequent). Therefore, to continue to manifest this behavior (for example, compulsive eating) the patient has to accept, in some fashion, first that it is a reasonable or desirable reaction to the antecedent (for example, frustration), and second, responsibility for its consequents (for example, obesity and additional unhappiness). To the extent that either of these is not acceptable, the behavior in question may be expected to diminish in availability to him. Generalizations, then, operate on the causal chains in the patient's image and in this way enter into the modification of his plans and subsequent behavior.

In many instances it is sufficient for therapeutic purposes to stop at generalization; behavior is modified in the desired fashion and the effect appears to be a stable one; there is no point in going further and attempting to impart some constructive interpretation to the patient. This is, perhaps, the most frequent course that interpretation takes in psychotherapy. There is little or no change in the patient's image of himself or his surround, or of the relationship between the two, especially as these might bear upon his behavior or the generalization interpretations that have been communicated

to him. Such changes are dependent upon constructive interpretations.

Constructions in psychotherapy have three possible main
effects:

1. They provide support for generalizations, making them
plausible by providing an explanation for the relationship
purported to exist.

2. They alter the patient's image of himself, his surround,
or his relationship with his surround, with the result that
certain behaviors, feelings, and attitudes become either dissonant or consonant with the altered image, and hence either
less or more available to him.

3. They may initiate changes in the patient's images as these
are portrayed by the construction and found dissonant with
other prepotent images.

Any construction may have one or more of these effects; let
us examine each of them a little more closely. The therapist
may offer the patient an interpretation in the form of a generalization, which on the face of it seems unlikely, or which,
for defensive reasons, the patient cannot readily accept. In
such instances a construction that accounts for the generalization may tip the balance. Consider, for example, a resistance
interpretation: a patient who is seen regularly at two o'clock
in the afternoon reports feeling drowsy during a series of
interviews focused primarily upon his childhood feelings about
his mother. He ascribes the drowsiness to the afternoon hour
and the effects of the preceding lunch hour. The therapist
observes that the drowsiness might be a form of avoidance
since it only developed during a particular phase of treatment,
and that perhaps it represents an attempt to avoid thinking
about or revealing certain thoughts or feelings, or to avoid
changing in certain respects. The patient complains that this
generalization—whenever he turns to a consideration of his
childhood experiences with his mother he becomes resistant—

does not make sense to him: he wants to get better; he wants to understand himself better; he is a cooperative person; he is laying out his own money for treatment. The interpretation appears to be dissonant with his plans for treatment and with his image of his role in the treatment process. He therefore rejects it.

The therapist then offers a construction that saves the day. He does not question the patient's desires to get well and to understand himself, or his intention to be cooperative, or the financial effort he has made to support his treatment; he is not impugning his motives by the interpretation. But he has made this observation, which he thought it well to share with the patient, and he thinks that it might be useful to speculate upon what might lie behind the pattern described, why he might be doing this. In a sense the generalization has served a Phase One function, increasing dissonance and thereby setting the stage for construction. Then, with appropriate introductions and qualifications, the construction is offered that the pattern described may be due to his attempt to protect his mother, to his fear of thinking anything or saying anything which would cast her in a bad light, that to do so would arouse guilt which might be unbearable for him at this time. Furthermore, when the therapist suggests that all of this is occurring at an "unconscious" level, the patient is relieved of some of the onus of the resistance, which now becomes understandable and also less dissonant. The constructive interpretation has made the generalization plausible and has also introduced additional cognitive elements into his image of himself vis-à-vis his mother.

Any change in any portion of the patient's image should, according to Miller, Galanter, and Pribram (1960), make itself manifest by change in *some* aspect of his functioning. This is so, it will be recalled, because all behavior must pass a test for congruence before passing out of the TOTE system. The locus of behavioral change will be dependent upon the locus of salience of whatever aspect of the image is changed: the effect will be to make those behaviors that are congruent with the changed image more probable of occurrence; those that are incongruent, less probable of occurrence.

Changes in images can come about in one of two ways: first, through the addition of new cognitive elements, and second, through a change in valence of the image itself whereby it becomes incongruent with some prepotent image, thus instigating operations that will result in appropriate changes in it. The first type of change, essentially an evolutionary one, would occur either through normal, unplanned, experience and learning in the course of the individual's daily life or through planned psychotherapeutic interpretation. The effect is one of bringing the image into sharper focus, enlarging upon or extending its realm of salience, or exploring hitherto darkened aspects of it. The image which emerges is *different* from that previously reigning, but not necessarily any more or less desirable; it is simply different.

Illustrative of this first way in which images may change and hence alter behavior is the case of a mother of a newly born child, her first, who requested clinic services because of fears that she might kill the infant. In the first stages of psychotherapy, she could admit of nothing but love for the child and for her husband; although marriage had interrupted a promising professional career, she could not admit of any misgivings on this score; the only jarring note in the whole situation as far as she was concerned was this recurrent fear that she might kill her child. Clearly, this was a woman whose image of herself contained no negative elements; she had never had to cope with ambivalence before, and so the coming of the child with its new demands upon her time— constantly reminding her of the choice she had made and that there now could be no turning back to her career—produced feelings which were markedly alien to this image of herself. In the protected and permissive environment of the consulting room she came to see that her fears represented genuine resentment toward the child; that she was a person who, in addition to desiring a family and being capable of strong feelings of love and affection, was also ambitious and capable of feelings of hatred; and that neither type of feelings was any the less genuine because of the existence of the other. Furthermore, she came to see that possessing both types of feelings was consistent with her image of herself as a fully sentient being. In this way her image of herself changed, it grew as it encompassed more elements, and as a result she was now able to experience and express negative feelings as well as positive ones without fear of being overwhelmed by either; the incongruity between her negative feelings and her self-image had been removed.

What might be thought of as more of the order of revolutionary change in the patient's image comes about when constructions are offered that cause the image itself to become dissonant or incongruent with some other prepotent image. This, for example, could occur in the case of the young man referred to earlier, whose postprandial somnolence was interpreted as resistance. In the course of buttressing this interpretation the construction was offered that he was involved in a symbiotic relationship with his mother. While he had never seen the relationship in this light before, many things fitted into place as a result of it, and so he came to accept it as a valid addition to his image of his relationship with his mother. The fact that he was involved in this sort of relationship with his mother had, of course, certain inescapable implications for his image of himself as well. Neither the image of the kind of relationship he had with his mother nor the image of himself that emerged were very attractive to him; they were dissonant with the image he wished to maintain of himself as a mature, masculine, self-actualizing individual. Since, in his case, this latter image was prepotent, he had no course open to him in reducing the dissonance but to alter his behavior, including his relationship with his mother, in such a fashion that the image of himself emerging from the constructive interpretation was no longer valid.

All interpretations at the propositional stage are in the nature of hypotheses proposed to account for certain observations, and therefore the strictures regarding tentativeness of expression hold no less here than they do for interpretations at the semantic stage. The forms that interpretations at this stage might take, while placing more emphasis upon recognition of patterning in the case of generalizations, and more explicitly adopting either an inductive or deductive attitude in the case of constructions, may still be thought of as falling into one or more of the categories found to account for semantic interpretations: tentative assertions, normative references, suppositions or invitations to speculation, and invocations of alternative perspectives. For this reason, no special illustrations seem necessary.

Generally, it will be found that a construction will only be accepted, or stand a chance of being accepted, if it has been preceded by a generalization which has gained acceptance. At times, however, acceptance of the generalization itself is contingent upon the presence of a construction to back it up. Therefore, from the standpoint of practice, the only generalization which can be made vis-à-vis strategy and the relationship between generalizations and constructions, is that it would not be wise to attempt the latter without having laid a foundation in the former, and that the therapist in offering generalizations should always be prepared, if he is intent upon their gaining acceptance, to offer also a construction which will support the generalization.

Constructions, challenging the patient's fundamental beliefs as they often do, should not be offered until the psychotherapist is certain of the effects they might have and, in any event, not until the therapeutic relationship is sufficiently well developed so that the patient does not misinterpret them as either criticism or rejection. Thus, as a kind of crude ordering, we might say that generalizations may be made earlier in the therapeutic relationship than constructions, and that both should come a good while after the therapist has found that he can make semantic interpretations without any untoward effects.

Properly conducted, interpretation does not end at this point. Although the patient appears satisfied with, and accepting of, an interpretation, for the therapist to rejoice at this point would be vain indeed. Interpretations that are found momentarily serviceable may not continue to be so unless they are given full field tryouts and the kinks worked out of them. That is, to ensure that the patient derives the maximal benefit from each interpretation, and that each interpretation is firmly integrated into the patient's system of plans and images, there must follow a final phase in interpretation which we shall call consolidation and testing.

Phase Three: Consolidation and testing

The events for which an interpretation is developed do not exist *sui generis;* they are related in many ways to other events and aspects, past and present, of the individual's experience; they are but those particular strands of the whole warp and weft of the individual's existence that happen to have come under scrutiny at one particular moment in the psychotherapeutic situation. Any interpretation should therefore be expected to have implications beyond those events immediately under consideration at the moment of interpretation; we should expect meanings of other events as well to change in the light of the interpretation as the individual begins to integrate the interpretation into his over-all system of plans and images. This is Phase Three of the interpretive process in psychotherapy, consolidation and testing, and upon it depends the final fate of any interpretation, whether it will be left to wither with genteel acceptance on the vine or exist as an isolated and rather useless nugget of wisdom, or whether it will be exercised and exploited to the fullest over the widest possible range of events and circumstances in the individual's life. Only in the latter instance is the interpretation likely to have any significant therapeutic effect; and only in the latter instance has the interpretation been thoroughly tested for adequacy.

Phase Three, although we can define its function and can speak of it as a specific phase in the interpretive operation, is not a one-time affair with regard to any single interpretation. Once an interpretation is made, Phase Three activities frequently continue for the duration of psychotherapy. These activities are part of what is commonly referred to as "working through" and occur in connection with each new topic brought up, with each new problem encountered, and with each new interpretation considered. In each case the question is raised as to the implications of the interpretation for the topic, problem, or interpretation currently under discussion, how these should be understood in light of the interpretation and how valid the interpretation is in light of these new considerations.

These activities should encompass both a forward and backward temporal perspective. That is, they should be concerned with the implications of the interpretation for the patient's planning and expectancies for the future ("How do you think you will feel next time your boss criticizes your work?") as well as with his perceptions of his past ("Now I can see why I could never . . ."). And as psychotherapy progresses they should be concerned with contemporary events of the patient ("But isn't this another example of what we understood earlier as your tendency to . . . ?") and the extent to which his current behavior is consistent with the interpretation ("If we were right about your really wanting to . . . , I wonder why you have now done . . . ?). In this way, as the implications of an interpretation are traced through each of these temporal perspectives, and as they are found relevant, and sometimes revelatory, the interpretation becomes more firmly consolidated as an integral part of the patient's constantly evolving plans and images, and hence becomes a more salient determinant of his behavior.

Much of Phase Three will occur spontaneously in the hands of the patient as he seeks to determine how much increased dissonance the interpretation is likely to cost him, and as he tests it for serviceability in understanding some of the perplexities with which he has been struggling and in providing him with greater freedom of movement than he has enjoyed in the past. This spontaneous activity is all the more likely to occur when the patient wholeheartedly accepts an interpretation, when it seems like a true illumination to him, than when he feels that it has been foisted upon him or when he is at least dubious of its value to him. Nevertheless, the responsibility for Phase Three cannot be left entirely to the patient; the therapist must be ready at appropriate times to implement this phase also, and in the final analysis it is his responsibility to see that this phase of the interpretive process is carried through.

The testing that occurs in Phase Three is of a different sort for the therapist than it is for the patient. For the therapist the testing here consists of his observations of the patient's behavior during this phase, the extent to which he engages in the activities just described, the quality of these activities, and the extent to which his behavior, attitudes, complaints, and symptoms change in the manner expected as a result of the interpretation. Testing for the therapist is, then, in reference to the adequacy of his interpretation for the particular patient with whom he is working. In order to make this evaluation, the therapist must have a thorough understanding of the nature of psychological interpretation, and he must know how much he can realistically expect of an interpretation in any particular case. Only after Phase Three has been completed for the therapist, as well as for his patient, can he close his books on the interpretation.

A word remains to be said about the matter of approach to Phase Three. I pointed out earlier that Phase Three activities with regard to a given interpretation may be expected to appear from time to time for the duration of psychotherapy; now I would like to say a word about when and how these activities should begin following Phase Two.

Although the therapist has the ultimate responsibility for seeing that this phase is executed in connection with each interpretation, this is not to say that he must follow up each interpretation, immediately, with Phase Three operations. To do so would create an atmosphere of inexorability more appropriate to a class in logic or geometry than to psychotherapy, and would remove much of the spontaneity and freedom essential for successful treatment. Furthermore, although this is the therapist's responsibility it is also the patient's, and should the therapist always be the first to wade in he will soon discourage the very independence and initiative he would hope the patient would develop in the course of his contact with him. For the therapist always to take the initiative with respect to Phase Three would also have the effect of suggesting that the interpretation was more for his benefit than the patient's, that he has more invested in it than the patient, and, in fact, that psychotherapy is really his show and the patient a privileged spectator. Clearly, this we do not want.

There are two additional reasons why Phase Three should not be pursued hot on the heels of Phase Two by the therapist. The first is that in turning the initiative over to the patient he has an opportunity to assess the patient's evaluation of the interpretation. If the patient seizes upon it and begins to apply the interpretation quite spontaneously, and sometimes with avidity, the therapist can be assured that the interpretation was appropriately timed and expressed, and that it has met with favorable reception. If, on the other hand, the patient shows no enthusiasm for initiating Phase Three, the therapist should be concerned about how the interpretation was received; this could be an expression of general passivity and dependency or it could reflect indifference or worse on the part of the patient vis-à-vis the interpretation.

Even the best of communications channels have some noise in them, some distortion occurs in the course of message transmission, and this is no less true for interpretation in psychotherapy. Phase Three permits the therapist to determine how much distortion has occurred in the interpretation between his intention and the patient's understanding and application. This is the second reason for letting the patient take the initiative here. It is one way in which the therapist receives feedback upon the effectiveness of his communication with the patient, particularly with reference to the interpretation. It permits him, if he wishes, to institute corrective procedures if he feels the patient has gone too far astray in his understanding of the interpretation. All of this would obviously be cut off if the therapist assumed full responsibility for Phase Three; some of this is cut off if he takes the initiative.

Of course, not all distortion is detrimental; some may well be benign. And so, again, permitting the patient to take the initiative here provides him with some freedom to introduce changes in the interpretation that may suit his case somewhat better than did the original version. The therapist in a sense hands the patient his first approximation to the correct interpretation and it is the patient who molds it into its final and most useful form for himself. One of the interesting and instructive things to observe in psychotherapy is the changes interpretations undergo over time. We can only assume that these are needed, and so the therapist, instead of decrying the changes wrought in his handiwork, should try to learn from them. The therapist must never be so vain as not to recognize that "distortion" is both a prerogative of the patient's and a necessary aspect of the interpretive endeavor.

Where the patient does not take the initiative in Phase Three, then the therapist must step in. The point to remember here is, perhaps, best made by emphasizing that Phase Three must be truly collaborative, just as is the rest of psychotherapy, with the therapist being active, attentive, encouraging, and sympathetic throughout, but with a bit more readiness than elsewhere to give the patient his head.

SOME PROBLEMS OF INTERPRETATION

In this section we shall consider a number of common problems of interpretation from the standpoint of the theory proposed in the preceding chapter. These are problems with which many writers and practitioners in the field have been concerned and I do not pretend to come up with any more original or persuasive solutions to many of them than have been offered in the past. Rather, my aim here is simply to show how they are approached from the present point of view. While in many instances the practice advocated will be no different from that which is now accepted and common, an advantage derives from the presence of a systematic rationale to which questions of practice can be referred, and it is this which represents the distinctive contribution I hope to make in this section. Again, insofar as the theory of interpretation in psychotherapy provides this rationale, its right to demand our serious consideration is increased.

Contraindications

When should the therapist refrain from interpretation? Under what circumstances are certain types of interpretations contraindicated? To begin with, it will be helpful to remember Postulate I: *The effect of interpretation is predictable to the extent that therapist and patient possess a common core of language meaning and usage.* This would suggest as a first contraindication for interpretation any signs, psychotic, cultural, or intellectual, that patient and therapist do not possess a common core of language meaning and usage. Because the effects of interpretation depend upon a delicate balance between pre- and postinterpretive dissonance (Postulate III), unless the therapist can predict fairly accurately how the language of his interpretation will be interpreted, he is just as likely to produce an unfavorable balance as a favorable one. Should the balance tip in the unfavorable direction, we would expect from Postulate IV (*Events or conditions present at the time of increases in dissonance will themselves take on aversive qualities; events or conditions present at the time of decreases in dissonance will themselves take on appetitive qualities.*) that the therapist's relationship with the patient—indeed, the entire psychotherapeutic endeavor—would be placed in jeopardy. In the degree that patient and therapist, for whatever reason, do not possess a common core of language meaning and usage, interpretation is contraindicated.

Because interpretation is productive of dissonance (Axiom 6), the therapist must gauge the extent to which the patient can handle the increased demands placed upon his controls by any interpretation. Should the therapist judge the patient to be on the verge of emotional decompensation, or should he judge him unable to handle the threat engendered by the content of a particular interpretation, this would contraindicate interpretation. Where controls are tenuous, interpretation should not be made unless the therapist is certain that it will serve to reduce the strain presently placed on the patient's adjustive resources.

A third, less serious, contraindication is the case where the patient is experiencing little dissonance, essentially a case where Phase One has not been successfully executed. To offer an interpretation under these circumstances is to court its, and one's own, rejection (Postulate IIIA) by the patient. This contraindication probably becomes less serious as the psychotherapeutic relationship develops, but still it is not very desirable to have one's record studded with too many failures, even if each in its own right is inconsequential.

Because it is likely that interpretations at the propositional stage demand greater intellectual competence of the patient than do interpretations at the semantic stage, the former would be contraindicated in cases of limited intellectual capacity, whether this be of endogenous or exogenous origin. To offer a propositional interpretation to a patient suffering from chronic brain syndrome would probably be to so overwhelm him in perplexity as to render the remainder of the psychotherapy hour valueless. This is much less likely to be the case with a semantic interpretation; the patient either takes it or leaves it, it either makes sense immediately or it does not, and that is it.

A final contraindication for interpretation, and probably the most difficult to recognize or acknowledge, is that where the interpretation is intended as a tour de force, where it is made more to enhance the therapist's ego than to rescue the patient's. Too many such indulgences on the part of the therapist, and the patient will soon come to feel, and rightly, that he is being exploited by the therapist, that his own welfare is a secondary consideration. There can be no denying that a successful interpretation is gratifying to the therapist; this recognition should occasion no defensiveness or guilt. But the problem always exists that such gratifications may become an end in themselves, and then there is good reason for guilt. As we have seen, the interpretation enters a system of delicately balanced forces; if any of these are misjudged the interpretation may fail and the patient may suffer. The therapist who is more acutely tuned to his own need system than to the patient's is also more likely to make errors of judgment with regard to the effect of an interpretation upon this balance of forces. Hence, where the therapist finds himself approaching an interpretation with relish, regretting only that his audience is so limited, where he views the interpretation as evidence of his own brilliance, there the interpretation is likely to be made to the detriment of the patient and so is contraindicated.

Timing and gauging readiness for interpretation

In one sense, the patient is ready for interpretation as soon as he enters psychotherapy. In entering into such a relationship he is tacitly admitting that there is something about his interpretation of events which is causing him trouble and so he looks to the therapist to suggest alternative interpretations. Despite this, however, interpretation as a discernible event, as one aspect of the therapeutic transaction, is more appropriate under certain circumstances than under others, will be more effective under certain circumstances than under others, and here we consider what these might be. This is obviously related to the problem of contraindications, and so we should not be surprised to find some of the same considerations coming up again here.

It is generally agreed that the ideal point at which an interpretation should be made is when the patient is on the verge of making it himself, or at least where all of the elements going into the interpretation are apparent to the patient, or close to being so. This certainly makes good sense, for under such conditions the interpretation is most likely to gain a favorable reception. The only question that might be asked in this regard is why not let the patient, himself, make the interpretation, why not let him experience the benefit of discovering that he is able to reduce his own dissonance (Corollary IVE)? There is therapeutic value in the patient's making his own interpretation and so where this seems likely to occur, it should be encouraged.

Beyond this, timing and readiness depend upon estimates of the level of dissonance the patient is experiencing, whether this is sufficient to provide incentive to him to expose himself to the hazards of interpretation; the quality of the psychotherapeutic relationship, whether it is such that it can weather the stresses and strains of the endeavor; and lastly, the therapist's understanding of the patient, whether he believes that he knows his patient well enough to be able to predict how the interpretation will be received. It would be unrewarding to attempt to describe all the possible signs that the therapist might use in making these estimates—this is where experience counts—but these do suggest some general principles that may be of value.

While an individual might be described in terms of some over-all general level of dissonance, it is helpful also to think in terms of areas of functioning and levels of dissonance within those areas. For example, a patient may seem to have little or no dissonance in the area of heterosexual relations, but quite a bit in the area of work and achievement. Another point which should be recognized in this connection is that interpretations will vary in the amount of dissonance they are likely to produce (Postulate II). Hence, it would be most desirable for the therapist to make his decision on readiness in terms of level of dissonance in the area in which interpretation is to be offered, and level of dissonance likely to be produced by the interpretation. The higher the dissonance likely to be produced by an interpretation, the higher the dissonance should be in the area of its application (Postulate III).

Here is an illustration of one of those many nice judgments the therapist is called upon to make. There is a limit to the extent to which the above principle holds; as dissonance increases within a certain area, a point is reached beyond which *any* interpretation is contraindicated. A proper metric by means of which such judgments may be guided will be a long time coming, hence estimates of how much dissonance is enough, but not too much, depend upon the experience and astuteness of the therapist. This being the case, it might be suggested that for the neophyte the safest course is to leave a wide margin for error: refraining from interpretation whenever he has *any* doubt as to whether the level of dissonance in an area is either too high for the patient to tolerate the added strain of the interpretation, or too low for the magnitude of dissonance likely to be generated by the interpretation.

Of course, as a concomitant of duration of the relationship, the therapist's understanding of his patient may be expected to increase, so that he should be better able to predict how an interpretation will be received in the middle and end stages of psychotherapy than in the early stages. But even here, the importance of this consideration depends upon the significance of the interpretation being offered. If it is a minor one and not likely to incur much dissonance the risks of offering it early in psychotherapy are minor also. In fact, I believe that a case might be made for the use of minor interpretations as a way of gauging the patient's readiness to entertain interpretations as an aspect of the therapeutic enterprise, and as a way of introducing him to the proper set for this aspect of psychotherapy. And again, to be able to use interpretations in this way, the therapist must have sufficient experience and astuteness to recognize what is minor and what is not for the patient. Unless he can make this kind of judgment with a high degree of accuracy, he is best advised to follow the general rule of refraining from any interpretation early in psychotherapy.

Over the course of psychotherapy, regardless of duration, the nature of the relationship is likely to fluctuate from warm to cold, from intense to tepid, and from positive to negative. In the language of psychoanalysis, there are likely to be alternating periods of positive and negative transference. Unless the interpretation is directed at the relationship itself, at the transference, it is generally undesirable to offer it during a negative period. This is so, first, because during such periods the patient is already questioning the motives and competence of the therapist and so is more prone to use this as a means of dissonance reduction than he would be otherwise (Postulate IIIA), and second, because being in something of a state of disrepair, the relationship itself cannot help the patient over the increased dissonance produced by the interpretation —there is little he can turn to in the relationship as compensation for the increased discomfort occasioned by the interpretation. If the therapist has decided to interpret the transference itself, then there is no help for it but to proceed whether the transference is positive or negative. This will make maximal demands upon both patient and therapist and is not for the faint of heart, for the going will be rough. If the storm is weathered, however, the patient may have made gains that would have been denied him otherwise, or at least would have been much longer in the making. Putting this whole thing a bit more positively, we might say that interpretations are best made during periods of positive transference or when the relationship between patient and therapist is not itself a source of distress; if the relationship itself is to be the object of interpretation this stricture does not hold.

Frequency

We can really not make any definite statements about how frequently interpretations should occur in psychotherapy, although this is a legitimate cause for concern and speculation. However, stating what some of the general considerations should be in this regard may have some heuristic value.

In many respects the problem here is not unlike that of massing and spacing in learning. Fundamentally, it would seem that the optimal frequency for interpretation should depend upon two factors: the over-all level of dissonance under which the patient is operating, with especial consideration for the degree to which dissonance from each interpretation has been dissipated; and the rate at which each interpretation is integrated into the patient's system of plans and images. The therapist should be able to make crude estimates of both of these factors.

Lacking operations for the measurement of dissonance at this point, we know nothing of the form of the growth curve for dissonance with each succeeding increment. Nevertheless, it would seem reasonable to suggest that it would be unwise to pile on additional increments until the patient has begun to meet with some success in coping with the dissonance already produced by interpretation. The patient must not come to feel that he is caught in a squirrel cage. Otherwise, besides taxing his adjustive resources to the utmost, an unrestrained rate of interpretation is likely to be highly demoralizing for him.

The same points might be made with regard to the rate at which interpretations are being integrated into the patient's system of plans and images. As we implied in our discussion of Phase Three of interpretation, integration is a continuing process and so we cannot suggest that each interpretation be fully integrated before the next one is offered, even if operations could be found which would tell us when this has happened. The point is that the therapist should have *some* evidence that the patient has made *some* progress toward integration of one interpretation before another is offered. People differ in the rates at which they are able to process information, and this depends also upon the kinds or amounts of information involved, and so it is with interpretation. The optimal point here is likely to vary from patient to patient and from one interpretation to another, but this does not relieve the therapist of responsibility for striving to determine this point for his particular patient and for each particular interpretation.

Each interpretation involves a suggested exchange of the therapist's point of view for the patient's. Hence each interpretation contains an implied challenge to the validity of the patient's perception of reality. This too should be taken into consideration in thinking about frequency of interpretation. For involved here is the question of the rate at which we should proceed with the dismantling of some of the patient's most fundamental beliefs and values, the very images upon which he has built his sense of identity and his plans for coping with reality. Too fast a rate and the patient, unless he protects himself by some form of resistance, could well be panicked into a psychotic episode. Thus interpretation should never proceed so fast that we leave the patient on a sea of shifting sands.

Rejection of an interpretation

Understandably, rejection of an interpretation is disturbing to the clinician; it may or may not be so to the patient. The therapist has invested something of himself in the interpretation—this is not necessarily a question of vanity—and so to reject the interpretation is also to reject him in some degree. Few therapists can take this with complete equanimity. The result is that we have developed various ways of protecting ourselves in such a situation. Generally, these all have in common the placing of the onus for rejection of the interpretation entirely upon the patient, and the viewing of this as evidence either of how resistant he is, or of how really sick he is. From the present point of view, these allegations are unfair to the patient and obscure any beneficial understanding of what the rejection might mean.

Let us begin with the suggestion that rejection of an interpretation in *any* situation is a *benign* response. The reasons for this are not far to seek.

While some, because of a curious model of man as being infinitely perverse, would take rejection of an interpretation as conclusive evidence of its aptness or truth, I would prefer that such judgments be made upon a more positive basis: whether it accomplishes what the therapist intends it to. In any event, the truth of the interpretation should not be the major issue here. If we eschew this kind of reverse logic we can only conclude that when an interpretation is rejected it is because this was the best possible response in the situation in which the patient found himself. The therapist's job then is to find out why the interpretation was rejected, what this means in terms of this particular patient.

It will be remembered that according to Corollary IIIA, rejection of interpretation is *one* of the means by which the patient may cope with the situation where postinterpretation dissonance is greater than preinterpretation dissonance. The important point here is that this is but one of the means, the other two being distortion of the interpretation and devaluation of the therapist. Hence, where the patient rejects the interpretation we can at least be fairly certain that he has not resorted to one of these other means, the first of which might be quite difficult to detect and time-consuming to correct, and the second of which could seriously affect the therapist's effectiveness. Therefore, granted that the patient rejects the interpretation, we may assume that the therapist erred in his judgment somewhere, that the dissonance incurred by the interpretation was too much for the patient to bear at the moment, and that he has chosen this means of reducing it. And of the three means available to him, rejection of the interpretation seems by far the most desirable.

That the patient has chosen this means of dissonance reduction, means, of course, that he was unable to follow through on the implications of the interpretation, changing his plans, images, and behavior accordingly, and the therapist will want to find out why. Assuming that the therapist did not intend his interpretation to be rejected, he can conclude that his understanding of the patient was somewhat less than he thought it was. Beyond this, however, the therapist should also take the patient's use of this approach as evidence of certain strengths in the patient and in the relationship. Specifically, I would suggest that when a patient rejects an interpretation rather than resorting to either distortion or devaluation of the therapist, he is presenting evidence that he feels secure enough in the relationship to adopt an evaluative attitude and to communicate his judgments to the therapist. He is adopting a truly collaborative role in the relationship. The less secure the patient is, the less he is able to do this. Therefore, if the therapist can accept the rejection in this spirit, as part of his joint endeavor with the patient, nothing will be lost by an occasional rejection of interpretation, and in fact, something might be gained.

To be sure, there are cases where rejection of an interpretation does not betoken a collaborative attitude at all, where it is instead intended as a thwarting of the therapist motivated by the nature of the patient's perception of himself vis-à-vis the therapist. But this interpretation of rejection, like that which treats it as evidence of the truth of the interpretation, must be established on the basis of other supporting evidence; it cannot be assumed merely on the basis of the rejection itself. To counter rejection of one interpretation with another interpretation—especially if this is to be expressed to the patient—will not do unless the evidence is quite compelling: if having one interpretation rejected is bad, having two rejected is worse.

When the patient rejects an interpretation the therapist should invite him, without any attempt at argumentation, to consider his reasons for doing so. Frequently these will be given spontaneously. Ideally, such a discussion should revolve around other competing interpretations for the same events and the evidence supporting these. Some attention might be given to the fact of rejection per se, what this means for the patient, his motives and feelings. The therapist should be alert to feelings of guilt aroused in the patient by the rejection and should be careful not to imply in any way that he takes the rejection personally. In this way the patient may come to learn something very important: that it is possible to disagree with someone and yet not jeopardize one's relationship with him, that disagreement does not necessarily mean hostility, that it is not necessarily destructive, and that it need not necessarily arouse counterhostility or destruction. And this would be no mean gain. Whether or not this gain is realized depends entirely upon the skill and tact of the clinician as well as on his own personal feelings about the rejection. Skill and tact will not be able to cover up feelings of rejection or hostility by the therapist if they are present, nor will "proper" feelings carry him through if skill and tact are absent. We cannot go beyond this in the present context.

Distortion

This is a problem that will become apparent only to the degree that Phase Three has been adequately covered in the interpretive sequence. I would define distortion as the patient's giving an interpretation any meaning or import other than that intended by the therapist. By this definition, intellectualization with respect to an interpretation becomes distortion to no less extent than does blatant misrepresentation, as when the patient takes the therapist's interpretation that he provokes hostility from others as meaning that he is the victim of others' hostility toward him. What does distortion mean when it occurs and what can the therapist do about it?

While it should not be overlooked that a certain amount of distortion may be the result of the impaired cognitive functioning of the patient, because of the very processes which brought him into psychotherapy, more often distortion is a form of defense, a way of avoiding the threat implied by the content of the interpretation or the dissonance that would result from accepting the interpretation into his presently existing system of plans and images. The patient is neither able to reject the interpretation outright nor does he choose to devalue the therapist, and yet he has this interpretation to deal with which for some reason he is unable to handle. His only recourse therefore is to change the nature of the message in some fashion—distortion.

As dismaying as it may be when discovered, the therapist must not view distortion as evidence of the patient's perversity or stupidity, but rather as evidence that something in the interpretation was very disturbing and that this was the patient's attempt to make the best of a bad situation. For this the patient deserves credit.

The therapist has two alternatives at this point: he can either point out the distortion to the patient or he can let it go by the board, temporarily. Which alternative he chooses should depend upon his purposes at the moment and his assessment of the case and the reasons for distortion.

If the therapist is interested in pointing up the patient's resistances, and if he has assured himself that the patient can tolerate this, then he may well decide to point the distortion out to the patient. In doing so his aim is not only to correct the distortion, but also to use this as an object of interpretation in its own right. He invites the patient to join him in speculation upon the reasons for the distortion and as a result the interview may take a turn quite different from that being pursued by the original interpretation. Two things must be guarded against here: first, the patient's inability to tolerate the added stress inherent in this approach, and second, the appearance that the therapist is calling the patient on the carpet, that he is criticizing him for his obtuseness or his capriciousness.

Should the therapist not be seeking opportunities to interpret the patient's resistances to him, then he would be well advised to take a different approach to distortion. Fundamentally, this involves taking the view that interpretation involves a process of successive approximation; if the patient has distorted the interpretation on first try, at least he has not rejected it outright, and the therapist will seek subsequent opportunities for making the same interpretation again, perhaps with different events involved and perhaps in different terms. In this way, the therapist accepts the patient's distortion as necessary at the time it occurs and seeks for an ultimate accommodation between his view of the events involved and a view which the patient can accept. The primary demands upon the therapist here are for patience and flexibility.

Interpretive bewilderment

Not infrequently material will present itself for interpretation for which no apparent or adequate interpretation seems forthcoming. This is likely to occur in connection with dreams reported by the patient, but might also involve other experiences of the patient as well that seem incongruous, dissonant, and in need of interpretation. The patient asks for interpretation; he explores interpretations; and the therapist might well agree that interpretation is called for but cannot come up with one with which he, at least, is satisfied. This is interpretive bewilderment.

This need not be a problem at all. It comes about simply because of the multidimensional nature of all events (Axiom 2) and can actually be turned to good advantage in helping the patient recognize that events are subject to more than one interpretation, in effect loosening the ties by which some of his own interpretations are now bound to events, thereby making him more amenable in the future to other interpretations. If the therapist does not appear disturbed by this state of affairs neither will the patient, and as a result he will come to be more tolerant of ambiguity and of divergent perspectives. The patient has an opportunity here to learn of the probabilistic nature of all knowledge and of the world in which we live. If he learns this in the company of a therapist who accepts this knowledge with equanimity, he too will come to do so. If the therapist sees this state of affairs as one offering freedom and opportunity, so will the patient. This also presents the patient with an opportunity for learning that the therapist is human just like himself, that he is not either omniscient or omnipotent. In this way the basis for a realistic psychotherapeutic relationship may also be formed out of this state of affairs.

If, on the other hand, the therapist sees himself as a prophet, if he subscribes to a naive realism, and if he conceives of interpretation as uncovering the "real truth," then interpretive bewilderment poses a serious problem. He is apt to experience frustration and accuse the patient, or his unconscious, of perpetrating this state of affairs so as to obscure matters, and attempt various ruses so as to cover up his discomfiture in front of the patient. As a result the patient will become anxious, he may (rightly) question the ability of the therapist, and he will surely avoid bringing up any other material that is likely to be bewildering. The patient becomes confirmed in his view that he is living in an enigmatic and threatening world.

After considering all the possible interpretations and finding none acceptable, or after employing each of the interpretive perspectives described in Chapter 3 and finding none that will yield a plausible interpretation for some event, the therapist would be well advised to state in a matter-of-fact fashion that it seems that at present the meaning of the material confronting them cannot be determined. He might cite the various alternatives at present available to them, and then suggest that perhaps the wisest course would be to defer any further attempt at understanding the material until some later date, when perhaps they will have more information to guide them. This, in fact, is all that he can do. As additional information comes in, the context of the events in question becomes filled out and so will lend its support more strongly to one interpretation rather than another. At present this context is just too sketchy for the job before it.

This leaves the patient with probably as much dissonance as before, but with one difference. The therapist is sharing this dissonance with him; he must no longer shoulder this burden alone. And the situation has changed for the patient from one of "my problem" to one of "our problem"; he is no longer quite so isolated, and a truly collaborative relationship is in the making.

To be sure, if too many instances of interpretive bewilderment arise in the course of therapy the patient may begin to wonder about the value of his new-found collaborator, as indeed his therapist might also. When this point is reached, of course, will depend upon the personalities of both patient and therapist, and we must also always acknowledge the possibility that in some cases this questioning, at whatever point it arises, will be well founded. While there is some hope of rescuing the situation if the former is the case, if the latter is true it would be just as well admitted early in the course of therapy rather than late. However much it may hurt the therapist, it is far better for the patient, so far as his expectations of psychotherapy are concerned, for the therapist to admit that he seems unable to work with him and to suggest that the patient might do better with someone else than for the patient to have to take the initiative in this regard. I would not wish to suggest that such cases occur very often, but when they do the patient will leave with greater respect for the therapist and for psychotherapy if the issue is faced squarely by the therapist. If nothing else, the patient has met an adult who can admit his own inadequacies without being crushed by them and it holds out hope to him that he may also be able to do so some day.

What to interpret

Having already spelled out in detail in several parts of this book the nature of material to which interpretation is appropriately addressed, this should not be a question at this point. Although much has been written about the merits of interpretation of resistances, instincts, transferences, dreams, and other content, I am inclined to agree with Fromm-Reichmann (1950), who, after considering these questions, concludes with her characteristic candor: "In the last analysis the question of how to go about the process of interpretation depends to a great extent upon the psychiatrist's and the patient's personalities and upon the general nuances of their psychotherapeutic collaboration" (p. 88).

Yet the theory of interpretation in psychotherapy proposed in the preceding chapter does have at least one implication that merits consideration with respect to this problem. It is this: regardless of the nature of the content, which is the proper concern of a theory of personality, material selected for interpretation should form a graded series over the course of psychotherapy in terms of the amount of dissonance aroused. That is, interpretations coming early in psychotherapy should confront the patient with minimal amounts of dissonance as compared to those coming later. Put this way, this stricture might sound as though it were simply part of the folk wisdom that suggests "little steps for little feet." If it does, so much the better. But let us look at the theory and see where the rationale for it arises.

The greater the amount of dissonance an interpretation is likely to produce, the greater the risk involved. However, the more the therapist knows about the patient, and the greater the degree to which they share a common language system (Postulate I), the less this risk should be for any given amount of dissonance. Hence, since both increased understanding of the patient and increased sharing of a common language system may be expected to be concomitants of increased duration of psychotherapy, it follows that for a given amount of dissonance the risk will be less as therapy progresses.

As a consequence of the increased sharing of the therapist's frame of reference that comes about as psychotherapy continues, interpretations made by the therapist become more plausible, with the result that, for a given amount of dissonance, they are less susceptible to rejection (Corollary IIIA) in the later stages of psychotherapy than they are in the earlier ones. At the same time, as psychotherapy progresses the status and phoric differentials between patient and therapist become more firmly established, thereby minimizing devaluation of the therapist as a route through which the patient might attempt to reduce dissonance. He is left, therefore, with only distortion or appropriate revision of his plans and images as ways of reducing postinterpretive dissonance, and in the later stages of psychotherapy the patient is much less likely to engage in distortion and much more likely to revise his plans and images appropriately.

The third point at which the theory supports the idea of a gradual increase in dissonance in interpretations over the course of psychotherapy is Corollary IVD: *To the extent that increases in dissonance following interpretations tend to precede further increases in postinterpretive dissonance, or failures in reduction of preinterpretive dissonance, dissonance itself will suffer a further increase in its aversiveness. To the extent that the reverse is true, dissonance will undergo some diminution in aversiveness for the patient.* If, therefore, we begin with interpretations that arouse minimal amounts of dissonance and that therefore stand the best chance of being followed by subsequent reductions in postinterpretive dissonance, we should, according to this corollary, expect to build up the patient's tolerance for dissonance itself, since he comes to learn that any build-up of it immediately following an interpretation is likely to be a precursor of a subsequent reduction. It would seem that in this way Fenichel (1941) was right—although for different reasons—when he argued that there is a "correct sequence" in making interpretations in psychotherapy just as there is in releasing cables in launching a ship from its moorings.

Having begun this chapter with the caveat that there was more to psychotherapy than interpretation, let me end it on the same note. Treated with respect, interpretation will be a rewarding enterprise; demand too much of it and we are bound to be disappointed. Interpretation can be heady medicine and is best used with care in all cases. When the therapist is in doubt about making an interpretation he is best advised *not* to make it. Interpretation can mobilize anxiety as well as reduce it; can help tighten a patient's thinking as well as loosen it; can obscure as well as illuminate. If one is not sure which the effect will be in a given case, it is best to refrain from interpretation entirely. This is not the only means by which behavioral change might be instigated. Some patients will improve without interpretation, some will improve because of interpretation, and some will improve in spite of interpretation. The therapist should always have more than one string to his bow.

SUMMARY

Having proposed a theory of interpretation in psychotherapy, in this chapter I have tried to indicate its practical consequences. It seems that interpretation in psychotherapy is best understood as consisting of three phases. Phase One involves preparing the ground for interpretation. Here the therapist, through a variety of techniques, juxtaposes two or more items of information or observations, which have the effect for the patient of increasing dissonance, thus making the need for interpretation apparent to him. Phase One also gives the therapist an opportunity to determine the patient's readiness for interpretation. Phase Two consists of the interpretation proper. Consideration was given to the different effects the various types of interpretation might be expected to have, and questions of when one type or the other might be most appropriate were considered. Phase Three involves consolidation and testing, in which therapist and patient together determine the acceptability and utility of the interpretation and attempt to integrate it into the patient's general cognitive structure.

Also discussed in this chapter were a number of practical problems involving interpretation, such as its contraindications and timing, and criteria for gauging readiness for interpretation, determining frequency of interpretation, and handling rejection of interpretations. In each case an attempt was made to relate consideration of the problem to particular aspects of the theory proposed in Chapter 8.

Finally, the point was stressed that interpretation is merely one of the means by which behavioral change may be induced in psychotherapy, that it may be harmful as well as beneficial, and that the competent therapist will use it with discretion.

Epilogue

As diffidence gave way to commitment, and I could no longer deny either to myself or to others that I was WRITING A BOOK, the most frequent question asked after that of the topic was, "Interpretation of what?" This, of course, reflected one of the problems that led to writing this book in the first place: to my way of analyzing the process of interpretation, the question was a meaningless one, for the principles and assumptions of interpretation were the same regardless of the "what." The very fact that this question was asked so frequently, however, further convinced me that this was a very real problem, that people did indeed think that it made a difference to what interpretation was being applied, that somehow the principles of interpretation varied with its subject matter. If such particularism were the case, teaching, practice, and research dealing with interpretation would be futile. This book was an attempt to demonstrate otherwise.

It may appear that in this attempt I have described the process of interpretation in such fashion as to make it indistinguishable from cognition and thought in general. If this is the case, so much the better. Psychological interpretation has been viewed too long as a semicharismatic activity by some and as intrinsically dependent upon psychoanalytic theory by others. Neither of these views, I believe, is correct.

I have therefore argued that the only scientifically defensible conception of interpretation is that it is a transformation of data, an exchange of frames of reference, and nothing more. Truth in any absolute sense is never an issue except within a particular frame of reference, and there it is better understood as consistency. I have attempted to divorce interpretation from any particular personality theory by showing that as an activity it can be accounted for by a model which itself is not tied to any single personality theory, that theory enters only in connection with the language and focus of interpretation, never with its justification or use. As a result, one's use of psychological interpretation should no longer be taken as indicative of his theoretical allegiance, only of his strategic and pragmatic decisions in the given instance.

In the process of achieving this theoretical asepsis of interpretation, I began with an analysis of the assumptions and principles that were implicit in the work of the interpreter. These, it was seen, were not in any way dependent upon any particular personality theory. Following this, we considered the case for interpretation in psychodiagnosis and testing, detailing the particular contribution that interpretation might make in these activities and illustrating the operation of the assumptions and principles of interpretation discussed earlier. Finally, in connection with interpretation in psychotherapy, a theory drawing upon recent work in cognition and communication was constructed to account for several phenomena commonly attributed to interpretation, and the implications of this theory for practice in psychotherapy were traced out in some detail. It now remains to make a few concluding observations.

Although my intent was not to write a handbook of psychological interpretation, it would be incorrect to state that I did not intend this book to have some practical value. The most practical need in clinical psychology today is for theory and research; we can no longer continue to justify our practices on the basis of testimonials, case studies, or "clinical evidence"; the clinician must be alert to, and curious about, the intellectual and scientific issues involved in his practice if he is not to become a mere technician or hack. Thus, the practical value of the present work comes, I believe, in giving the clinical psychologist an orientation to his work, or at least to one aspect of his work, that should help him to recognize the continuity between the problems and knowledge with which he works and those of psychology as a whole. He is still a psychologist first, a clinician, a diagnostician, or a psychotherapist second.

We have seen that recent work in cognition and communication is relevant for the clinician in understanding the process of interpretation, and, by the same token, it would appear that the work of the clinician should be seen as a valid area of interest for those working primarily in cognition and communication. We may hope that if this view is shared by others it would help to forestall the forces of parochialism long enough to permit a more studied decision to be made as to just where the lines of demarcation should be drawn—if, indeed, they should be drawn at all—between clinical and general psychology.

The fact that I have denied psychological interpretation any special status among the arts and have attempted to lay bare the logic underlying this process does not mean that I believe that anyone understanding this logic can be assured of success in its application. At various points in this book I have pointed out the demands made upon the clinician's personality by psychological interpretation and the ways in which his personality may affect his practice. This undoubtedly represents one of the major uncontrolled sources of variation in psychological interpretation, and an extremely subtle one as well. But beyond this, although I have maintained an avowedly—perhaps even aggressively—positivistic viewpoint with regard to psychological interpretation in this book, I should like to conclude by conceding that there is still another type of personal element which probably no amount of abstract knowledge of the interpretive process can seriously alter, and which may, in the final analysis, differentiate between the successful and the unsuccessful, the mediocre and the brilliant, application of interpretation. This is *style*. In interpretation, as in diplomacy, it is quite likely that style may often count for as much as, if not more than, content in making the difference between success and failure.

To what extent style can be taught and developed we do not know because heretofore it has been confounded with so many other factors. But it seems likely that even when we have finally explicated and learned to control all the other parameters of the interpretive process, style may still remain as the ultimate winnower among men. And perhaps this is as it should be, perhaps this is the province within which we should seek for the distinguishing marks of the great interpreter and the master therapist if such exist, for this is a uniquely personal and human dimension of existence, the means by which we express our identity and individuality, and which, perhaps, is best left untouched in this great era of homogenization. If psychology needs a touch of romanticism, perhaps this is where it should be.

References

Adler, A. *The practice and theory of individual psychology*. New York: Harcourt, 1927.

Allport, G. W. *Personality: A psychological interpretation*. New York: Holt, 1937.

Auld, F., Jr., & White, Alice M. Sequential dependencies in psychotherapy. *J. abnorm. soc. Psychol.*, 1959, *58*, 100–104.

Ayer, A. J. *Language, truth, and logic*. (2nd rev. ed.) London: Gallancz, 1946.

Bartlett, F. C. *Remembering*. New York: Cambridge, 1932.

Barzun, J. *The house of intellect*. New York: Harper, 1959.

Beck, S. J. *Rorschach's test:* I. *Basic processes*. New York: Grune & Stratton, 1944.

Bender, Lauretta. *Instructions for the use of the Visual Motor Gestalt Test*. New York: Amer. Orthopsychiat. Assoc., 1946.

Berg, C. *Psychotherapy: Theory and practice*. New York: Norton, 1948.

Berg, I. A. Response bias and personality: The deviation hypothesis. *J. Psychol.*, 1955, *40*, 61–72.

349

Bergman, D. V. Counseling method and client responses. *J. consult. Psychol.*, 1951, *15*, 216–224.

Blum, G. S. A study of the psychoanalytic theory of psychosexual development. *Genet. Psychol. Monogr.*, 1949, *39*, 3–99.

Blum, G. S., & Miller, D. R. Exploring the psychoanalytic theory of the "oral character." *J. Pers.*, 1952, *20*, 287–304.

Boder, D. P. The adjective-verb-quotient: A contribution to the psychology of language. *Psychol. Rec.*, 1940, *3*, 310–343.

Boring, E. G. *A history of experimental psychology.* (2nd ed.) New York: Appleton, 1950.

Braithwaite, R. B. *Scientific explanation.* New York: Cambridge, 1955.

Brown, F. An exploratory study of dynamic factors in the content of the Rorschach protocol. *J. proj. Tech.*, 1953, *17*, 251–279.

Bruch, Hilda. *The importance of overweight.* New York: Norton, 1957.

Bruner, J. S. Going beyond the information given. In *Contemporary approaches to cognition.* Cambridge, Mass.: Harvard University Press, 1957.

Bruner, J. S., Goodnow, Jacqueline J., & Austin, G. A. *A study of thinking.* New York: Wiley, 1956.

Brunswik, E. *Systematic and representative design of psychological experiments.* Berkeley: University of California Press, 1947.

Brunswick, E. The conceptual framework of psychology. Chicago: University of Chicago Press, 1952. (*Int. Encycl. Unif. Sci.*, Vol. 1, No. 10.)

Buhler, Charlotte. The ball and field test as a help in the diagnosis of emotional difficulties. *Charact. & Pers.*, 1938, *6*, 257–273.

Buhler, Charlotte, Buhler, K., & Lefever, D. W. *Development of the Basic Rorschach Score with a manual of directions. Rorschach standardization study.* Los Angeles: Author, 1948.

Cattell, R. B. *The description and measurement of personality.* New York: Harcourt, 1946.

Cattell, R. B. *Personality and motivation structure and measurement.* New York: Harcourt, 1957.

Chapple, E. D. The interaction chronograph; its evolution and present application. *Personnel*, 1949, *25*, 295–307.

Cohen, M. R., & Nagel, E. *An introduction to logic and scientific method.* New York: Harcourt, 1934.

Cronbach, L. J., & Meehl, P. E. Construct validity in psychological tests. *Psychol. Bull.*, 1955, *52*, 281–302.

Deutsch, M. D., & Murphy, W. F. *The clinical interview.* New York: International Universities, 1955.

Dittman, A. T. The interpersonal process in psychotherapy: Development of a research method. *J. abnorm. soc. Psychol.*, 1952, *47*, 236–244.

Dollard, J., & Miller, N. E. *Personality and psychotherapy.* New York: McGraw-Hill, 1950.

Dollard, J., & Mowrer, O. H. A method of measuring tension in written documents. *J. abnorm. soc. Psychol.*, 1947, *42*, 3–32.

Edwards, A. L. *The social desirability variable in personality assessment and research.* New York: Holt, 1957.

Elizur, A. Content analysis of the Rorschach with regard to anxiety and hostility. *Rorschach Res. Exch.*, 1949, *13*, 247–285.

Feldman, M. J. An evaluation scale for shock therapy. *J. clin. Psychol.*, 1958, *14*, 41–45.

Fenichel, O. *Problems of psychoanalytic technique.* New York: Psychoanalytic Quarterly, 1941.

Fenichel, O. *The psychoanalytic theory of neurosis.* New York: Norton, 1945.

Festinger, L. *A theory of cognitive dissonance.* New York: Harper, 1957.

Fiedler, F. E. The concept of the ideal therapeutic relationship. *J. consult. Psychol.*, 1950, *14*, 239–245. (a)

Fiedler, F. E. A comparison of therapeutic relationships in psychoanalytic, nondirective, and Adlerian therapy. *J. consult. Psychol.*, 1950, *14*, 436–445. (b)

Fiedler, F. E. Factor analyses of psychoanalytic, nondirective and Adlerian therapeutic relationships. *J. consult. Psychol.*, 1951, *15*, 32–38.

Finney, B. C. Rorschach test correlates of assaultive behavior. *J. proj. Tech.*, 1955, *19*, 6–16.

Fisher, S. Plausibility and depth of interpretation. *J. consult. Psychol.*, 1956, *20*, 249–256.

Frank, J. D.   The role of influence in psychotherapy. In M. I. Stein (Ed.), *Contemporary psychotherapies*. New York: Free Press of Glencoe, 1961.

Frank, L. K.   Projective methods for the study of personality. *J. Psychol.*, 1939, *8*, 389–413.

French, J. R. P., Jr.   A formal theory of social power. *Psychol. Rev.*, 1956, *63*, 181–194.

Frenkel-Brunswik, E.   Intolerance of ambiguity as an emotional and perceptual personality variable. *J. Pers.*, 1949, *18*, 108–143.

Fromm, E., *et al.* (Eds.), *Zen Buddhism and psychoanalysis*. New York: Harper, 1960.

Fromm-Reichmann, Frieda.   *Principles of intensive psychotherapy*. Chicago: University of Chicago Press, 1950.

Fulkerson, S. C., & Barry, J. R.   Methodology and research on the prognostic use of psychological tests. *Psychol. Bull.*, 1961, *58*, 177–204.

Gough, H. G.   Tests of personality: questionnaires. A. Minnesota Multiphasic Personality Inventory. In A. Weider (Ed.), *Contributions toward medical psychology*. New York: Ronald, 1953.

Greenbaum, M., Qualtere, B., Carruth, B., & Cruickshank, W. M.   Evaluation of a modification of the Thematic Apperception Test for use with physically handicapped children. *J. clin. Psychol.*, 1953, *9*, 40–44.

Hammer, E. F.   The role of the H-T-P in the prognostic battery. *J. clin. Psychol.*, 1953, *9*, 371–374.

Haugen, G. B., Dixon, H. H., & Dickel, H. A.   *A therapy for anxiety tension reactions*. New York: Macmillan, 1960.

Heider, F.   *The psychology of interpersonal relations*. New York: Wiley, 1958.

Helson, H.   Adaptation-level as a basis for a quantitative theory of frames of reference. *Psychol. Rev.*, 1948, *55*, 297–313.

Hendrick, I.   *Facts and theories of psychoanalysis*. (2nd ed.) New York: Knopf, 1948.

Henry, Edith M., & Rotter, J. B.   Situational influences on Rorschach responses. *J. consult. Psychol.*, 1956, *20*, 457–462.

Henry, W. E.   *The analysis of fantasy*. New York: Wiley, 1956.

Henry, W. E., & Guetzkow, H.   Group projection sketches for the study of small groups. *J. soc. Psychol.*, 1951, *33*, 77–102.

Hobbs, N. Group-centered psychotherapy. In C. R. Rogers, *Client-centered therapy.* Boston: Houghton Mifflin, 1951.

Hovland, C. I., Janis, I. L., & Kelley, H. H. *Communication and persuasion.* New Haven: Yale University Press, 1953.

Hovland, C. I., & Pritzker, H. A. Extent of opinion change as a function of amount of change advocated. *J. abnorm. soc. Psychol.,* 1957, *54,* 257–261.

Hull, C. L. Differential habituation to internal stimuli in the albino rat. *J. comp. Psychol.,* 1933, *16,* 255–273.

Jackson, D. N., & Messick, S. Content and style in personality assessment. *Psychol. Bull.,* 1958, *55,* 243–252.

Jessor, R. The problem of reductionism in psychology. *Psychol. Rev.,* 1958, *65,* 170–178.

Johnson, W. *People in quandaries.* New York: Harper, 1946.

Josselyn, Irene M. Psychotherapy of adolescents at the level of private practice. In B. H. Balser (Ed.), *Psychotherapy of the adolescent.* New York: International Universities, 1957.

Jung, C. G. *Modern man in search of a soul.* New York: Harcourt, 1933.

Kelly, G. A. *The psychology of personal constructs.* New York: Norton, 1955.

Kinget, G. M. *The Drawing-Completion Test.* New York: Grune & Stratton, 1952.

Klein, Melanie. *The psychoanalysis of children.* London: Hogarth, 1933.

Klopfer, B. Introduction: The development of a prognostic rating scale. *J. proj. Tech.,* 1951, *15,* 421. (Abstract).

Klopfer, B., Ainsworth, Mary D., Klopfer, W., & Holt, R. R. *Developments in the Rorschach technique.* Vol. 1. *Technique and theory.* New York: Harcourt, 1954.

Klopfer, B., & Kelley, D. M. *The Rorschach technique.* New York: Harcourt, 1946.

Lesser, G. S. The relationship between overt and fantasy aggression as a function of maternal response to aggression. *J. abnorm. soc. Psychol.,* 1957, *55,* 218–221.

Levy, L. H. A note on research methodology used in testing for examiner influence in clinical test performance. *J. consult. Psychol.,* 1956, *20,* 286.

Levy, L. H. Anxiety and behavior scientists' behavior. *Amer. Psychologist*, 1961, *16*, 66–68.

Lindner, R. M. The content analysis of the Rorschach protocol. In L. E. Abt & L. Bellak, *Projective psychology*. New York: Knopf, 1950.

Lindzey, G. Thematic Apperception Test interpretive assumptions and related empirical evidence. *Psychol. Bull.*, 1952, *49*, 1–25.

Machover, Karen. *Personality projection in the drawing of the human figure*. Springfield, Ill.: Thomas, 1948.

Masling. J. The influence of situational and interpersonal variables in projective testing. *Psychol. Bull.*, 1960, *57*, 65–85.

Maslow, A. H. Deficiency motivation and growth motivation. In M. R. Jones (Ed.), *Nebraska symposium on motivation*. Lincoln, Neb.: University of Nebraska Press, 1955.

May, R., Angel, E., & Ellenberger, H. F. (Eds.) *Existence: A new dimension in psychiatry and psychology*. New York: Basic Books, 1958.

McClelland, D. C., Atkinson, J. W., Clark, R. A., & Lowell, E. L. *The achievement motive*. New York: Appleton, 1953.

McReynolds, P. The Rorschach concept evaluation technique. *J. proj. Tech.*, 1954, *18*, 60–74.

Meehl, P. E. *Clinical versus statistical prediction*. Minneapolis: University of Minnesota Press, 1954.

Meehl, P. E. Wanted—A good cookbook. *Amer. Psychologist*, 1956, *11*, 263–272.

Meehl, P. E., & Dahlstrom, W. G. Objective configural rules for discriminating psychotic from neurotic MMPI profiles. *J. consult. Psychol.*, 1960, *24*, 375–387.

Meehl, P. E., & Rosen, A. Antecedent probability and the efficiency of psychometric signs, patterns, or cutting scores. *Psychol. Bull.*, 1955, *52*, 194–216.

Menninger, K. *The theory of psychoanalytic technique*. New York: Basic Books, 1958.

Miller, G. A., Galanter, E., & Pribram, K. H. *Plans and the structure of behavior*. New York: Holt, 1960.

Miller, J. S., & Scodel, A. The diagnostic significance of usual and unusual TAT stories. *J. consult. Psychol.*, 1955, *19*, 91–95.

Morris, C. E. Foundations of the theory of signs. Chicago: University of Chicago Press, 1938. (*Int. Encycl. Unif. Sci.*, Vol. 1, No. 2.)

Munroe, R. L. Prediction of adjustment and academic performance of college students. *Appl. Psychol. Monogr.*, 1945, No. 7.

Murray, H. A. *Thematic Apperception Test: Manual*. Cambridge, Mass.: Harvard University Press, 1943.

Murray, H. A., *et al. Explorations in personality*. New York: Oxford, 1938.

Mussen, P. H., & Naylor, H. K. Relationships between overt and fantasy aggression. *J. abnorm. soc. Psychol.*, 1954, *49*, 235–240.

Nagel, E. Methodological issues in psychoanalytic theory. In S. Hook (Ed.), *Psychoanalysis: Scientific method and philosophy*. New York: Grove, 1960.

Newcomb, T. M. *The acquaintance process*. New York: Holt, 1961.

Orr, D. W. Transference and countertransference: A historical survey. *J. Amer. psychoanal. Assoc.*, 1954, *2*, 621–670.

Osgood, C. E., & Tannenbaum, P. H. The principle of congruity in the prediction of attitude change. *Psychol. Rev.*, 1955, *62*, 42–55.

Phillips, E. L. *Psychotherapy: A modern theory and practice*. Englewood Cliffs, N.J.: Prentice-Hall, 1956.

Piotrowski, Z. A. The Rorschach ink-blot method in organic disturbances of the central nervous system. *J. nerv. ment. Dis.*, 1937, *86*, 525–537.

Powers, W. T., & Hamlin, R. M. Relationship between diagnostic category and deviant verbalizations on the Rorschach. *J. consult. Psychol.*, 1955, *19*, 120–124.

Price, H. H. *Thinking and experience*. Cambridge, Mass.: Harvard University Press, 1953.

Purcell, K. The TAT and antisocial behavior. *J. consult. Psychol.*, 1956, *20*, 449–456.

Rabin, A. I., & Haworth, M. R. (Eds.) *Projective techniques with children*. New York: Grune & Stratton, 1960.

Rapaport, D., Gill, M., & Schafer, R. *Diagnostic psychological testing*. Vol. 2. Chicago: Year Book, 1946.

Raush, H. L., Sperber, Z., Rigler, D., Williams, J., Harway, N. I., Bordin, E. S., Dittman, A. T., & Hays, W. L. A dimensional analysis of depth of interpretation. *J. consult. Psychol.*, 1956, *20*, 43–48.

Reichenbach, H. *The rise of scientific philosophy*. Berkeley: University of California Press, 1951.

Reik, T. *Listening with the third ear*. New York: Grove, 1948.

Rogers, C. R. *Counseling and psychotherapy*. Boston: Houghton Mifflin, 1942.

Rogers, C. R. *Client-centered therapy*. Boston: Houghton Mifflin, 1951.

Rogers, C. R. A theory of psychotherapy with schizophrenics and a proposal for its empirical investigation. In J. G. Dawson, H. K. Stone, & N. P. Dellis (Eds.), *Psychotherapy with schizophrenics*. Baton Rouge: Louisiana State University Press, 1961.

Rogers, L. S., & Hammond, K. R. Prediction of the results of therapy by means of the Rorschach test. *J. consult. Psychol.*, 1953, *17*, 8–15.

Rorschach, H. *Psychodiagnostics, a diagnostic test based on perception*. (Translated by P. Lemkau & B. Kronenberg) New York: Grune & Stratton, 1942.

Rosen, J. N. *Direct analysis*. New York: Grune & Stratton, 1953.

Rosenzweig, S. *Psychodiagnosis: An introduction to tests in the clinical practice of psychodynamics*. New York: Grune & Stratton, 1949.

Rosenzweig, S., & Fleming, E. E. Apperceptive norms for the Thematic Apperception Test. *J. Pers.*, 1949, *17*, 475–503.

Rotter, J. B. Thematic Apperception Tests: Suggestions for administration and interpretation. *J. Pers.*, 1946, *15*, 70–92.

Rotter, J. B. *Social learning and clinical psychology*. Englewood Cliffs, N.J.: Prentice-Hall, 1954.

Rotter, J. B. Some implications of a social learning theory for the prediction of goal directed behavior from testing procedures. *Psychol. Rev.*, 1960, *67*, 301–316.

Sarbin, T. R. Clinical psychology—Art or science. *Psychometrika*, 1941, *6*, 391–400.

Sarbin, T. R., Taft, R., & Bailey, D. E. *Clinical inference and cognitive theory*. New York: Holt, 1960.

Saslow, G., & Matarazzo, J. D. A technique for studying changes in interview behavior. In E. A. Rubinstein, & M. B. Parloff

(Eds.), *Research in psychotherapy*. Washington: American Psychological Association, 1959.

Saul, L. J. The psychoanalytic diagnostic interview. *Psychoanal. Quart.*, 1957, *26*, 76–90.

Sechehaye, Marguerite A. *Symbolic realization*. New York: International Universities, 1952.

Secord, P. F. Objectification of word-association procedures by the use of homonyms: A measure of body cathexis. *J. Pers.*, 1953, *21*, 479–495.

Seeman, W. "Subtlety" in structured personality tests. *J. consult. Psychol.*, 1952, *16*, 278–283.

Seeman, W. Concept of "subtlety" in structured psychiatric and personality tests: An experimental approach. *J. abnorm. soc. Psychol.*, 1953, *48*, 239–247.

Shneidman, E. S. *Thematic test analysis*. New York: Grune & Stratton, 1951.

Slater, R. Karen Horney on psychoanalytic technique: Interpretations. *Amer. J. Psychoanal.*, 1956, *16*, 118–124.

Speisman, J. C. Depth of interpretation and verbal resistance in psychotherapy. *J. consult. Psychol.*, 1959, *23*, 93–99.

Stein, M. I. *The Thematic Apperception Test. An introductory manual for its clinical use with adults*. (Rev. ed.) Reading, Mass.: Addison-Wesley, 1955.

Stirt, S. S. Overt mass masturbation in classroom. *Amer. J. Orthopsychiat.*, 1940, *10*, 801–804.

Strupp, H. An objective comparison of Rogerian and psychoanalytic techniques. *J. consult. Psychol.*, 1955, *19*, 1–7.

Sundberg, N. D. The practice of psychological testing in clinical services in the United States. *Amer. Psychologist*, 1961, *16*, 79–83.

Swensen, C. H., Jr. Empirical evaluations of human figure drawings. *Psychol. Bull.*, 1957, *54*, 431–466.

Taylor, Janet A. The relationship of anxiety to the conditioned eyelid response. *J. exp. Psychol.*, 1951, *41*, 81–92.

Thompson, C. E. *Thompson modification of the Thematic Apperception Test*. Cambridge, Mass.: Harvard University Press, 1949.

Tolman, E. C. Cognitive maps in rats and men. *Psychol. Rev.*, 1948, *55*, 189–208.

Vernon, P. E. *Personality tests and assessments.* London: Methuen, 1953.

Watkins, J. G., & Stauffacher, J. C. An index of pathological thinking in the Rorschach. *J. proj. Tech.,* 1952, *16,* 276–286.

Wertheimer, M. On the supposed behavioral correlates of an "eye" content response on the Rorschach. *J. consult. Psychol.,* 1953, *17,* 189–194.

Whorf, B. L. *Language, thought, and reality.* New York: Wiley, 1956.

Windle, C. Psychological tests in psychopathological prognosis. *Psychol. Bull.,* 1952, *49,* 451–482.

Wolpe, J. *Psychotherapy by reciprocal inhibition.* Stanford: Stanford University Press, 1958.

Zubin, J., Eron, L. D., & Sulton, F. Current status of the Rorschach Test: 1. A psychometric evaluation of the Rorschach experiment. *Amer. J. Orthopsychiat.,* 1956, *26,* 773–782.

Author Index

359

Subject Index

Event-occurrence probability function, 57
Events, 7
  and their interpretation, 7–10, 280–281
Ex cathedra interpretations, 312
Existentialism, 146
Expressive dimension, see Instrumental and expressive dimensions of behavior

Faculty psychology, 23
Fear-arousing appeals, 263, 269
Figure-drawing, 229–230
"Flop-over" point, 263
Forms of interpretation
  invitations to speculation, 310, 319
  invoking alternative perspectives, 310, 319
  normative references, 310, 319
  suppositions, 310, 319
  tentative assertion, 310, 319

Gambler's fallacy, 50n
Generalizations, 118–122, 124, 125, 135, 138, 141, 147–148, 152–155, 174, 210, 222, 280, 308, 314 ff.
  basis for anticipation and decision-making, 120–121
  effect on patient, 312–314
  prior to constructions, 121
  probabilistic nature, 127–129
  process in, 125–126
  role of schema in, 126–127, 132–133, 155
  and sample size, 128–131, 133
  sources of error in, 127–134, 148
  sources of observations, 131

Homonyms, use of, 101

Id, 20, 244
Image, 274–278, 280, 284, 287, 296, 297, 314, 320, 322, 331–332, 333, 336
  alterations, 287–290, 294, 297, 308, 310, 314, 316, 317–319, 334, 342
Imbalance, 258
  stressful nature of, 268
Incongruity, 258
Incremental probability implication, 55–56
Insight, 20–21, 29, 252, 289, 290
Inspection technique, 162
Instrumental and expressive dimensions of behavior, 204–209
  defined, 204–206
  and interpretive approach, 206
  and tests, 207–209, 239
Instrumental conditioning situation, 263
"Intellectualizedinterpretation," 246
Interpretation, art of, 84–85
Interpretation in psychotherapy, 242–244, 299 ff.
  classical conditioning paradigm, 270
  contraindications, 325–382, 344
  and dissonance, 269–272, 282, 284, 285–289, 296
  dual role, 248
  frequency, 331–333, 344
  phenomena of, 252–256
    affective consequences, 253–254, 271, 295
    behavior change, 252–253, 295

optimal frequency and timing, 254, 295

optimal relationship between interpretation and patient's conceptualization, 254–256, 295

as problem of

communication and influence, 244, 262–266

interpersonal relations, 244, 266–272

perception and cognition, 244, 272–279

rejection of, 285–288, 297, 311, 333–336, 344

a benign response, 333

status of, 245–248

theory, 279–298

requirements of, 248–252

timing and readiness for, 328–331, 344

see also Dissonance, preinterpretation *and* postinterpretation

Interpreter

demands upon, 70, 74, 76–77, 338, 347

as source of error, 133–134

as source of variance, 82, 107

Interpretive bewilderment, 338–340

Interpretive perspectives, 91–114, 154, 339

affect, 98–99, 114 218, 224

associations, 104–105, 114, 229

effect, 96–98, 99, 114, 211, 224, 227

frequency, 107–108, 111, 112, 114, 216

function, 95–96, 99, 114, 221, 224, 227, 229

intensity, 108–109, 111, 114, 224

logical extension and reversal, 101–102, 114

metaphor, 99–100, 114, 216, 218, 228, 229, 231

pervasiveness, 109–111, 114

phonetic analysis, 100–101, 114

reactions of the interpreter, 105–107, 114, 231

sequence, 102–104, 105, 114, 227, 229

structure, 94–95, 99, 114, 224, 227, 229

uniqueness, 111–112, 114

Inversion, 42

Journal of Projective Techniques, 198

Language

of theory, 25, 27, 39, 54

of data, 25, 26, 27

see also Semantic aspect of interpretation

Lawfulness of behavior, 58–60, 66

and relevance, 59

Learning theory, 107, 273, 282

Logical positivism, 9

Make A Picture Story (MAPS) Test, 228–229, 231, 232

Manifest Anxiety Scale (MAS), 184–185, 186

children's form (CMAS), 186

Mental mechanisms, 93, 115

as logical operators, 86

Minimax criterion, *see* Psychodiagnosis

Minnesota Multiphasic Personal-

ity Inventory (MMPI), 159, 162, 163, 198–204, 207, 208, 209
configural rules, 204
subtle and obvious items, 201–202

Overdetermination, 69
Operate phase, 275

Palo Alto Aggressive Content Scale, 223–224
Personality dynamics, 27, 116, 173, 174
Personalizing question, 194
Phases of interpretation in psychotherapy
consolidation and testing, 320–325, 344
interpretation proper, 307–320, 343
propositional, 312–320, 327
semantic, 308–312, 327
preparing the ground, 300–307, 343
exposure of discrepancies, 306–307
questioning, 304–305
recollection and observation, 305–306
Phoric differential, 258, 259, 261, 263, 267, 287, 288, 296, 297, 342
Plans, 274–278, 280, 284, 287, 296, 297, 320, 322, 331–332, 333, 336
alteration, 287–290, 294, 297, 308, 314, 334, 342
Postdiction, 137, 141, 144–146, 147, 149
and criterion contamination, 145, 149

Prediction, 6, 137, 141, 143–147, 149
Prestige, role of, upon suggestion, 262, 269
Principle of congruity, 266–267
Prognostic Rating Scale, 162, 203, 210
Progressive relaxation techniques, 248n
Projection, 87
Projective tests, as abortions, 237–238
see also Tests
Propositional aspect of interpretation, 31–36, 68, 73, 103, 104, 116, 147, 152–156, 210, 259
as assertion of relations, 59–65
empirically rooted, 60–65
role of theory in, 61–65
Propositional stage, see Propositional aspect
Propositional statements, 25, 28, 116, 222
role of theory in, 25–26, 35, 122–123
Psychic determinism, 58
Psychoanalysis, 15, 19, 20, 26, 34, 41, 49, 86, 106, 124, 134 ff., 224, 243, 250, 271, 279, 299, 330, 346,
diagnostic interview, 168–169
theory of psychosexual development, 48
Psychoanalyst, 20, 72, 251
Psychodiagnosis
bounded class of problem, 171–177, 179, 181, 188–189, 194, 196
and decision-making, 158, 177
formal approach, 160–189, 194–196

RC
469
.L45

RC
469
.L45